APPROACHES TO LEARNING

Volume 1, The Best of ACLD

APPROACHES

Edited by

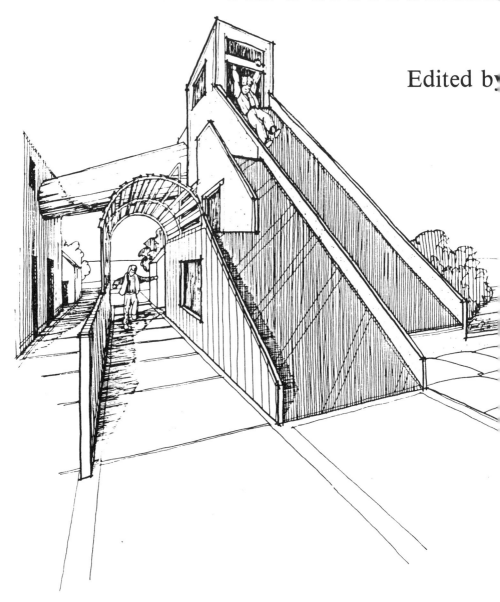

TO LEARNING

WILLIAM M. CRUICKSHANK

Selected Papers from the 15th and 16th International
Conferences of the Association for Children
with Learning Disabilities, 1978–1979

Syracuse University Press • 1980

Copyright © 1980 by Syracuse University Press
Syracuse, New York 13210

ALL RIGHTS RESERVED
First Edition

Library of Congress Cataloging in Publication Data

Association for Children with Learning Disabilities.
   Approaches to learning.

   Bibliography: p.
   1. Learning disabilities—Congresses. 2. Associ-
ation for children with Learning Disabilities.
I. Cruickshank, William M. II. Title.
LC4704.A88 1980   371.9   79-25638
ISBN 0-8156-2203-1

Manufactured in the United States of America

CONTENTS

CONTRIBUTORS

Ruth Angel is Director of Programs for Exceptional Children, Gaston County, North Carolina.

Bruce Balow is Professor of Psychoeducational Studies, University of Minnesota, Minneapolis, Minnesota.

Norma Barnaby is Psychologist, Department of Psychiatry, Ohio State School of Medicine, Columbus, Ohio.

James C. Chalfant is Professor of Special Education, University of Arizona, Tucson, Arizona.

Linda Charles is a research associate in the Department of Special Education, UCLA, Los Angeles, California.

William M. Cruickshank is Professor of Child and Family Health, Psychology, and Education, and Director of the Institute for Mental Retardation and Related Disabilities, University of Michigan, Ann Arbor, Michigan.

Jon Eisenson is Distinguished Professor of Special Education and Director of the Scottish Rite Institute for Childhood Aphasia, San Francisco State University, San Francisco, California.

Douglas Fuchs is Psychologist, Special Education Preschool Programs, Minneapolis, Minnesota.

Donald Guthrie is Coordinator, Computing Resources Group, Mental Retardation Research Center, UCLA, Los Angeles, California.

Rosa A. Hagin is Research Professor of Psychology, New York University-Bellevue Medical Center, New York, New York.

Merrill Hiscock is Assistant Professor of Psychology and Clinical Instructor in Psychiatry, University of Saskatchewan, Saskatoon, Saskatchewan, Canada.

George Hynd is Associate Professor of Educational Psychology, University of Georgia, Athens, Georgia.

Merle B. Karnes is Professor of Special Education in the Institute for Child Behavior and Development, University of Illinois, Urbana/Champaign, Illinois.

Marcel Kinsbourne is Professor of Pediatrics in the Faculty of Medicine and Professor of Psychology in the Faculty of Arts and Sciences, University of Toronto, Canada.

Attie Belle Liles is Director of Reading, Grades K-12, Gaston County, North Carolina.

Charles Meisgeier is Professor of Education and Director of the Child Service Demonstration Center, University of Houston, Houston, Texas.

Linda Menius is Training Coordinator at the Child Service Demonstration Center, University of Houston, Houston, Texas.

Gary T. Moore is Assistant Professor, School of Architecture and Urban Planning, University of Wisconsin, Milwaukee, Wisconsin.

Ann Obrzut is Coordinator of Special Education and School Psychologist, Weld County School District, Greeley, Colorado.

John Obrzut is Professor of Psychology, University of Northern Colorado, Greeley, Colorado.

Howell I. Runion is Associate Professor of Physiology, Pharmacology, and Electrophysiology, School of Pharmacy, University of the Pacific, Stockton, California.

Richard Schain is Professor and Head, Division of Pediatric Neurology, UCLA Center for Health Sciences, Los Angeles, California.

Jean A. Seabrook is Director of National Teacher Training, Christchurch, New Zealand.

Archie A. Silver is Professor of Psychiatry and Chief, Division of Child and Adolescent Psychiatry, College of Medicine, University of South Florida, Tampa, Florida.

Selma Thackery is Psychologist, The Seely Place School, Edgemont, New York.

Marty Williams is Program Coordinator for National Learning Disorders Assistance Project, the technical assistance agency which serves the Title VI-G network.

PREFACE

SINCE 1963, when the Association for Children with Learning Disabilities (ACLD) was first organized, hundreds of papers have been presented at annual international meetings. Proceedings of the early conferences through 1971 have been published, and selected papers from many of the conferences were included in an overview publication of papers in 1975. Since the 1974 conference, no permanent record has been made of the many and varied presentations. In 1978, the board of directors of ACLD approved the publication of a careful culling of papers from future conferences. This is the first book of this series, representative of the best of ACLD.

The ACLD Editorial Committee determined that only a few of the total number of presentations could be included within the covers of a single book. We sent a letter to each of the nearly 400 participants listed in the 1979 International Convention Program, telling them of ACLD's book publication plans. After excluding panel discussions, each member of the Editorial Committee examined the preliminary convention program and indicated those authors who might be expected to prepare a scholarly paper. A second letter was sent to approximately 150 people, inviting them to submit their papers for publication.

Many conference presenters responded from this latter group—some enthusiastically, others indicating a commitment to publish elsewhere, and, too often, still others saying that they would not be preparing a paper, but would be speaking extemporaneously or from notes. Some fifty papers were submitted before or immediately following the 1979 Convention. Each member of the Editorial Committee read and made publishing recommendations about each paper. Three papers presented in 1978 at Kansas City, one presented there in cooperation with the newly organized International Academy for Research in Learning Disabilities, were also selected by the Editorial Committee members for inclusion in this 1978–79 book.

Why another book? First, important ideas are often presented at the International Conference which should be preserved for historical reasons, for use by students, and as stimulants to others in future research. Second, members of the ACLD Executive Committee and Editorial Committee expect that the publication of selected papers will have the effect of raising the professional quality of future conferences. ACLD is a strong organization. Its annual convention serves as a forum where new ideas should be presented, as an arena where discussions are held out of which new or renewed efforts in behalf of the growth and development of children with learning disabilities should be experienced by researchers and practitioners. The members of the Editorial Committee hope that the publication of these papers will serve as an incentive to future conference participants.

The papers included here represent a variety of points of view and subject matter. Some are directed toward the educational scene; others pertain to psychology and neurophysiological dysfunction. Each is important in its own way, and each contributes to the ever-enlarging body of literature and research.

The thirteen chapters of this book have been organized in the following manner for the convenience of the reader: Chapter 1 serves as the prologue or foreword. Chapters 2 through 7, inclusive, are concerned with reading and cognitive development. Chapters 8 and 9 focus on pediatric pharmacology. Chapters 10 and 11 are particularly important statements regarding cerebral lateralization and dominance. Chapter 12 concerns itself with play environments outside the school building which reflect the internal educational philosophy and program. Chapter 13 constitutes the epilogue or afterword.

A research thrust permeates the papers presented in this collection. We hope that future publications will bring forth more research which sharpens the cutting edge of practice, and new practice which wields the new knowledge specifically and effectively.

The Editorial Committee
William Cruickshank, Ph.D., Chairman
Janet Lerner, Ph.D.
Archie Silver, M.D.
Eli Tash, Ph.D.

APPROACHES TO LEARNING

Volume 1, The Best of ACLD

1

"When Winter Comes, Can Spring . . . ?"

William M. Cruickshank

At the outset we must put forward the premise that there is nothing so rotten in Denmark that honorable men cannot put right. If learning disabilities be our Hamlet's Denmark, the honorable men are those who today listen and tomorrow may read and put right what we say here. Someone has said, however, that "The best intentions of honorable people do not preclude bias." The best intentions of honorable people also do not always work out. Shakespeare's definition of the word *rotten,* honorable people with biases, the intentions of honorable people falling short of their mark—these are the developmental characteristics of the professional field of learning disabilities as it is and can be viewed today.

I entered into the preparation of this paper with a spirit of positive anticipation and purpose. Spring does follow winter as Shelley reminded us so long ago. But winter is upon us now. Heavy snows cloud our vision of the road ahead. One philosophical ice-bound river charges into another with neither of them blending. As two incompatible chemicals they stay at their own levels as hostile mixtures. This is as it is in learning disabilities.

In the minds of men, winters are often long. Reformation thinking of Luther, Wesley, Comenius, Rousseau, Knox, Calvin, Cromwell, and others foamed for a century or more before men accepted new ideas on a more or less intellectual and universal basis, and even now there are those opposed to two- or three-century-old "new ideas." Sixty years have passed since the wrenching birth pangs of the Soviet Union spawned forth a new body politic and since Mao Tse Tung and his friend, as beggars, trudged through the vastness of China. Still their political ideation grows and remains unacceptable to more than half the world. The music of Stravinsky, the art of Dali, the choreography of Joffrey, the rock sound of the sixties—all of these were initially rebuffed except by the avant-garde of their individual fields, and over the better part of a century they have had to fight as ideas and art forms for their places in the sun.

Keynote address, ACLD International Convention, Kansas City, 1978; reprinted with permission of *The Exceptional Child* (Australia), 25 March 1978: 3-25.

If one looks into history, one can become terribly disturbed by the events which men have allowed to happen, by the carnage and human waste which selfishness has produced. In the long view, however, the best of human endeavor has usually won out and a better life has sometimes appeared. Like Keats in the "Grasshopper and the Cricket," I believe that "The poetry of earth is never dead." Leonard Bernstein goes farther and says this is true so long as "spring succeeds winter, and man is there to perceive it." This is learning disabilities. Aligning our beliefs with those of Shelley, Keats, and Bernstein, let us examine the Winter of Learning Disabilities, and see ourselves what icy rivers must be caused to melt in order that this generation of children no longer is buffeted by professional politics, by theoretical ineptitude, by the mouthings of court fools, or by the hollow and soundless speech of cathedral gargoyles. For in less poetic terms these elements characterize the field of learning disabilities, and children are those who suffer. How has the confusion of the present been created by the efforts of honorable men in years recently passed?

The great Spanish and Argentinian poet, Jorge Luis Borges, says it appears that "The goal is oblivion. I have arrived early." This is my thought as I often muse sadly over the chaotic field of learning disabilities and see around me today those exploiting an idea and children in their grasping for selfish ends, whether it be yoga as a solution to the neurological problems of learning disabilities, Transcendental Meditation as a panacea for faulty neurophysiological circuits, those who would put down perceptual-motor training as fruitless, those who would put it up as the end-all and be-all of a regimen, those who espouse mainstreaming as the sole solution to all the problems of childhood, those who ignore the presence of learning disabilities in children of low intelligence and state that such doesn't exist, those who equate learning disabilities with Julie Andrews' concept of normalcy, those who for whatsoever reason feel driven to protect areas of territoriality in the false belief that through such barrier-building attempts the problems of children will be solved, often those who present the most complicated of all learning difficulties in the whole spectrum of human growth and development. Bernstein in his addresses to the undergraduates of Harvard University says, to paraphrase him considerably, expressive distinctions in points of view and positions depend ultimately on the dignity and passion of the individual creative voice. In learning disability, passion too often exists without dignity, and the individual creative voice is subject to put-down by those whose future is superficially secured by climbing over the bodies of their professional colleagues. The politics of academia are horrible, not worthy of the minds of those who occupy scholarly chairs. Yet this is the environment in which learning disabilities is set. In more specific terms, what are our problems? These are not all new ideas; I have spoken and written of them before.

THE TERM

An essential problem, fundamental to the directions in which this field so blindly moves, is the failure to understand historically what learning disabilities as a plural noun is, and from whence it came. The result, as Santayana has suggested, is the redoubling of one's efforts when you have forgotten your aim. In the case of learning disabilities, too many have never read Lee Wiederholt (1974), and have never understood the historical antecedents to our aim. The acccidental impress which learning disabilities as a term was given in 1963 has opened a Pandora's Box, so large and so frightening that one wonders if logic will ever prevail. We fail in this consideration to make the necessary separation of learning disabilities as a neurophysiological entity from problems of learning in children which are environmentally produced. Indeed, if one were initially and accurately planning for this field in 1978—if one could be omnipotent—one might well create an organization called the Association for Children and Youth with Learning Disabilities and another called the Association for Children and Youth with Environmentally Produced Problems of Learning. This would provided a dynamic focus on two quite dissimilar problems which are now considered as one and permit an appropriate attack on each. Congress would be happier, for quite possibly legislative vision appropriate to the specific needs of the two groups would become clear in the minds of those who must legislate. Administrators at the executive levels of both state and national departments of education might then really perceive what the impact is of PL 94-142 and its state-level counterparts on educational programming.

A contributing factor to the Winter of Learning Disabilities is the fact that the term "learning disabilities," accidental as it was in its inception, is inaccurate in describing the problems of the children under our consideration. It permits the inclusion of too many quite disrelated educational, adjustment, and learning problems whose origins and educational attack are different from the basic issue. And it permits every educator in the world without training to identify with the problem, because *as a teacher* it goes without saying that he or she is a specialist in learning disabilities.

The comedy of errors so accurately perceived by Shakespeare is full blown on the stage of learning disabilities. The term is not functional. It leads nowhere. It clouds the real undergirding issues. It permits hassling which is observed on all sides as one writer after another has attempted to put the issue straight. The number of articles which has appeared in the literature during the past decade and which attempt to explain this term is nearing encyclopedic proportions. Until a term can be defined accurately and understood, it is worthless. Where would our colleagues in other sciences be if their basic vocabularies were as misunderstood, colleague-to-colleague, discipline-to-discipline, as those terms are in this field of learning disabilities: atom, space, neutron, fusion, upper atmosphere, element, or molecule. Even with the accuracy imbedded in these terms, fatal errors involving human beings have been made. Compare the accepted accuracy of these few words with "learning," with "disabilities," "dysfunction," "impairment," "perception," "deficit," or with "brain injury," "minimal cerebral dysfunction," "hyperkinetic," or with a myriad of other terms which are accepted without real understanding, thought, or definition by the untold number of "experts" in the field of learning disabilities.

Is it time to put our terminology and the definitional house in order? An agreed-upon toxonomy is badly needed. No field can accurately progress with the semantic confusion which educators and psychologists appear to accept as a necessary, but burdensome fact. Not so. While perhaps more difficult to present in defined form, terminology can be made more exact, words can have accurate meanings, and solidarity of effort can be a reality as a result.

Recently, on the first day of meeting with a large graduate class which was to be devoted to the neuropsychological aspects of learning disabilities, I asked this group of select students—no one of whom was naive—to write a definition of learning disabilities for me. The results were astounding. One student had moved ahead of his fellows and had read a book written by the instructor, a copy of which he had with him. He turned into me my definition! But the others, perhaps more honest in sharing their lack of understanding, defined learning disabilities as "remediation," as "emotional," as "related to normalcy and high intellectual level," as the "result of poor parental home controls," as "always related to birth injury," as the "result of poor teaching in the very early grades," as the "result of conflict in the home between parents or siblings," and as other results of, but not a definition of, this significant childhood and adolescent problem. I like students—love them indeed. We get along well. Dare we let advanced graduate students move into the professions unable to define accurately the field which will soon provide them sustenance? I hope those students in the group about which I speak will not perpetuate inaccuracies. But this is not typical of the professions as a whole. At times it appears that individuals are driven by some unseen hand to disagree and to find personal satisfaction in intellectual recalcitrance. I appeal to good will, to negotiation, and to compromise toward that which is correct. Professional people who cannot function within these established boundaries do not deserve to be placed in a leadership position.

I was recently having lunch with one of my university professors of forty years ago, the renowned William Clark Trow. He left me with a copy of a book which at the age of eighty-four he had recently published, *Gulliver's Visit to Walden III.* I commend it to you. In Walden III he finds his narrator working on six errors of present concern in the Mental World. Each of these is so specific to the field of learning disabilities as to prompt me to include them here.

My professor is concerned with the—

— *"Error in identifying the cause* [italics added] of some event as if there were but one, confusing a causal sequence with a merely temporal one.

— *"Error in identifying a cure* for some undesired condition, often thought to be a punishment of some sort.

— *"Error of considering only one value* in some situation without regard for those that are of the chief concern to other people and to other worlds.

— *"Error of assuming that to follow a prescribed program of instruction necessarily qualifies one for some academic or vocational certification* for which it constitutes the requirement. . . .

— *"Error in believing that an authority* in one field of knowledge is to be accepted as such in other fields.

— *"Error in arbitrarily placing learners in groups* . . . and then evaluating them by comparing their performance with that of the others in their group" (Trow 1976).

If those of us working in the field of learning disabilities can deal with these errors of identification, assumption or belief, we can cut to the heart of most of the confusion in our field and provide a focus which will go far in providing an attack on the problem which when logically pursued will result in growth, success, and happiness for children and their families. To do otherwise is to perpetuate the icy confusion in which we as parents and as professional workers are today ensnarled.

TEACHER EDUCATION

A contributing factor to the Winter of Learning Disabilities is the issue of teacher training, or we might add of professional preparation in any of the professions related to learning disabilities. Pediatrics has recently discovered the problem, and frantically grasps to make it its own. Pyschology and its subalterans of neuropsychologists are sure that they discovered the problem first and before all others. Social workers, speech patholo-gists, nutritionists, each in their own time, have suddenly burst upon the scene with flags waving their advance into a problem about which they, in reality, frequently know little. Occupational therapists have trod more cautiously under good leadership; physical therapists are just awakening to the issue; administrators, of course, must know and understand it all in order to maintain their pinnacled position in the professional hierarchy. But to return to teacher education.

Few places in the educational scene in the United States, and few places elsewhere, under the leadership of a professor who is knowledge-able in depth, is a student prepared through didactic instruction, clinical experience, and research exposure to the nature and needs of what learn-ing disabilities in its true form is. Since very few professors have been pre-pared for the roles which they now perform, most must of necessity retreat to the security of secondary sources and the sanctify the Eclectic Approach as the essence of learning disabilities. An eclectic approach, unevaluated for the most part, leaves the student with a little information about several things, but insufficient in-depth understanding of any of them to be able to transplant his knowledge into a dynamic attack on the problems of children when these children present themselves as live, kick-ing, and, as most often, lovable beings five days a week for 180 days in a school year for as long as their needs necessitate special treatment regi-mens. Professors who have come to their present posts also via an eclectic approach can ill but do otherwise.

Unfortunately, few of the faculty members espousing learning dis-abilities today have lived long enough to be able to understand and prac-tice with this complex group of children. While on the one hand, we at present have children who, because of the nature of their disabilities, pre-sent subtle complexities, we have, on the other hand, among the youngest of our present professorial group those who as recently as 1963 were but fifteen years old. With all due respect, where have these professors, now turned thirty, received their preparation? Where is the evidence that these young persons have worked daily with these children? Where is the re-search experience so necessary to permit them to put the field into a logi-cal perspective for their students? Where is the psychoeducational clinical experience which is required before one can truly feel comfortable with this problem and assist students to achieve a similar balance? Too often these requisites to scholarly instruction do not exist, and at the college or university level our present students are exposed too often to the aura of a dilettante rather than to the secure wisdom of one who has been there. Too often the superficially prepared college professor will of necessity attack the child from a single point of view where a multifaceted thrust is required. Permit me, very liberally, to paraphrase Arnold Gesell. He said that one cannot begin to study any part of the child without immediately becoming aware that there is a lot more attached which has to be accounted for. It is always a source of fun and satisfaction when I have the opportunity to watch a young person approach a child with learning disabilities, push Button No. 1 and find a reaction from Responses No. 33, 37, 39, and 83, when Response No. 2 was supposed to have been produced. When the student's quizzical expression and frustration is replaced with the question, "Why?", I know that growth is possible and that ultimately this student may become the master. Unfortunately, when the situation I describe here is seen, too often educators fail to look at themselves and quickly displace the responsibility for the child's failure on uncooperative parents, too little or too much medication, failure of early discovery, genetic factors which are little understood as yet, stress between father and mother, or a myriad of other possible causative factors other than the teachers' own lack of understanding, training, or experience. Part of the Winter storm in which we find ourselves is due to the instant learning disability specialist, to youth and inexperience, and to inept preservice preparation in our colleges and universities. We will address this issue more positively in a latter part of this paper.

Rest assured that amidst mediocrity, I do find a nucleus of outstanding professors and teachers, teachers on whom the lives of some children rest, and from whose guidance and secure understanding parents draw their own security and reason in an often unreasonable parent-child world. During the past two years I have been spending almost one day a week in the rural schools of Michigan. From time to time, I find educational greatness there, perhaps the single thing which draws me in an otherwise very busy schedule to continue to do this work. There is a teacher in Jeddo, Michigan, whose work I would match with any teacher anywhere. There is a young teacher in Marlett, Michigan, whose understanding of emotionally disturbed adolescents belies his age. There are others, and they constitute the strength of the educational system. There are hundreds of these teachers, but not enough, who have drained the best of their preparatory years, who have mixed this with insight and intelligence, and who have been able to translate what they have read, heard, and assimilated into dynamic programs for children. They give us evidence that Winter will be followed by more favorable seasons for children and youth. But the ice melts too slowly, and inadequate teacher preparation based on fad and fashion rather than on basic theory, experience, research, and clinical observations continues into this day and will unfortunately continue until a rigorous change is demanded by those who now are so poorly served. Is it revolutionary to ask that child deviance be addressed with the best by the best?

Part of the Winter of Learning Disabilities is found in the tremendous amount of diagnostic data which never becomes translated into action for children. It is not uncommon for me to be handed clinical records of children with suspected learning disabilities, and to find that these records are between twenty and 200 pages long. In a school situation recently I examined, in a cursory fashion, a dozen child records; the psychological reports in each were never less than thirteen pages long. Yet when I asked the young psychologist to accompany me to the firing line, and to work with me and the teacher in translating his data into an action plan, he was mute. Teachers do not need more diagnostic information. They need instructional assistance and leadership. Information flows to educators from psychologists, social workers, neurologists, nutritionists, pediatricians, audiologists, communication experts, biochemists, dentists, electroencephalographers, ophthalmologists, otorhinolaryngologists, occupational therapists, physical therapists, and, of all things, perceptual-motor diagnosticians—each discipline included in a recent set of clinical records I was given to examine. To say the least, this sets the stage for confusion. What if the arrow pointed not to the educator, but to the psychologist and all of this vast amount of often disrelated information went to that office? What would the psychologist do with it? What if it all went with the addition of a good educational diagnostician's report to the electroencephalographer? You know as well as I what he would do with it. The teacher, however, if she gets the material at all, is supposed to "integrate it in behalf of the child," said one administrator to me on a recent school visit. The teacher in question was twenty-three years old, had one year of experience, and was a resource teacher with twenty-eight exceedingly complex children. He wanted tenure and he really wanted to be a coach. He actually sobbed when he found in me someone who was sympathetic to the unholy situation in which he was, and who might be able to give him some instructional assistance couched in educational four-letter terms that he understood.

Diagnosis is important. Reports are often helpful. But teachers and school administrators cannot be expected to take the wisdom of professions foreign to their own, expounded in a professional taxonomy which is fully disrelated to that of education, and be able to translate this into an educational management plan which benefits children. It cannot be done, and those who expect that it will are foolish. I do not talk down to teachers here. The good ones have my highest admiration as the record for many years shows. However, the onus of responsibility is on the shoulders of the interdisciplinary diagnosticians to indicate the implications of their professional findings for classroom management and for instruction. Educators can at least expect this reaching out to them from the other disciplines which claim an involvement.

Here are some quotations from a single record I had received in the mail, one which is far from unique. It is not atypical. I will admit that these statements are taken out of context, but a half dozen sentences on either side of the ones I have selected would make the situation no clearer to the educators to whom the data had been sent originally.

"The Dd scores from the Rorschach fully illustrate the compulsiveness which Joe shows, and likewise indicate the nature of his needed learning experiences. On the other hand, the high Z-score belies the results of the Leiter Test, but still further evaluation is needed to determine which is more nearly accurate. In the meantime the schools should probably provide Joe with materials requiring high organizational ability at a low mental age level." "This is a young man who is characterized by dissociation, perseveration, sequencing difficulties, closure problems, and cross-hemispheric inconsistencies. It is rare what one sees such a classical problem of learning disabilities. This boy should challenge any teacher to do her best." It is fortunate indeed that psychology is such a young discipline. The poetry of some psychologists would place Byron, Longfellow, Keats, and Whitman on the defensive and cause them to be completely tongue-tied for all of their words would have long since been used up! The audiologist who saw Joe is much more succinct, although probably no more helpful to Joe's teacher or parents. He said, "Decibel level: No positive findings. Frequency disturbances: No positive findings. Auditory perception: Did not test for." We later found that he didn't test for auditory perceptual processing problems because he didn't know how, and had no equipment to search for problems in this area! I could go further and carry you through statements made by the ophthalmologists regarding diopters and peripheral vision; by neurologists regarding the cerebellum, the left parietal lobe, and the extrapyramidal system; by the electroencephalographer regarding spiked waves and readings taken under sedation. No one of these persons ever suggests that curriculum, teaching reading and number concepts, skill-development with eye-hand coordination, geometric forms, handwriting or other daily activities, are important or that their findings might be translated in such a way as to be meaningful to the one who will have this child for more hours per day, more days per week, more years per child-life than any one other person except the parents who are likewise kept in the dark by the cacaphony of disciplinary terminology. Simple, unadorned English is rarely used to transmit between people clear-cut ideas, suggestions, and rational statements.

RESEARCH

Although there are other contributing factors to the maze in which learning disabilities children and youth find themselves, time and space preclude the mention of but one other. Then we must turn our attention to other things. One issue deserves recording and that is of concern or should be of concern to others as well as to ourselves who are working with the learning disabilities problems. Universities and university faculty promotions committees are a thing of wondrous awe to me still even though I have lived in university settings all of my professional life. Faculties have permitted themselves, as professors of old, to continue to count the number of angels who periously hang onto the head of a pin. Much modern faculty research and doctoral research is no better. If one reads, as I must periodically, lists of research titles which are submitted in defense of a faculty member seeking promotion, or review the dozens of book or article manuscripts or research proposals which cross my desk in a year's time, one is awed by the extent to which inconsequentia becomes world-shaking in its import. On the other hand, when someone produces a report of significance, it immediately spews a multiplicity of small attacks on insignificant details or aspects of the major issue, the latter each contributing to the plodding steps of the individual up the academic promotional ladder. While not all the problems of the world are to be solved in a given master's or doctoral thesis, one is often sickened when reading a commencement program to contemplate the excessive amount of energy that has been spent by well-intended young people which leads to nowhere for the professions. Stringfellow Barr, late the President of St. John's College in Annapolis, in his delightful novel, *Academically Speaking,* finds one of his characters saying, "I don't know whether teaching is any longer possible in universities. At least American universities. I won't bore you with the reasons. I'm not even sure that they're good places to write books in" (1958). Too true, except they appear to be good places for the ever-increasing flow of inconsequentia and the repetitive writing which paraphrases that which has gone before it through the fingers of wiser minds.

Kirk, McCarthy, Bateman, and others who were then colleagues, have developed a splendid instrument for, if not quantitative, then qualitative, assessment of the child's capacity to deal with input stimuli and a variety of expressive responses. Is it necessary that these splendid people be asked constantly to defend themselves by those who are married to standard deviations, chi-squares, and parametric statistics? The ITPA has value in the hands of those who know how to use it cautiously. The amount of time which men of stature must spend in defending themselves against minutiae is staggering. Why must we have any more pseudo-research defending the professions against perceptual-motor training when sound educators have known for decades where, why, and with whom this detail fits into a total program of instruction? Why the constant put-downs? Master's degrees have been won, promotions earned, and salary increments obtained through the publication of something called research which studied as isolated factor the impact on learning of eight heterogenous children which occurred in a cubicle for ten minutes per day over a three-week period! Taking a single element out of the total instructional context, and using it as the sole controlled variable in a manner never previously recommended is hardly research, nor does it smell any sweeter by any other name. Ideas should be challenged, but they should be challenged in a manner which permits the profession to grow and children to be served, not in the self-serving manner which in virulent form is so common today. It would appear that the price of standing for what one believes also requires academic crucifixion. But then that may be the price which Skinner, Kirk, Ayers, Myklebust, Frostig, and others who *believe in something* have to pay, and perhaps that is the way of human nature down through the ages of intelligent man. One regrets the energy which these remarkable people must pay, however, in whisking aside the gnats which constantly hover around in the reflected glory of Attack. Some of this would be obviated completely if the earlier issues of exact focus on the problem of what learning disabilities is would be solved. Then those who get their recipes mixed would no longer, at least, have that issue as one to divert their research from purposes of academic advancement. The problems of children with learning disabilities might be solved, because there would be so much time left over from writing inconsequentia and from the necessity of sounder minds defending against it.

This is the Winter of Learning Disabilities. It is not a kind winter such as portrayed in a Grandma Moses *naiveten* painting. It is not the "over-the-hills-and-through-the-woods" winter of our childhoods. It is a vicious winter of non-analytical thinking, of power hunger, and of selfishness for one's position rather than selflessness for a group of children who must be served accurately. It is a winter of childishness rather than one for childhoodness. One state department of education special education administrator, speaking in a petulant manner, told me in a public meeting that he could define learning disabilities in any way he wished. On examination of that state's definition, one sees this to have happened, for the definition excludes those whose problems challenge the educator. The definition, so often replicated in other states, also contributes to the most flagrant types of discrimination. If this were not true, why is it that so many of our so-called children with learning disabilities in large city school systems are white; so many of our so-called retarded children, black? This is an example of Winter when educational blinders have become a fixed piece of professional equipment. But Bernstein continues his lectures to the Harvard undergraduates and says that following winter, "I believe that from that earth emerges a musical poetry, which is by the nature of its sources tonal." In his Nobel lecture, Saul Bellow said, "On occasions like this I have no appetite for polemics." And later, "But I am interested in the question of the artist's priorities" (1977).

". . . CAN SPRING BE FAR BEHIND?"

The Spring of Learning Disabilities will come when we truly get our priorities established, and make them operational, organizationally and personally. Although there are many needs in the field of learning disabilities, I speak here only of priorities—the priorities which will move us to the ultimate solution of needs which here time permits to be mentioned only in a catalogued way. What are the priorities which I view as essential mandates for the profession world-wide, and specifically in the United States, because so many, perhaps unwisely, assume our leadership capacity? I see four priorities, the achievement of which is absolutely essential before this vast national and international program can go forward with secure steps. These are not necessarily in the order of importance, for all are equally important: (1) the achievement of true interdisciplinary research and programmatic functions; (2) the agreement on an accurate definition of the problem we espouse, perhaps even modifying its name in the long haul; (3) the implementation of a national program for the preparation of college professors as the first step in the sound preparation of the next generations of teachers; and (4) the achievement of a new ethic among professional people which makes possible the other priorities which we have mentioned. Let us examine each of these briefly.

Interdisciplinary Functions

At the risk of being criticized, I am going to approach the first priority, interdisciplinary functions, as I did sometime ago in another setting, paraphrasing my own words to fit this occasion, for basically, although time has passed, they contain truisms for today equal to those of the time when they were first uttered (1970).

During the past several years many have watched with keen interest the growth and maturation of the young Japanese musician and conductor, Seiji Ozawa. Mr. Ozawa, a protégé of Bernstein and now a conductor of renown, was interviewed with respect to his perception of a symphony orchestra. "An orchestra, after all," Ozawa is reported to have said, "is a very unnatural thing. An impossible thing, almost. A musician naturally wants to play alone, or in a group where he can be heard, appreciated, and still express his individuality . . . the musicians must submerge themselves into an orchestra to make the necessary sound and let one musician tell them how to play. Whenever it goes well, I am happy, because it is surprising that it ever works at all" (March 1969).

In the sensitive statement of this colorful musician is to be found the nature of some of the problems of interdisciplinary action. If Ozawa's few sentences are considered each alone, a fuller meaning to our problem may be perceived. "An orchestra, after all, is an unnatural thing." This is perhaps more the case in the United States and certain other western countries than it might be in Mr. Ozawa's native Japan. Our cultural heritage has been one of individual initiative and enterprise. The price has been high in the United States, for people like Sinclair Lewis' Babbitt, or his Dr. Peckerbough in opposition to his Dr. Gottlieb or Arrowsmith. The repeated pleadings of Horace Greeley who urged young men to go West and as individuals to prosper and succeed, characterized and moulded the thought of both young and old in the United States for many years. The aggressiveness of the railroad combines, the mining interests, the oil consortiums, and the Henry Fords of this land has produced a type of individualism which contains few precedents for the cooperative effort required in the interdisciplinary solution of the problems of mankind. That we may now be paying the high costs of individualism in the interdisciplinary challenge to environmental rot may become more evident within the next decade than it now is. Be that as it may, an interdisciplinary partnership, like Ozawa's orchestra, may indeed be an unnatural expression in the individualistic society and the political and social philosophy of the United States. This in truth may be the reason why so few interdisciplinary models have succeeded. While leaders in the disciplines have urged the interdisciplinary model, their own ingrained experience and long-standing operational model has been that of the homesteader of earlier decades who stakes out his plot and as an individual with his wife and children struggles to achieve. This model has been held before youth and man alike in the United States for two centuries. It is unrealistic to expect that the individualism of generations, in the short span of a few decades, could change into a type of allocentrism which would allow one to encompass others as equals in the solution of man's problems.

"A musician naturally wants to play alone." As a psychologist, I am not sure that Ozawa's use of the adverb "naturally" is correct. I suspect that there is no instinct for solo action. I am sure, however, that the training and guidance which children and young people have had in American schools over the past decades have moved them more in the direction of soloists than as members of a group capable of action in concert. Unilateral action rather than multilateral action has been the order of our individual and collective thinking. The validity of this statement is supported and expounded by Urie Bronfrenbrenner in his recent comparison of children in the U.S. and U.S.S.R.

As professional persons, irrespective of our area of personal training and concern, we want to play alone or in a small group where each of us can be heard. Witness any discussion group, and note the number of references to "*my* program," "*my* department," "*our* school," "in *my* university," "in *my* experience," "from the point of view of *my* profession," "*my* idea," "*my* efforts," "*my* system," *ad infinitum*.

Group action is not the only way to insure progress; certainly individual efforts in behalf of mankind have historically played a significant role. There is a place for both types of actions and activities. One of the causes of ineffective interdisciplinary action is the failure to realize that there is a place for the soloist and the belief that all things must be solved in concert. The mark of wise leadership is to determine which approach is most appropriate for which activity. An orchestra is sometimes needed, and when this mechanism is demanded to release the beauty of a composer's ideas, then this model of interdisciplinary trust is called. But on many occasions, the soloist has an equally significant contribution to make and his place in the niche of human history cannot be denied.

When I was a young boy I lived in a suburb of Detroit. An interurban trolley car connected us to the large city and it cost ten cents to ride the sixteen miles which would bring us to the Detroit Art Institute. Diego Rivera was then painting the remarkable murals which adorn the four walls of the beautiful interior court. Huge canvas curtains hung over the doors preventing the general public from disturbing the gigantic Mexican mind which was at work. My mother used to give me a dime, and with another friend or two, I would take the trolley and go to the Museum. I am sure that many knew what we were doing, but we were pleased to think that we were able to sneak in between the canvas drapes and squeeze quietly against the wall and watch the artist at work. He and his assistant, on scaffolds hung many feet above our small heads, would mix colors and then Rivera would apply them in all his artistry to the sketches which he had previously placed on the huge walls. He saw us sitting there, and once in awhile would wave a brush in our direction to acknowledge his awareness. As long as we were quiet, he said nothing nor did anyone else regarding our intrusion. Once he called us, and said in his very heavy English, "You like?" On another occasion, his assistant pointed out to us the many, many concepts contained in the murals: industry, religion, art, music, life, death, happiness, sadness, and many other fundamental concepts which because of our youth we could not fully appreciate. He once said, in referring to Rivera, "the artist must have many interests and know much and love many things." Rivera's biography and his paintings, in the Detroit Institute of Art, in the Prado Hotel of Mexico City, on the wall of the decaying municipalidad in Cuernevaca, and on the walls of other public places, show him to have been a man intimately interested in and concerned with engineering, military matters, "popular culture," science, surgery, children, social concepts, death, funerals, education, Anglo-Saxon cultures, history, communism and political thought, and many other matters. His was a life of versatility and his remarkable paintings show it. There is here another element in the interdisciplinary mind. The man who functions in the interdisciplinary model must not only be allocentric in his view of life and people, but he must be one who is capable of dealing with many facets in the spectrum of human effort. Closed systems have no place in interdisciplinary work. Open systems and systems which include many subsystems are required.

The system of interdisciplinary attack requires that "the musicians must submerge themselves into an orchestra to make the necessary sound." In its fullest this requires a type of personal discipline and self control of which through the ages philosophers have written. It requires a mentality which can focus on the goal, but simultaneously is appreciative of all which goes on around it. It demands a person who can bring, from all which human development has created, those things which illuminate the issue and clarify its solution. John Romano, the psychiatrist at Strong Memorial Hospital in Rochester, New York, is a remarkable example of this ability. In once discussing a schizophrenic patient whose problems were complex, he had the facility and wisdom to draw on Chinese literature for what it could contribute, on the life of Picasso, on Byzantine history, on the Industrial Revolution, on the writings of Bertrand Russell, on the obvious and the illusive, and from each to draw a thread which when woven into a new fabric brought a new insight into a man's problem. Interdisciplinary function requires a personal depth and understanding of the ways of men and what they have done. Members of an interdisciplinary movement must be of great breadth and must draw on many and often seemingly unrelated fields in their search for solutions. While the Riveras and the Romanos would probably in and of themselves not make good interdisciplinary agents, they represent a mentality which the interdisciplinary participants must use and must seek for themselves. Perhaps as an aside, their breadth of understanding of the ways of people make it unnecessary as well as impossible for them to function as a member of a group. They epitomize the group action in their broad grasp of ideas and things. As an individual each is indeed a group.

To this point, the interdisciplinary model which we seek to build requires individuals willing to submerge themselves into the greater effort of the group. It requires, secondly, individuals of great personal strength and capacity to understand and draw the best from many areas of learning. "The musicians must submerge themselves into an orchestra to make the necessary sound and let one musician tell them how to play." A third characteristic of the interdisciplinary model is the act of sacrifice—personal sacrifice. The model is not without the leader. The model is not necessarily the essence of democracy. The operative model seeks but does not necessarily require that for the moment all disciplines are equals. From the backdrop of understanding in which all disciplines are equals among equals, there must emerge, in an ever changing fashion, one musician to tell them how to play, one disciplinary leader who for the moment is entrusted with the act of coordination, direction, redirection, or if necessary complete restructuring of the model. That leader is one of the most crucial cogs in the entire chain of events. The interdisciplinary leaders, the case conference chairpersons, the team captains, or whatsoever these may be called, must be possessed of a unique blending of egocentricity and allocentricity. They must be respecters of other personalities, and yet firm in an unyielding effort to achieve the goal. They must be able to draw out the best from the minds of colleagues without stunting the creativeness of any one. They must be the catalytic agents to group action and to group decision without stultifying the imagination and vitality of any member of their groups. They are indeed paragons of virtue, but not to such an extent that they are unobtainable. Were they as a paragon unobtainable, the issue to which we address ourselves might better be left as wishful thinking. I am of the mind to believe that man, more often than not, can be conditioned to the type of leadership of which we here speak to the end that the reservoir of interdisciplinary captains, orchestral or choir conductors, leading actors and actresses of the theater, political shoguns, and university deans and presidents—each both a soloist and a member of a team if he is effective—can be available to tackle the complex issues of our society, learning disabilities among them.

The team leader of which Ozawa speaks must have traits of compassion and understanding as well as a firm resolve to unite the group into a common action. To this end, the goal to be attained is the first priority, not the fact that he is a pianist, a cellist, a psychologist, a physician, a lawyer, or an educator. To the end of concerted action, far greater in its implications than the contribution of a single discipline, will be drawn the best from each whatever may be its contribution. Under this concept, historical roles of medicine, for example, cease to be important. The historical roles of education, psychology, law, and other significant disciplines of our time change. Legal responsibilities of a given profession can be accepted or may need redefinition and modification. The concept of paramedical is soon understood to be no more fundamental or important than any other disciplinary term. Sometimes education is paramedical; but equally as often if not more so, medicine is "paraeducational." When this is learned and understood, interdisciplinary power is ready to be released in the appropriate solution of human problems. The leader of the interdisciplinary team understands this delicate balance and deals with it. The team members know that the disciplinary leader of today's group may not be the appropriate person for the same role for tomorrow's problem by the same group of people. Leadership flows from discipline to discipline and falls when and where it is appropriate on a given discipline. Leadership never remains fixed, nor is it the property of a given discipline. In the interdisciplinary team, medicine may one day be the focal point of the team; occupational therapy, nutrition, nursing, speech pathology, education or other, the core profession of the next day. Position in the interdisciplinary structure is of little import; each discipline uses its skills of the moment in the best possible way to seek solution to the problem before it. The leadership role is not defined by historical prerogatives, regulation or law, by length of academic preparation, salary schedule, or chronological age, but by the pertinence of the discipline to the agenda before the team and by the capacity of the individual representing that discipline to weld the other members into a force for the problem's solution, whatever it may be. This is what learning disabilities must expect from professional people.

Ozawa represents in his final comment what is so necessary in every disciplinary situation, a sense of humor. "When it goes well, I am happy, because it is surprising that it ever works at all." Often a Rube Goldberg construct, never a smoothly operating mechanism, it is surprising when the interdisciplinary team works. It works better if the individuals on the team do not become either too serious about what they are doing or too enamored of the roles they play. Each must be devoted to the goal he or she seeks, but each member must also maintain a perspective. In a tense professional operation, the wheels grind more smoothly when there is also an individual who can bring high academic purpose and lofty pronouncement to the level of the mundane and instill into the minds of those who struggle with ideas a smile—that person is worth his or her weight in gold.

As a student at the University of Chicago in 1937, I was privileged to experience a seminar on governments in crisis lead by the great Eduard Benes, who had recently been the President of Czechoslovakia. In the face of the personal and political tragedies of himself, his family and his country, Benes used to caution us as we listened to him quietly speaking at the end of a long oval table, "Never lose your sense of the enjoyment of things. Never forget that at the basis of the good life there must be humor." Humor in the interdisciplinary model is an ingredient, the absence of which will quickly bring the house down.

Accurate Definitions

The Canadian Association for Children with Learning Disabilities, through its courageous Project Consensus, is seeking the adoption of a definition of learning disabilities which is predicated on historical fact and psychoneurological accuracy. Both historical accuracy and psychoneurological accuracies must be taken equally into consideration, for if one part of the equation is omitted, serious misunderstanding and misdirection will be forthcoming. Learning disabilities cannot be all things to all vested interests, any more than the category of "communicable diseases" can be considered as a single entity to be treated in a single manner. If learning disabilities is merely a catch-all term for a tremendous miscellaneous collection of childhood problems, then we should accept the term for just that. If, however, learning disabilities is a more favorable term to the consumer for what initially was called something else, then we must look to that and sharpen our current understanding of what that is. If in the doing, some of the fellow-traveler problems are caught short or dropped by the wayside we must be sufficiently courageous to recognize what we are doing, and to seek ways in which those different problems can be solved in other more compatible arenas. Without going further, *learning disabilities* when it is accurately defined are:

1. problems in the acquisition of developmental skills, academic achievement, social adjustment, and secondarily emotional growth and development, which are the result of perceptual and linguistic processing deficits.
   Further defined, *learning disabilities*
2. may be of any etiological origin;
3. may be observed in children and youth of any age, and
4. of any level of intellectual function;
5. are the result of perceptual processing deficits which, in turn,

6. are, or may be, the result of a (diagnosed or inferred) neurophysiological dysfunction occurring at prenatal, perinatal, or (in the case particularly of linguistic dysfunction) at the post natal periods of development.

This definition negates the too-often-heard statement by the uninitiated that the problem cannot be defined. Of course, learning disabilities can be defined. When it is as we have done here, it provides a focus which permits bona fide research to be undertaken; it permits epidemiological studies to be initiated and completed; it provides a decent structure for the preparation of teachers; it provides a bridge between and among professional disciplines to foster good interdisciplinary cooperation; and it provides for parents, not a discouraging problem filled with fatalistic immovability, but an orientation around which positive programs of treatment and education can be organized to bring the child to the maximum of his potentials as a youth entering adulthood. There is nothing wrong with having a central nervous system impairment. There are many positive vectors in the issue, the primary one being that we know or suspect the springboard from which, with the child, we have to jump. Planning of a positive nature becomes possible with accurate orientation. The Winter of Learning Disabilities becomes Spring with alacrity, and with a common orientation to the problem, an attack for all seasons becomes a reality.

If learning disabilities in its present unsatisfactory conception, is to be continued as an inclusive, generic term, then an alternative to what we have just suggested is definitely in order. The toxonomy we have said is missing must be forthcoming. Simultaneously, a classification system of learning disabilities is then warranted in which the subsets are easily identifiable and are defined. Such a system of learning disabilities would include among others the following major heading:

1. perceptual processing deficits,
2. environmentally determined problems of learning,
3. minimal cerebral dysfunction,
4. dyslexia,
5. aphasia,
6. hyperkinesis,
7. multiple disabilities to be elaborated, i.e.,
   a. learning disabilities and mental retardation,
   b. mental retardation and environmentally determined problems of learning,
   c. perceptual processing deficits and cerebral palsy, and
   d. others.

This list is not intended to be inclusive, merely suggestive of the way we might proceed to seek clarity. Each of the topics mentioned can be defined just as we have defined perceptual processing deficits—historically the grandfather syndrome of the total learning disability family. Professional unanimity and a meeting of the minds might be forthcoming and hopefully will be. Were such unanimity to be achieved, think of the energies which could then be directed toward appropriate research and services to children.

A Corps of University Professors

I know that I will be criticized for suggesting as I have done here that college and university professors in the area of learning disabilities are not uniformly well-prepared. Many of them, with all due credit, have reached out to try to fill a void when they indeed did not possess all of the basic preparation to do so. We have already spoken to this issue, and need not repeat our deep concerns for the future of the field in the face of this situation. How can the ice of Winter be cracked, and a warm breath of competency begin to make itself felt?

On May 22, 1968, after discussing the background of the issue fully, I wrote a high official in the United States Office of Education as follows:

> Let us first concentrate on a corps of trained college professors. I would recommend that the U.S. Office of Education set up fifty two-year post-doctoral fellowships. These fellowships, ample in amount of the stipend, would be granted to professors-now-in-service who would be granted a leave of absence at half-pay from their university or college. The stipend would equal their other half of pay and would also permit a salary increase during the second year. These fifty professors would be brought together in one or two (possibly three) centers in the United States where they would undergo an intensive preparation in the total issue of the learning disability problem. I have done enough investigation to ascertain that several of the leaders currently in the field would be willing to join these "centers" as a part of the visiting faculty for long enough periods of time to be able to make a contribution. In my experience, I believe that two academic years . . . would be required. . . . It takes [this length of time] because of the unique elements which have to be "lived with" for a while before they are assimilated.

> I believe if fifty stipends were established, two groups of twenty-five in two major university centers could be worked into a dramatic crash program which would have the capacity to go far. I would certainly mean that in two years a corps of well-oriented professors would be found in fifty teacher

education centers in the United States capable of organizing appropriate teacher education programs in their institutions. We would put a stop to the messes we see currently in many places.

It might be that the U.S. Office of Education could follow-up the professor-training period with a modest planning grant in those universities which had participated in the training phase. . . . If what I am saying has meaning, it should be discussed. I know that I and my colleagues would be happy to co-operate in the development of this idea. If someone else would like to run with the ball, my cooperation with them would be insured. I have no vested interest in insuring my point of view or involving the University (in which I am employed) as one of the two centers. We would, if this seemed appropriate.

We continued with some additional elaboration. That letter never received a reply, nor did an inquiry regarding it which was made some years later. Think of the potential which has been missed, and which yet might be captured. While I cannot and do not speak for the persons I name here, I have a suspicion that some or all of them could be brought into such a national crash program. Dr. Samuel Kirk, Dr. Marianne Frostig, Dr. Charles Strother, each retired or semi-retired, could, I suspect, be enticed to serve as a visiting faculty member for a semester or a year. Dr. Helmer Mykelbust, Dr. Doris Johnson, and Dr. Gerald Getman might be able to obtain leaves from their employment to participate. Dr. Klaus Wedell of England could likely obtain a leave or a Fulbright lecturership if appropriate steps were taken. Dr. Ray Barsch, Dr. Katrina de Hirsch, Mrs. Elizabeth Freidus, are others who could probably be involved in some manner. Since I am so easily suggesting the names of others who have spent their lives with these problems and still have much to contribute, I must also include my own name. I would be available in whatsoever manner my efforts could best be utilized. Since 1968, when I first made this offer, we have lost the services of Newell Kephart (who worked with me on the idea and hoped to co-develop it), Sam Rabinovitch, and Herbert Birch. Those living are a few of the giants whom I would involve in the development of a program which would crack the unholy containment which represents the total field today, typified by much of the inconsequentia we have already lamented. They are not as the late Gilbert Highet said, "quiet, weak men who want to creep into some little niche"; they are people of purpose and authority who can yet provide direction to this field. In these efforts, not only a Spring and its budding efforts would result, but there would be a growing Summer making possible deep national roots to take hold in behalf of those children to which we are devoting so much needed attention.

Research

In discussing the interdisciplinary model, we referred to research. Both interdisciplinary and disciplinary research are needed, but these issues have been discussed by others and in many others places. Today as we are thinking about a Spring for Learning Disabilities I should like to report and record what we hope will be a significant event which took place on March 1, 1978.

A very small group of the world's leaders in many aspects of research which impinge on learning disabilities organized themselves on that date into the International Academy for Research on Learning Disabilities. At the current session representatives from Canada, Argentina, and the United States attended. An identical organizational meeting was held in Amsterdam on May 18, 1978, and representatives from Canada, the United States, the United Kingdom, Belgium, Poland, Denmark, the Netherlands, and West Germany attended. The Academy will eventually number about 150 persons from all disciplines which are concerned with learning disabilities. It now includes the disciplines of pediatrics, psychology, neuropsychology, special education, neurology, neuroradiology, speech pathology, biochemistry, nutrition, otology, and others. Who are some of these who are agreeing to devote their energies in this effort? They include a significant list of scientists all of whom are typical of the few illustrative examples here included:

Dr. Klaus Wedell, United Kingdom, Educational Psychology
Dr. Abraham Epstein, Denmark, Speech Pathologist
Dr. Joaquin Cravioto, Mexico, Pediatric Nutritionist
Dr. Julio B. de Quiros, Argentina, Pediatric Otologist
Dr. Ryuji Ito, Japan, Special Educator
Dr. Heinz Bach, West Germany, Special Educator
Dr. Jacob Valk, the Netherlands, Neuroradiologist
Dr. William Gaddes, Canada, Neuropsychologist
Dr. Marcel Kinsbourne, Canada, Pediatric Neurologist

A few weeks prior to his death, Dr. Alexander Luria of the USSR expressed his wish in a personal letter to me that he could participate.

What do we of the Academy hope to accomplish? Obviously 150 men and women cannot accomplish all, nor is it the intention of them to do so. One hundred and fifty persons of the world's leadership in learning disabilities can do much, however. Initial efforts will include among other things the following:

1. the Academy membership will seek to influence governments to make investments in research on learning disabilities;
2. the Academy membership will seek to develop ways in which there can be arranged appropriate exchange of research personnel between countries;
3. the exchange of promising graduate students will be a central focus of the Academy membership; and
4. task forces will undertake the preparation of research status reports, each one of a major contribution to a specific discipline. These should serve as guides to future disciplinary research.

It has been my considered opinion during the years and months when a few of us have been working to bring the Academy into its initial state of being, that the efforts of a few international giants can have a beneficial effect in both the long and short term. The membership also includes a number of promising young researchers for obvious multiple reasons to insure longevity of the effort. The Academy to me is a bright spot in the Spring of Learning Disabilities.

A Professional Ethic

Learning disabilities will come into its fullness when all of us who work in the field adopt a personal and professional ethic which is allocentric rather than egocentric. We have referred earlier to those whose reputation is seemingly self-enhanced by put-downs of their peers or elders. Professional differences of opinion often result in strengthening the profession. Personalities which are pitted against one another produce little which is positive, but do much to enhance a negative reputation for those who initiate such ineffective controversy.

The issue to which I address myself here may be a function of immaturity. In connection with the development of the Academy, letters of invitation were sent to these international leaders. Replies spawned humility if anything. Luria of Russia wrote, "I would have so little to contribute." A world leader from The Netherlands wrote, "I know so little, but could learn." One of the leading psychologists of Poland responded by writing, "I could suggest several persons far more competent than I." A pediatrician from the United Kingdom whose name is familiar to the literature, wrote, "This is a field to which I have devoted my professional life. I certainly join you and the others. No one yet has the answer, I above all, but perhaps in a collegial effort we can achieve and take at least one important step."

There is no sarcasm here. No comparisons between self and others detract from the reputation of the writers. The keynote is allocentricism and a reaching out to others who have a common goal irrespective of the disciplines which are involved. Galileo centuries ago spoke of the "humble reasoning of a single individual," a characteristic to be sought and prized if it is achieved.

There is so much to be done. So many children and youth, their families and future generations wait for questions to be answered. So many new developments in so many disciplines are appearing so frequently that acceptance of others, tolerance, cooperation, and interdisciplinary endeavors can through the efforts of well-intentioned men and women, bring understanding and better lives to those who suffer. Less we cannot expect from leadership.

REFERENCES

Barr, S. (1958). *Academically Speaking.* New York: Simon and Schuster.

Bellow, S. (1977). "The Nobel Address," *The American Scholar* (Summer): 316–25.

Bernstein, L. (1976). *The Unanswered Questions: Six Talks at Harvard.* Cambridge: Harvard University Press.

Cruickshank, W. M. (1970). "An Interdisciplinary Model for Manpower Development for Mental Retardation." In J. S. Cohen, ed., *Proceedings of the 1st Annual Spring Conference of the Institute for the Study of Mental Retardation.* Ann Arbor: ISMRRD.

March, R. C. (1969). "Ozawa in Transit." *Saturday Review* (September 27): 631.

Trow, W. C. (1976). *Gulliver's Visit to Walden III.* Kappa Delta Pi Press.

Wiederholt, L. (1974). "Historical Perspectives on the Education of the Learning Disabled." In Mann, L., and Sabatino, D., eds., *The Second Review of Special Education.* Philadelphia: JSE Press.

2

Reading and Language Problems
Two Sides of the Coin

Jon Eisenson

THE PROCESS OF READING

THIS ESSAY might also have been titled "Reading Difficulty as an Aspect of General Language Disability." However worded, and before I try to support my assumption, I will offer two basic definitions and make several statements about the nature and processes involved in reading.

"Reading" is a mental process by which a person derives meaning from events other than auditory through an avenue other than hearing. Initially, the avenue is usually visual, but it may be tactile, as it is for the blind. In a more limited sense, reading is a process by which a reader decodes events that are representations of or related to other events that constitute a linguistic system. Most frequently these "other events" are visual. Psychologists who are students of language do not pretend to know all the mental processes and mental events that take place when a listener understands a speaker, even when the utterance is comparatively simple. They, and by identification I, certainly do not know all that goes on in the mind when we are engaged in reading. Whatever reading may be, it comprises a great deal more than decoding and translating or redecoding from sight to sound. Furthermore, as Goodman indicates, (in Smith 1973) reading is a psycholinguistic guessing game that involves the reader in selecting visual cues and predicting messages provided by visual symbols in the form of a representational display. Such a display may be or appear to be alphabetic or ideographic as in Chinese or a combination of the two as in Japanese. It may also be pantomimic and/or alphabetic as in manual-visual systems used by the deaf where the display is sequential and transient rather than fixed as with printed forms. It may, of course, also be tactual as in Braille and other systems employed by the blind. I shall, however, limit my discussion to the visual systems used by sighted persons. I will try to limit what I have to say to written languages such as English that employ alphabetic representational systems rather than ones that employ ideographic characters.

25

In a written language system such as English the reader is exposed to a visual system that has three sub-systems. The most obvious sub-system is the one that somehow relates sight to sound. In American English, even if differences in dialects are not considered, there is at most a 50 to 60 percent correspondence between letter arrangements and sounds (phoneme-grapheme correspondence). This cue system is *graphophonic*.

The second cue sub-system that the reader uses is *syntactic*. In English the *syntactic system* includes pattern markers such as function words and inflectional affixes and modal-auxiliary words to create structures that are cues to meaning.

The third sub-system is *semantic*. The semantic system is in the mind of the reader rather than in the visual material. It is what, at any given moment, a reader can bring to and apply to the visual events in his psycholinguistic guessing game. To paraphrase Goodman, the semantic aspect goes beyond word recognition and word meaning and beyond syntactic knowledge. It is a matter of experience and cognitive-conceptual background that a reader can bring to bear at a given moment when engaged in reading. Goodman reminds us that "all readers are illiterate in some senses, since no one can read everything written in his native language" (p. 25). At some moments, by reasons of psychodynamics, some meanings may be blocked (repressed) and not derived despite adequate experience and knowledge of the language and the subject on the part of the reader.

Proficient readers as well as proficient listeners are good at the psycholinguistic probability game. "Proficient readers make generally successful predictions, but they are also able to recover when they produce miscues which change the meaning *in unacceptable ways*" (Goodman, p. 26).

When children learn to read, or perhaps better when they are taught to read, they are likely to rely heavily on orthographic features. As they become proficient in reading, the information from the orthography becomes subordinate to the syntactic and over-all semantic cues, that is, semantic cues beyond the level of individual word meaning. Misspellings are overlooked or not perceived. Unless engaged in proofreading, broken letters or unusual letter forms as well as other "typos" do not enter significantly in the reading process.

READING DISABILITY

Now, what is reading disability, or better when does a child have a reading disability?

I consider a reading disability to be present if, despite what is presumed to be adequate mental capacity, sensory equipment, motivation, and intelligent attempts at instruction, a child has difficulty in deriving meaning from visual-representational (symbol) material. The degree of difficulty, if measurable, should be two or more years behind what we may expect based on an individual's age and mental capacity. So, for the sake of maintaining my position, a child should be at least seven or eight years of age before we should even consider designating him or her as having a reading disability. It is, of course, more likely to be a *him* rather than a *her* who presents a severe reading difficulty.

This does not imply that we who are teachers or clinicians may not begin the disabling process earlier, even at the very first opportunity provided. Often the potentially disabled reader indicates by a lack of interest in looking at pictures and at books, or listening to stories, or even watching television that a promise of reading disability may be anticipated. However, to insure reading disability takes time and continued application to the task. Two years of judicious effort is usually sufficient. Teachers, parents, and the children themselves contribute to this effort.

Dyslexia

The epitome of the disabled reader is the dyslexic child. Critchley (1964) considers dyslexia as "a defect in the visual interpretation of verbal symbols—an aphasia-like state: part of an inherent linguistic defect" (p. 10). Critchley considers *developmental* dyslexia an organically determined cerebral impairment—essentially a failure to associate sight and sound. *Symptomatic dyslexia,* Critchley believes, may be caused by a diversity of factors, organic as well as psychiatric, and is often associated with a visual-perceptual lag.

In 1968 the World Federation of Neurology agreed to the following as a definition of *specific developmental dyslexia*: "a disorder manifested by a difficulty in learning to read, despite conventional instruction, adequate intelligence, and socio-cultural opportunity. It is dependent upon fundamental cognitive disabilities which are frequently of constitutional origin."

As early as the 1930s, in his book on *Reading, Writing, and Speech Problems in Children* Samuel Orton (1937) indicated that dyslexic persons suffered from a general lag in the acquisition and development of all language skills—perhaps in all verbal symbol functioning. This was in keeping with Orton's view that all language functions are somehow interrelated. Although we cannot always support this view in developmentally dyslexic children, we certainly find that dyslexia as an aspect of acquired aphasia is almost invariably associated with a variety of language deficits. The literature on children who presumably have minimal brain damage is replete with evidence that these children have a high incidence of language problems that are by no means limited to reading and writing.

Now, in keeping with my assignment, I will review some of the representative literature on the relationship of language impairment and reading disabilities.

SPEECH AND LANGUAGE DISORDERS AND READING DISABILITIES

What is the evidence that children who present themselves as having difficulties in speaking are also likely to have difficulties in reading? Much of the evidence is clinical observation from presumably sophisticated clinical observers. Fortunately, some of the recent evidence is supported by investigative studies. Others are based on surveys of the literature. I shall present a few observations by writers who are accepted as authorities. We will note that the relationship between reading disability and speech and language improficiencies include a broad array of problems. In fact, only *vocal difficulties per se* are not included.

Arnold (1960) views cluttering as a disorder of *central language imbalance* that comprise features of delayed language onset, dyslalias, and reading and writing difficulties.

Weiss (1964) takes the same position as Arnold to the effect that cluttering is a disorder of central language imbalance featured by an initial delay in language acquisition, continued delays and deficiencies in language development, articulatory defects, rhythm defects, and reading and writing difficulties.

Based on a review of the literature and my own (1977) observations, clutterers as well as stutterers often have a history of delayed onset of speech and slow development of language, especially in syntactical proficiency. Several recent studies, including one of our own at the Institute for Childhood Aphasia, support this observation.

Mykelbust (1975) sums up the consensus of observations and his own position on the relationship of dyslexia to oral and written language proficiency.

That dyslexia is a complex condition, however, is apparent because of the evidence that many of these children also have deficiencies in spoken language. They might fall 2 to 3 years below average in facility with the spoken word. Moreover, they are severely limited in use of the written word; they write fewer sentences, less words per sentence, and are inferior in use of syntax. Factor analysis and inter-correlation studies show that dyslexics vary from the normal in various cognitive processes; they are less able to relate the auditory and visual facets of letters, syllables, and words. In addition, and perhaps of considerable consequence, they are deficient in ability to integrate meanings, although interneurosensory processing was achieved (p. 426).

Powers (1971) reviews the literature on the relationship between language skills and reading, and particularly on articulation and reading. In general Powers found that studies reported a positive relationship between severe articulation disorders and reading, a tendency for poor articulation to be associated with difficulties in oral reading, but no consistent evidence that children with articulatory defects were not proficient in silent reading. Powers cites a study by Van Demark and Mann (1965) who analyzed language samples of 50 children in grades three to six who were identified as being defective in articulation. This group was compared with a matched population of children who had no speech defects. Van Demark and Mann observed: "It appears that children with defective articulation are not inhibited in terms of the amount of verbal output, but they do perform less well in areas of grammatical completeness and complexity of responses." I present this study because of the possibility that children who are deficient in syntactic production may also be deficient in reading. An ongoing study at our Institute suggests that this is a likely correlate.

A series of studies by Quigley and associates at the Institute for Research on Exceptional Children, University of Illinois investigated the acquisition and development of a variety of syntactic structures in deaf school-age children, age range 10–19. The general findings are that deaf children are deficient in their knowledge and application of grammatical rules as judged by their written productions. In regard to the use of *wh* questions, Quigley, Wilbur, and Montanelli (1974) observe "Even the youngest hearing students consistently obtained higher scores than most of the deaf students." In a more recent study (1976) the same investigators found that deaf children made many errors in judging the grammaticality of sample sentences that contained infinitival or gerundive complements. Again they observed "Even the youngest hearing students consistently obtained higher scores than most of the deaf students."

Silverman (1971, p. 411) reports that "By age 16, an age at which most hearing children who attend school are in the third grade of high school, the majority of deaf children are at about the level of the eighth grade." On the basis of standardized test results, Silverman reports "Deaf children do not score equally well on all tests. The poorest scores are found in reading tests (paragraph and word meaning) and in arithmetic reasoning or problem solving."

Winitz (1969), after his survey of the literature and a review of five studies involving children, notes that "it seems reasonable to conclude that the reading skills of articulatory defective children are delayed." The delays are found for both oral and silent reading.

THE RELATIONSHIP BETWEEN READING
AND LANGUAGE DISORDERS

Now, for the other side of the coin, the side viewed by authorities in reading and learning disabilities.

Gibson and Levin (1975), in discussing the nature of dyslexia, include minimal brain dysfunctions as a possible cause. On the basis of Clements' (1966) criteria for MBD, Gibson and Levin say: "The abnormal functioning may result in various combinations of deficits in perception, conceptualization, language, memory, or control of attention which will interfere with the reading process" (p. 490). Gibson and Levin cite Bannatyne (1971), who described a group of dyslexic children who perform very poorly on such language-related tasks as the discriminations of sequences of sounds, the discrimination of speech sounds, and sound blending in their attempts at reading.

I will make an editorial note at this point that the discriminative difficulties cited by Gibson and Levin have very little to do with reading for meaning. I suggest that the children who showed such difficulties were also telling us that they were being taught by the wrong method. This is a point emphasized by Smith in his provocative book *Psycholinguistics and Reading* (1973).

Money (1966) observes: "it is rare that the child who is retarded in reading can be shown to be acoustically impaired. He may, however, have been slow in general language development, with unduly prolonged persistence of baby talk and other errors of articulation" (p. 33).

Rutter (1975), on the basis of his review of the literature and his own studies summarizes his observations about retarded readers:

> there is a well-established tendency for retarded readers to have impaired verbal skills . . . This finding is in keeping with the extensive evidence that

speech and language difficulties are strongly associated with reading retardation. A characteristic story is that the child has been delayed in learning to speak, then showed great difficulties learning to read. . . . Other developmental delays are also significantly associated with reading retardation. One of the most important concerns verbal coding and sequencing . . . poor readers have difficulty matching either auditory or visual dot-and-dash patterns. This may be because they do not find it so easy to produce verbal codes for the patterns . . . but have to remember the pattern as a picture. Indeed many have problems with any kind of task that involves putting things into an order of sequence. (pp. 275–76)

The difficulties children who are retarded in reading have with sequential events, with reproducing an order of events compared with their tendency to recall and reproduce patterns or totalities (*gestalten*) has an important implication for how some poor readers can be helped to become more proficient readers.

Sanders (1977) as well as Mattingly regard learning to read as a language processing task. Sanders cites Mattingly as follows. Reading is: "a deliberately acquired language-based skill, dependent upon the speaker-hearer's awareness of certain aspects of primary linguistic activity. By virtue of this linguistic awareness, written text initiates the synthetic linguistic process common to both reading and speech, enabling the reader to get the writer's message and so to recognize what has been written" (Mattingly 1972).

Further, Sanders says: "We might also hypothesize that, since the processes of speech perception and reading are dominated by the generative language abilities of the listener, subtle neural dysfunction or faulty early learning could conceivably account for many of the highly persistent problems in speech and in reading" (p. 225).

Vogel (1974) found that children with reading disabilities—*dyslexic children* by her definition—were deficient in syntactic ability as measured by oral-aural auditory productions. Her investigation compared a group of twenty children who were deficient in reading comprehension with twenty children who were "normal" readers. The children were in attendance in Evanston, Illinois, elementary schools.

Vogel posed three research questions:

1. Are dyslexic children significantly different from normal readers in the syntactic components of language?

2. Which measures best differentiate the dyslexic children with syntactic deficits from the normal readers?

3. What relationship is there in abilities in reading comprehension and syntactic, semantic, and decoding abilities in the two populations?

Vogel used a variety of standardized tests and some specially devised tests for her assessments. Her major hypothesis was confirmed. Dyslexic children with comprehension difficulties were found to be significantly deficient in oral syntax when compared with normal readers. *Syntax,* Vogel believes, *carries* the burden of a written message. Hence the relationship between poor comprehension and deficient syntax.

At this point I will cite from a few sources—mostly from psycholinguists—as to the relationship of an oral language system such as English to the written system. Essentially I will try to bring out that the two, however related, are not parallel systems. Further, that some apparently surface similarities between the two systems may be misleading and so cause some teachers and teacher-clinicians (or clinician-teachers) to use approaches that are ineffective for dyslexic children.

Derek Sanders, cited earlier, accepts Mattingly's thesis that learning to read requires knowledge of what language is about but is, nevertheless, a separate and different language skill from speaking. Sanders is emphatic that the syllable rather than the sound—the individual phoneme—is likely to be the minimum linguistic unit that a child can process. The perception of single phonemes, if they are perceived at all, can take place only after a syllable containing a given phoneme has first been perceived. If we accept this position then it follows, as Sanders argues, that "teaching approaches that place a heavy emphasis on the ability to blend sounds into wholes will fail with children experiencing speech and/or reading problems" (p. 226).

Mattingly (1972) speculates that inner speech may simply be "a kind of auditory imagery, dependent upon linguistic awareness of the sentence already synthesized, reassuring but by no means essential to synthesis (any more than actual utterance or subvocalization), and rather time-consuming" (p. 144).

Mattingly poses the question "Why should reading be, by comparison with listening, so perilous a process?" Speculatively, he also provides an answer:

> If our view of reading is correct, there is plenty of reason why things should often go wrong. First, we have suggested that reading depends ultimately on linguistic awareness and that the degree of this awareness varies considerably from person to person. While reading does not make as great a demand upon linguistic awareness as, say, solving British crossword puzzles, there must be a minimum level required, and perhaps not everyone possesses this minimum; not everyone is sufficiently aware of units in the phonological representation or can acquire this awareness by being taught. In the special case of alphabetic writing, it would seem that the price of greater efficiency in learning is a required degree of awareness higher than for logographic and syllabary systems, since as we have seen, phonological segments are less

obvious units than morphemes or syllables. . . . In a society where alphabetic writing is used, we should expect more reading successes, because the learning time is far shorter, but proportionately more failures, too, because of the greater demand upon linguistic awareness. (p. 144)

Mattingly also points out that usually the written text is less redundant than speech. (I assume that some primers of a previous decade and Gertrude Stein are exceptions. On the other hand the possibility that the redundancies of primers are not maintained may be a source of difficulty for children with a low level of linguistic awareness.) So, Mattingly observes that however sloppily a speaker may speak or a listener may listen, the redundant and sometimes outright reduplications of utterances serve to get messages through. Thus, according to Mattingly, "the listener who misinterprets a single speech cue will often be rescued by several others. Even a listener with some perceptual difficulty can muddle along. The reader's tolerance of noisy input is bound to be much lower than the listener's, and a person with difficulty in visual perception so mild as not to interfere with most other tasks may well have serious problems in reading" (p. 145).

To sum up Mattingly's position, reading is *not viewed* as an activity and function in the visual mode parallel to speech perception. There are disparities that cannot be explained in terms of the differences in modalities. To reiterate and cite Mattingly again: "They can be explained only if we regard reading as a deliberately acquired language-based skill, dependent upon the speaker-hearer's awareness of certain aspects of primary language activity."

Vellutino (1977), based on his own investigation and a review of the literature, agrees that a verbal-deficit hypothesis is the most plausible explanation for dyslexia. Vellutino conceptualizes reading disability as resulting from one or more aspects of linguistic functioning that include semantic, syntactic, and phonological components. He is aware that most dyslexic children may have no readily apparent language problems that can be detected in spoken discourse. However, Vellutino cautions that "We should not . . . discount the possibility that more subtle deficiencies in grammatical competence may impede the development of reading skill. This would certainly apply to the deciphering of connected text, and it might also cause problems in developing efficient word recognition" (p. 348). Vellutino concludes: "Thus children who lag behind their peers in general language ability—for example, those who have difficulty with grammatic transformational rules, who are unable to make morphophonemic generalizations, who cannot perceive the syntactic invariants and redundancies characteristic of all natural languages—can be expected to have difficulty in one or more aspects of reading. The little available research suggests that some poor readers may be of this description and that the study of basic syntactic deficiencies would be a worthwhile pursuit."

Although we are aware that many deaf children are poor in reading ability, some are not. Certainly deaf children do not learn to read by associating reading with speaking. I assume that they must learn to read through the visual modality alone. If we would somehow learn precisely how deaf children who are proficient readers accomplished this, we might well be able to help dyslexic children to raise their level of achievement.

Before presenting my position statement I will discuss briefly a study by P. Rozin, S. Poritsky, and R. Sotsky. In an article originally published in *Science* (1971): 1264–67, and reproduced in Smith (1972), the authors demonstrated that "American Children with Reading Problems can Easily Learn to Read English Represented by Chinese Characters." Eight children in the second semester of the second grade were selected as subjects. No child in the group had a reading level better than middle first grade. IQs ranged from 83 to 107 and ages from 7-5 years to 8-8 years. The children had particular difficulty in sound blending; many had difficulty in alphabetic symbol-sound correspondences.

The Chinese characters (ideographs) were presented and read directly in their English equivalents. Chinese was never spoken. After approximately four hours of instruction the children not only learned to read the individual Chinese characters but were able to arrange the ideographs into a sentence. There was no evidence that this reading achievement was related to any improvement in reading the English alphabet or in reading that employed the English alphabetic system.

Rozin and co-investigators are not certain about what aspects of their investigation produced the positive results and enabled young poor readers to associate Chinese characters with spoken English words. They speculate that the novelty of the task may have motivated the achievement. Another possible factor is in the nature of Chinese orthography which has no association or mapping into or onto a sound system. So, children who had difficulty in making phonemic-graphic correspondences had no such task to contend with in their reading of Chinese characters.

Following is my position for the teaching of children who have difficulty in learning to read. First and foremost, we need to do careful assessments of the language proficiencies of our severely disabled readers. It would not, of course, hurt to do so for all children who have a significant degree of difficulty in learning to read, or whose comprehension for reading is below what we have a right to expect from other indicators of their intellectual functioning. Then, based on what we discover, we teach the children what they need to know about language so that they can begin to appreciate more completely what complex sentences mean and to be good at guessing at contextual meanings rather than becoming proficient word callers.

Beyond this, here is my position statement for the most severe of our problem readers—the dyslexic children:

POSITION STATEMENT

1. Many problem readers become so because first attempts to teach them to read take place at the wrong time and/or by the wrong persons and/or by an inappropriate approach to their (the problem readers') perceptual-cognitive style and capabilities.

Dyslexics—the most severe problem readers—probably have atypical neurological mechanisms that make the integration of linguistic visual and auditory events virtually impossible at the time children are expected to learn to read. Dyslexics probably have the equivalent of a congenital *disconnection syndrome.* This deviant neurological state has the effect of making it impossible by ordinary teaching means to integrate cross-modal input. The implication of this assumed deviant neurological system is that reading may be established on a visual-to-visual basis (look and decide) rather than on a visual-auditory basis.

2. Dyslexics may (really, I think *should*) be taught to read with their right cerebral hemispheres. For most of us the right hemisphere deals with contents or events that do not require analysis for their perception and evaluation. The right hemisphere deals with wholes, with organized entities, with *gestalten.* In contrast, the left hemisphere deals with events that are analyzable. To be sure, what is a total or holistic event for one person may be a decodable event for another. Most persons listening to clicks may identify them only as clicks, or possibly as a pattern of clicks. A telegrapher may decode the clicks as symbolic events with linguistic-semantic equivalents. A musician may listen to music with the left hemisphere; nonmusicians are much more likely to listen to music with the right half of the brain.

I conjecture that our dyslexics cannot decode visual events that comprise the words of a linguistic system with their left hemispheres. There is evidence that they can do so with the right. To recall, Rozin, Poritsky, and Sotsky (1973) found that American children who are problem readers were easily able to read Chinese characters (symbols) and associate them with English words.

So, I suggest that by insisting on teaching dyslexics as if they had normal brain connections, we prevent them from learning to read up to the full potential of their right hemispheres. Admittedly, this may be below the potential that most of us have whose brains are normal rather than different. However, when we continue to teach dyslexic children by persisting in addressing the left hemisphere, rather than the right, we reduce the ultimate potential for reading for at least 10 percent of our population. The ultimate potential of dyslexics may in some instances be no higher than the fifth or sixth grade equivalent. But this provides a considerable base for much useful and even enjoyable reading. It is certainly better than having 5 to 10 percent of our population reading no better than on a first or second grade level and hating every moment of involvement with what should be an entertaining and informative ongoing relationship with written language.

REFERENCES

Arnold, G. E. (1960). Studies in Tachyphemia I. Present Concepts of Etiological Factors. *Logos* 3: 25–45.

Bannatyne, A. (1971). *Language, Reading, and Learning Disabilities.* Springfield, Ill.: Thomas.

Clements, S. D. (1960). Minimal Brain Dysfunction in Children, NINDB Monograph 3, Washington, D.C.: U.S. Department of Health, Education, and Welfare.

Critchley, M. (1964). *Developmental Dyslexia.* London: Heinemann.

Eisenson, J. (1977). In Eisenson, J., and Ogilvie, M. *Speech Correction in the Schools.* New York: Macmillan, pp. 376–79.

Gibson, E., and Levin, N. (1975). *The Psychology of Reading.* Cambridge, Mass.: MIT Press.

Goodman, K. S. (1973). In Smith, F., ed., *Psycholinguistics and Reading.* New York: Holt, Rinehart & Winston.

Mattingly, I. G. (1972). "Reading: The Linguistic Process and Linguistic Awareness." In Kavanagh, J. F., and Mattingly, I. G., eds., *Language by Eye and Ear.* Cambridge, Mass.: MIT Press, pp. 133–49.

Money, J., ed. (1966). *The Disabled Reader.* Baltimore: Johns Hopkins University Press.

Mykelbust, H. R. (1975). "Learning Disabilities and Minimal Brain Dysfunction in Children." In Eagles, E. L., ed., *Human Communication and Its Disorders.* New York: Raven Press, pp. 421–28.

Orton, S. (1937). *Reading, Writing, and Speech Problems in Children.* New York: Norton.

Powers, M. H. (1971). Functional disorders of articulation. In Travis, L. E., ed., *Handbook of Speech Pathology and Audiology.* New York: Appleton-Century-Crofts, pp. 865–67.

Quigley, S. P., Wilbur, R. B., and Montanelli, D. S. (1974). Question Functions in the Language of Deaf Children. *Journal of Speech and Hearing Research* 17: 699–713.

Quigley, S. P., Wilbur, R. B., and Montanelli, D. S. (1976). Complement Structures in the Language of Deaf Students. *Journal of Speech and Hearing Research* 19: 448–57.

Rozin, R., Poritsky, S., and Sotsky, R. (1971) American Children with Reading Problems can Easily Learn to Read English Represented by Chinese Characters. *Science* 121: 3977, 1264–67.

Rutter, M. (1975). *Helping Troubled Children.* London: Plenum.

Sanders, D. (1977). *Auditory Reception of Speech.* Englewood Cliffs, N.J.: Prentice-Hall.

Silverman, G. R. (1971). The Education of Deaf Children. In Travis, L. E., ed., *Handbook of Speech Pathology and Audiology.* New York: Appleton-Century-Crofts.

Smith, F., ed. (1973). *Psycholinguistics and Reading.* New York: Holt, Rinehart and Winston.

Vellutino, F. R. (1977). Alternative Conceptualization of dyslexia: Evidence in Support of a Verbal-Deficit Hypothesis. *Harvard Educational Review* 47 (3): 334–54.

Van Demark, A., and Mann, M. (1965). Oral Language Skills of Children with Defective Articulation. *Journal of Speech and Hearing Research* 8: 409–14.

Vogel, S. (1974). Syntactic Abilities in Normal and Dyslexic Children. *Journal of Learning Disabilities* 7: 103–10.

Weiss, D. (1964). *Cluttering.* Englewood Cliffs, N.J.: Prentice-Hall.

Winitz, H. (1969). *Articulatory Acquisition and Behavior.* New York: Appleton-Century-Crofts.

3

The Relationship between
Reading Gain and School Behavior
among Intermediate Grade Disabled Readers

Douglas Fuchs and Bruce Balow

Mᴀɴʏ ᴄʜɪʟᴅʀᴇɴ who have reading problems also manifest disruptive behavior in their classrooms, a relationship which has been substantiated by much clinical and empirical evidence (Stavrianos and Landsman 1969; Swift and Spivak 1969 and 1973; and Zimet, Rose, and Camp 1973). Despite these findings, most descriptions and evaluations of remedial reading interventions do not examine the possible positive influences that improvement in reading skill may have on disruptive school behavior. Instead, they focus strictly on reading achievement.

The majority of the few investigations found to explore seriously this relationship did not employ controls. Among this group of evaluative rather than experimental studies, Lane, Pollack, and Sher (1972) trained eight "severely disruptive" adolescents in the use of the Intersensory Reading Method and Contingency Management to tutor younger pupils. At the end of seven months, the tutors showed a mean gain of 1.7 years in reading, while a comparison of guidance counselors' and classroom teachers' pre- and post-treatment responses on a behavior rating scale indicated that all eight subjects reduced the frequency of their disruptive conduct. In contradistinction, the reading gain of 182 third graders enrolled in the Broward County Schools' (1971) remedial reading program was not associated with positive behavior change, as evidence by classroom teachers' ratings.

In the first of only two studies found to use a control group, Dietrich (1972) assessed the differential effectiveness of perceptual motor training and individualized remedial reading instruction on reading and behavior of 48 reading disabled pupils, 7 to 11 years old. These students were randomly assigned to the experimental treatments and to a placebo group. On post-treatment measures, subjects in the corrective reading intervention demonstrated the highest reading scores. (Neither gain scores nor the specific reading instruments employed were reported.) Both the reading and control groups were significantly superior to the perceptual

39

motor group in behavior adjustment as assessed by teachers. The reading group showed a more positive raw score change in behavior than subjects in the control group but this difference was not statistically significant.

In the second experimental investigation Cloward (1967) randomly selected 356 fourth and fifth grade deficient readers to be tutored by high school students either two or four times each week for 26 weeks. Another 157 students constituted a control group. Pre- and post-treatment reading tests indicated that experimentals who were tutored four times per week over a period of 5 months showed a mean gain of 6 months; experimentals participating in the reading program twice each week for the same amount of time gained five months; controls made 3½ months progress. Pre- and post-treatment data from a pupil questionnaire revealed that reading progress was not associated with positive changes in the subjects' attitudes toward school or in their vocational aspirations.

Thus the findings are contradictory as to whether progress in reading achievement is associated with a positive change in school behavior among reading disabled children. This conclusion becomes stronger with the realization that the methodologies of the pertinent studies, of which the above investigations are representative, produce multiple treatment effects, show infrequent use of systematic, direct observations of pupil behavior by impartial observers, and generally lack control groups. The validity of data generated by such studies calls into question any conclusions that might be made. Another short-coming of the aforementioned investigations is that none measured school behavior in the setting in which the reading treatment occurred and in the regular classroom despite the evidence that much behavior is situation-specific.

The primary objective of the present study was to investigate the amount and nature of behavioral change in a remedial reading setting concomitant with change in reading performance. Assuming that improvements in class conduct were observed together with reading gains in this setting, a second purpose was to assess the extent of transfer of such behavioral change from the remediation room to the regular classroom. Because research suggests that improvement in behavior is often specific to the situation in which academic improvement takes place, the present study explored the possibility of transferring to the regular classroom the expected improved behavior in the remedial setting. Toward this end, teachers and parents of a randomly selected subgroup of experimental subjects received periodic, formal feedback on the pupils' reading progress in the corrective reading program.

Moreover, on the presumption that formal feedback would facilitate such a transfer of positive behavioral change, a procedure was followed to determine whether feedback had differential effects among experimentals grouped on the basis of varying amounts of disruptive behavior demonstrated in the remedial setting.

METHOD

Population and Setting

The population consisted of intermediate grade pupils who attended three elementary schools in an urban, Midwestern school district. Two of the three schools shared the same large physical complex. The remedial reading program used as an experimental treatment in the investigation was located at this complex as well as in the third study school. Many of the students in these schools came from comparatively poor families and a large number of pupils were Black and American Indian. Each of the schools is partially supported by Elementary and Secondary Education Act Title I funds.

Sample

Subjects were 147 fourth, fifth, and sixth grade students who were chosen by reading specialists and regular classroom teachers to be the poorest readers in their grades. They were reading two years or more below grade level on a criterion referenced test and at least one year backward on a standardized reading instrument for third grade students. Following this screening, subjects were randomly assigned within school and grade levels to an experimental reading program or to their regular classrooms for reading instruction; 87 and 60 subjects comprised the experimental and control groups, respectively. At two of the study schools, boys were dramatically over-represented in the experimental group and under-represented in the control group. In the course of the investigation, 25 subjects from the initial sample moved away from the communities served by the study schools. Another 29 pupils participated in additional, and potentially confounding, special education programs and were eliminated from the final sample.

Procedure

Reading Assessment

Equivalent forms of the standardized reading test employed to screen pupils were used to measure reading gain. These forms were administered prior to and immediately following the experimental treatment which lasted five months.

Observation in the Remedial Setting

After participating in the corrective reading program for two weeks, each experimental subject was observed systematically for 30 minutes in the remedial setting. They were observed for an additional one-half hour during the last three weeks of the investigation. Preceding the first, formal observation phase, two observers, certified as elementary teachers, trained together in one of the remedial settings for more than six hours on three successive days. Acceptable inter-observer reliability was defined as .80 or better. This criterion had to be met for each of the four behavior categories comprising the observational system; if observers failed to establish this level of reliability for any of the categories, the data collected concurrently in the remaining categories were discarded. During three weeks of pre-treatment observations, inter-rater checks were conducted once each week totaling 46 minutes. Three individuals with elementary teaching experience conducted observations for two weeks in the remedial settings during the post-treatment phase of the study. Three inter-rater checks were made at one site and one inter-rater session was conducted at the second location totaling 203 minutes. The criterion for inter-observer reliability set during the pre-treatment phase was employed during post-treatment observations.

Differential Assessment of Feedback

On the basis of the pre-treatment frequency of their disruptive behavior in the remedial setting, experimentals were assigned to one of three classifications: high frequency of disruptive behavior (High), medium, or middle, frequency of disruptive behavior (Middle); and low frequency of disruptive behavior (Low). These categories were formed by asking the remedial reading specialists to distribute independently 100 points among the four behaviors comprising the observation system employed in the study. This exemplified how much each behavior disturbed them in the remedial setting. Weights for each category were created by dividing by 10 the points assigned by the reading teachers. The frequency with which an experimental subject demonstrated each of the four disturbing behaviors was multiplied by these weights. The four resulting transformed scores were added across the behavior categories to produce a single, total behavior score for each pupil who participated in the experimental reading intervention. A distribution of these pupils' total behavior scores was created and High, Middle, and Low acting-out groups were established at rather arbitrary cutting points in the distribution. In deciding on whom among the experimentals formal feedback should be delivered, the experimental students comprising the Low acting-out group were eliminated. It was assumed that most of these pupils also behaved appropriately in the regular classroom and feedback effects would be unfairly suppressed because of the scant improvement possible among this group of comparatively appropriate behavers. Thus, experimentals were randomly assigned to feedback and no feedback conditions within High and Middle acting-out levels.

Observation in the Regular Classroom

Experimentals and controls in two of the three study schools were observed in their regular classrooms on a post-treatment basis only. The same observation system employed in the remedial settings was used in the regular classrooms. Observation in the classrooms lasted four weeks. Three basic rules governed the gathering of all data in this setting. First, observers were required to record pupils' behavior only during two kinds of regular classroom activities—language arts (defined as creative writing, grammar, and spelling) and social studies (which included either reading from a text or discussing subject-related topics). Second, the format of the language arts or social studies instruction could be either a group lesson, over which the teacher presided, or students independently working at their assigned seats. Lastly, experimental and control subjects had to be participating together in these activities during the recording of the disruptive behavior. The two observers in the classrooms recorded disruptive behavior without knowledge of students' treatment affiliations. Reliability of the observations in this setting was established by four inter-rater checks in the classrooms of one school and two checks at the second school. A total of 197 minutes was spent in such checks at the two study schools. The lower limit set for acceptable inter-rater agreement was .80.

Experimental Treatments

The experimental reading intervention was the Basic Skill Centers Reading Program (BSC). A locally created program, BSC instruction teaches pupils to analyze printed words for recurring visual patterns of letters. A typical lesson has four components: a film strip with audio cassette instruction; a language master exercise; worksheets; and a writing supplement. A more complete description of this corrective reading program is provided elsewhere by Balow, Fuchs, and Kasbohm (1978). Regular classroom instruction involved use of the Ginn 720 basal readers, an approach which combines phonetic, whole word, and linguistic techniques. The second experimental treatment consisted of formal feedback both to regular classroom teachers and parents concerning students' reading progress in the BSC program. Feedback information was supplied on a feedback form. This form relayed the number of BSC lessons a student completed in one week and, also, communicated the BSC teacher's general evaluation of the student's effort for that week. Feedback forms were delivered to regular classroom teachers on a weekly basis, while every two weeks two forms were mailed to the students' parents. Once each month (or in every other mailing) a short story booklet accompanied the feedback forms to parents. These booklets represented the level of reading material the students were currently able to read fluently. In a cover letter parents were encouraged to ask their children to read to them from this booklet. This second experimental treatment lasted three months.

Dependent Measures

Four dependent measures were employed. Three of these were reading instruments and the fourth was an observational system used to assess disturbing behavior in regular and remedial classrooms. Of the three reading measures, one—the Gates MacGinitie Reading Test, Primary C— was used on a pre- and post-treatment basis. Only the comprehension section of the Gates C was employed. This subtest measures a student's capacity to read and understand whole sentences and paragraphs. The Words in Isolation subtest of the Silent Reading Diagnostic Tests and an Informal Reading Inventory (Fuchs and Balow 1974) were employed on a post-hoc basis. The Words in Isolation subtest is comprised of 54 items that require the student to select among five choices the correctly spelled word that describes a picture. The Informal Reading Inventory uses the American Book Company's basal series to assess instructional levels for oral sight reading and silent reading comprehension. A modification of Deno's (1973) observation and recording system was utilized to assess disruptive school behavior. This system comprises four behavioral categories: noise; out of place; physical contact; and off task. These behaviors are recorded with respect to the frequency with which they occur per unit of time. The basic interval of recording time was 20 seconds. Pupils were typically observed in triads and in alternate fashion. In an effort to insure high inter-observer reliability, two additional procedures were followed. First, irrespective of the number of times a given behavior was observed in one 20 second interval, only the first occurrence of that behavior was recorded. Thus, the maximum number of tallies per unit of recording time was four—one tally for each of the four disturbing behaviors. Second, if two behaviors occurred simultaneously, the observer recorded the behavior which claimed the higher ranking in the following arbitrary, hierarchical arrangement of categories: (1) noise; (2) out of place; (3) physical contact; and (4) off task.

Methods of Analysis

The numerous groups used to assess the various effects of the study's two treatment conditions were comprised of varying numbers of subjects. As a means by which one could demonstrate representativeness by a subgroup of a "parent" group, pre- and post-treatment functioning by each of the groups on the Gates-MacGinite Reading Test were obtained. Also, whenever it was appropriate, sub-groups were compared to "parent" groups with respect to how often they demonstrated disturbing behavior in remedial and regular classrooms. Because such comparisons so infrequently uncovered important differences, it should be assumed unless otherwise noted that the smaller groups were representative of the larger groups. T-tests and three-way analysis of variance with unweighted means were used to explore the effects of the BSC Reading Program; two-way analysis of variance was used to evaluate the effects of formal feedback upon the functioning of High and Middle acting-out experimental subgroups. Hypotheses were rejected at the .05 level of significance.

RESULTS

The Effect of the BSC Reading Program on Reading Achievement

Experimental subjects achieved significant and dramatic gains in the BSC Reading Program. At the end of 5 months of remediation, their mean gain was a little greater than 1 year and 2 months. Controls also made significant and dramatic improvements in their reading performance (see Table 3.1). While the experimentals' mean raw score gain was 2½ months greater than the controls', analysis of variance on both groups' pre- and post-treatment reading performances revealed that this difference was not statistically significant. Experimental subgroups also demonstrated greater mean raw scores than control subgroups on post-treatment administrations of the Words in Isolation subtest and the Informal Reading Inventory. Again, these raw score differences were not significant. An additional post-hoc analysis revealed that the experimental boys and girls failed to demonstrate significantly greater reading achievement than their same-sex counterparts in the control group.

The Effect of the BSC Reading Program on Behavior in the Remedial Reading Setting

Table 3.2 shows that a subgroup of 78 experimentals significantly and importantly reduced the frequency of disturbing behavior in the BSC settings, as measured by pre- and post-treatment observations. These dramatic reductions were obtained in all four behavioral categories comprising the observational system.

The Effects of the BSC Reading Program on Conduct in the Regular Classroom

Raw scores suggested that 47 experimentals manifested disturbing behavior less frequently in the regular classroom than 41 controls during

TABLE 3.1

Reading Achievement (Expressed in Grade Equivalents)
on the Gates-MacGinitie Reading Test, Primary C

Trt. Group	N	Pre-Test $\overline{X}$	Pre-Test SD	Post-Test $\overline{X}$	Post-Test SD	$\overline{X}$ Diff	T Value
E	87	2.51	.93	3.74	1.48	− 1.23	11.43*
C	60	2.34	.84	3.31	1.35	− .97	7.49*

$*P < .001.$

TABLE 3.2

**Change in the Frequency of Disturbing Behavior among 78 Experimentals
in the Basic Skills Reading Settings**

Behavior Category	Pre-trt. $\overline{X}$	SD	Post-trt. $\overline{X}$	SD	$\overline{X}$ Diff	T Value
Noise	4.54	5.28	2.87	2.99	− 1.67	2.64*
Out of Place	1.56	2.26	.58	1.30	− .98	3.94†
Physical Contact	1.68	3.13	.29	.76	− 1.38	3.99†
Off Task	14.23	6.19	8.00	5.05	− 6.23	7.53†

*$P < .01$.
†$P < .001$.

post-treatment observations. "Physical contact" was the only behavioral category for which the experimentals' frequency of disturbing behavior was not less than the controls'. However, an analysis of variance of these raw scores on "noise," "out of place," and "off-task" behavior revealed no statistically significant differences. A post-hoc comparison of the frequency of disturbing behavior among experimental and control boys showed that experimental boys manifested "off-task" behavior significantly less often than control boys, $t(56) = 2.03$, $p < .05$. A similar comparison between experimental and control girls indicated no significant differences between their respective amounts of disturbing behavior in this setting.

The Effects of Formal Feedback

The mean raw score gains of 29 students (E_1) randomly selected from those participating in the BSC Reading program, and on whom regular formal feedback was delivered to parents and teachers, while greater than, was not significantly different from the reading achievement among 24 experimentals (C_1) whose parents and teachers did not receive formal feedback. Similarly, E_1 subjects did not demonstrate greater, positive behavioral change in the BSC settings in relation to the C_1 subgroup. (It should be noted that E_1 and C_1 subgroups demonstrated significantly more frequent disturbing behavior in the BSC than the "parent" group of 78 experimental subjects.) Two-way analysis of variance also revealed that there were not significant differences in reading achievement or conduct in the BSC among E_1 and C_1 subgroups when compared within High and Middle acting-out strata. However, in the regular classrooms the E_1 subgroup manifested significantly less noise than the C_1 subgroup, $F(1,25) = 9.28$, $p < .01$. There were no other important between-group differences, nor were there significant differences between subjects organized by High and Middle acting-out levels, regarding behavior in the regular classrooms.

DISCUSSION

Because experimentals and controls both demonstrated important reading gains, it is difficult to attribute the experimentals' improvement to the BSC Reading Program. This finding runs contrary to the literature which rather consistently shows that pupils in corrective reading programs make greater progress than those receiving reading instruction in regular classrooms.

The control group's dramatic gains encourage one to explore explanations for both groups' progress, since before the experimentation all of the sampled children were seriously delayed in reading skills. One possible explanation is that the experimental treatment was responsible for the experimental group gains and that the control group was not a control but a "contrast" group, receiving its own special treatment. Across the three sampled schools numerous special reading programs were offered and large numbers of children with poor academic skills were removed from the classroom for remedial work. Therefore, the availability of remedial programs may account not only for remedial students' gains, but also influence classroom students' rate of progress by reducing competition for available instructional time. In a recent review of research on the relationship between class size and achievement (Porwell, cited in Fiske 1978) it is evident that small class size positively affects achievement among disadvantaged children in lower grades.

As shown, the experimentals' reading gain was associated with dramatic positive behavior change in the remedial setting, suggesting anew that academic achievement may be an important precursor to positive change in school conduct among chronically underachieving pupils. Experimentals and controls, however, demonstrated no significant differences in frequency of disturbing behavior in the regular classrooms, with the exception that experimental boys manifested significantly less "off task" behavior than control boys. This finding suggests there was little carry-over in positive behavior change from the remedial setting to the regular classrooms. However, it is important to point out that because (a) both experimentals and controls achieved significant and dramatic rates of improvement in reading and (b) a baseline of neither groups' conduct in the regular classroom could be obtained, it is possible that experimental subjects *did* transfer their improved behavior in the BSC to their regular classrooms. That the data fail to reflect this may be because the controls' behavior in the regular classrooms *also* improved as they experienced notable success in reading.

Presuming the absence of positive behavior change among experimentals and controls in the regular classroom, we may conclude that formal feedback generally did not artificially induce a transfer of positive behavior change between school settings. (Assuming that observed, improved behavior in the remedial setting carried over—undetected—to the regular classrooms, formal feedback failed to make that behavior any more appropriate than it already was.) While it is possible that more extensive feedback (substantively changed and/or delivered more frequently) may still prove to be an effective general technique to promote positive behavior change, these findings suggest that perhaps a more powerful strategy needs to be employed to relocate positive changes in conduct. One such method may be to move the remediation activity itself into the regular classroom. While there may be numerous logistical problems associated with this strategy, it may facilitate greater continuity between the remedial room and regular classrooms with respect to: kinds of educational tasks required of the pupils; assessment of the current level of functioning in skill areas; and provision of adequate emotional support.

Contrary to initial expectations, formal feedback did not promote greater reading gains or more positive improvement in school behavior in Middle acting-out than High acting-out pupils. The data suggest that highly disruptive students and relatively more appropriately behaving students are equally responsive to formal feedback, as defined in the present investigation.

REFERENCES

Balow, B., Fuchs, D., and Kasbohm, M. (1978). Teaching Non-readers to Read: An Evaluation of the Effectiveness of the Basic Skill Centers Reading Program. *Journal of Learning Disabilities* 11(6): 351–54.

Broward County School Board (1971). *Evaluation of the Reading Center's Remedial Program for the 1970–71 School Year.* Fort Lauderdale, Fla. ERIC Document Reproduction Service No. ED 059 845.

Cloward, R. D. (1967). Studies in Tutoring. *Journal of Experimental Education* 36(1): 14–25.

Deno, S. (1973). "A Manual for Observing, Recording, and Charting Discrepancies in School Behavior." Manuscript, University of Minnesota.

Dietrich, C. (1972). *Changes in Reading Adjustment, Perceptual Motor Ability, and Behavior Adjustment as a Function of Perceptual Motor Training and Individualized Remedial Reading Instruction.* Stevens Point, Wisc.: Wisconsin University. ERIC Document Reproduction Service No. ED 063 575.

Fiske, E. B. (1978). Small Classes Do Not Always Lead to Better Education, a Study Finds. *New York Times,* July 30, pp. 1, 16.

Fuchs, D., and Balow, B. (1974). "Formulating an Informal Reading Inventory." Manuscript. Available from Douglas Fuchs, Special Education Preschool Programs. Minneapolis Public Schools, 3017 East 31st Street, Minneapolis, Minn. 55406.

Lane, P. R., Pollack, C., and Sher, N. (1972). Remotivation of Disruptive Adolescents. *Journal of Reading* 15(5): 351–54.

Stavrianos, B. K., and Landsman, S. C. (1969). Personality Patterns of Deficient Readers with Perceptual-Motor Problems. *Psychology in the Schools* 6(2): 109–23.

Swift, M. S., and Spivak, G. (1969). Clarifying the Relationship between Academic Success and Overt Classroom Behavior. *Exceptional Children* 36(2): 99–104.

——— (1973). Academic Success and Classroom Behavior in Secondary Schools. *Exceptional Children* 39(5): 392–99.

Zimet, S. G., Rose, C., and Camp, B. W. (1973). Relationship between Reading Achievement and Rosenzweig-Picture Frustration Study in Early Grades. *Psychology in the Schools* 10(4): 433–36.

4

Models for the Dissemination of a Program for the Prevention of Reading Disability

The New York-Edgemont-Gastonia-Columbus Connection

Archie A. Silver, Rosa A. Hagin,
Selma Thackery, Ruth Angel, Attie Belle Liles,
Norma Barnaby, Marty Williams

PROSPECTUS (ARCHIE A. SILVER)

THIS PAPER WILL DESCRIBE models for the replication and dissemination of a program for the prevention of reading disability. The basic program, an Interdisciplinary Model for the Prevention of Learning Disability, was developed and validated by the Learning Disorders Unit at New York University Medical School, as a Child Service Demonstration Center, funded by the Bureau of Education for the Handicapped of the U.S. Office of Education. It will be outlined by Dr. Rosa Hagin.

Models for dissemination must not only adhere to rigid statistical constraints, but also must be flexible enough to fit the varying needs, the overall facilities and levels of training found in participating schools, all without sacrifice to the integrity and validity of the basic program. This paper will describe three general models for such dissemination.

The first, which we call the Seely Place model, will be described by Selma Thackery. This is essentially a replication of the basic Search and Teach program. In this replication, the staff of the participating school is first trained by our Unit, our staff travels to the school for examinations *in situ,* case conferences are held in the school, intervention plans are drawn, responsibilities assigned, and ongoing supervision and consultation is provided by our Unit. This model has been successfully used in large complex school districts located within one hour travel time of our medical center. The goal is the eventual independence of the participating school from the Learning Disorders Unit. As our philosophy and methods are transmitted to the school, their key people can take over our role.

The second model, the Gastonia model, will be described by Ruth Angel and Attie Belle Liles. Because of the distances involved and the

number of people to be trained, workshops at the medical center are pro-
hibitive. The solution of course, is to have the medical center go to Gastonia, an arrangement made possible through the Gaston County Division
of Special Education.

The third model to be described is the Columbus model (described
by Norma Barnaby). This essentially is the basic Search and Teach program, transplanted to another medical school. In this model, key people
from the participating school come to our medical center for intensive
one to three day training. They then return to their own school to apply
their new knowledge, using us as *ad hoc* consultants. This model trans-
plants a part of us into new soil, where it in turn may function as a center
for training and dissemination.

Finally, in this paper, Marty Williams will review the programs discussed in terms of practical lessons to be learned.

THE NEW YORK CONNECTION (ROSA A. HAGIN)

The Learning Disorders Unit at New York University–Bellevue Medical
Center operates school based projects to locate five-year-old children
whom we predict will fail in reading, to diagnose their needs, and to inter-
vene before they have failed. Our model intervention projects are located
in inner city schools, with varied ethnic composition.

There are three main elements to the program. Scanning, the identification of children vulnerable to learning failure, is the first. The second
is diagnosis, the intensive examination of the children scanning identifies
as vulnerable to failure. The third program element is intervention, to
prevent failure.

The core of our scanning is a test called Search. Our intervention
program is a series of learning activities called Teach, designed to mesh
with educational needs as revealed by Search. Search predicts vulnerability, identifies children who need intensive examination, and provides information for setting intervention priorities and for building a teaching
plan. Diagnosis helps us to understand the reasons for vulnerability and
to make appropriate long-range intervention plans. The tasks of Teach
are organized sequentially in clusters to teach accuracy of perception and
inter-model skills, basic to learning. Scanning, diagnosis, and intervention, all take place in resource rooms in the schools. We are committed to
a mainstream philosophy, to maintain the child within the regular classroom, and to provide within the school clinical and educational services
to the child and his family.

The history of our program goes back to 1969. At that time, we studied intensively all the children in the first grade of 1969–70 and 1970–71 in a public school in Kips Bay, Manhattan. One hundred sixty-eight children had individual neurological, psychiatric, psychological, and educational study. These examinations produced baseline data about the range of normal development of five- and six-year-olds and was helpful in defining those measures that were the strongest and most reliable measures of vulnerability to reading failure. It is these measures which went into Search, a cost-effective scanning battery which could be given to large numbers of children, quickly, reliably, to yield valid results.

Search emerged a ten-component test, consisting of three visual components (visual discrimination, visual recall, and visual motor), two auditory (discrimination and auditory sequencing), two inter-model tasks (one called Initials which is based on the names of the children in the school, and the ability to associate the sound and symbol for the initial consonant of these names, and an articulation test), three body-image tests (directionality, pencil grip, and a test of finger schema). The final scanning battery, then, includes the same areas that were tapped in the original intensive examination. It yields a score as a measure of vulnerability and a profile of assets and deficits to guide intervention plans. We encourage schools to use local norms and assist them in computing local norms. It makes sense to us that children should be compared with their peers from the same school, rather than with some kind of national average.

Data on the predictive efficiency (false negatives and false positives) as well as the statistical characteristics of the test may be found in the test manual (Silver and Hagin 1976) and in our publications (Silver, Hagin, and Beecher 1978). Based on roughly 1200 observations, we found the percentage of false negatives to range from zero to 15 percent with the mean of 10 percent; and on data from 365 children who were found vulnerable to learning failure, but who did not receive intervention, a range of 0 percent to 5 percent false positives were found at the end of second grade.

Our intervention is school based, rather than a clinical model. Intervention activities are contained in Teach, the prescriptive approach designed to build the neurological and psychological skills we believe basic for progress in reading, writing, and spelling. These are directed activities which seek to build accuracy of perception within single modality at a time in so far as possible.

The impact of these intervention programs were studied on the various groups of children with whom we have worked.

1. Through analysis of variance, a group of 87 intervention children was compared with 39 control children from the groups in which

there was not enough teaching time available. Significant ratios favoring the intervention group were found in the areas of perception, of oral reading, of word attack on the Wide Range Achievement Test, of word identification on the Woodcock, of word analysis on the Woodcock.

2. Using a norm-referenced model, one looks at the differences between the expected and the actual scores for the intervention group, and then, using the t test, tests for the probability by which such changes would occur by chance. During the first year non-significant changes occur, probably because the emphasis in our intervention is on single modalities of perception. In the second grade, however, we began to see the impact with significant t test scores ($p < .005$). At the end of the third grade, a year after the child has completed the program, we still find the same probability level of .005. The general picture is that accelerated gain in reading occurs as a result of the program.

During the three years of the Child Service Demonstration Center funding, the Interdisciplinary Model for the Prevention of Learning Disabilities has been replicated in 22 school districts involving 79 schools. The staff of the Learning Disorders Unit has guided these replications through (1) demonstration of the model in the core projects located in public schools of Community School District II, Manhattan, (2) inservice training both at New York University Medical Center and at the replication sites, (3) monitoring of ongoing projects, (4) provision of diagnostic services where local services were not available, (5) sharing of scanning, diagnostic, and intervention procedures with replicating schools, (6) provision of products such as Search and Teach, slides, videotapes, and reprints of papers, (7) ongoing consultation on scanning, diagnosis, intervention, and program planning. The reports which follow show how the basic preventive model was adapted to the needs and resources of three replication sites.

THE EDGEMONT CONNECTION (SELMA THACKERY)

Seely Place is a relatively small school with only 450 children K–6. Our class size is good, we have a very low or generally low pupil to teacher ratio, always under 30, usually in the 20s. We are in a New York City suburb about 20 miles north of the city. We have a very mixed but generally affluent population. Our teachers are uniformly well trained, generally very dedicated, and well supplied so we are in a good position to try new things and to work with our youngsters intensively. We have good support staff. In addition to myself as psychologist four days a week, we have two learning skills language arts coordinators, one for grades K–3 and the other for 4–6. We have a full-time nurse teacher, a part-time speech pathologist, a part-time math consultant, and parent volunteers. Our board of education is very sophisticated and for many years has been supportive in our efforts to help children with learning problems.

I was very impressed when I came to Seely Place in 1973, that my predecessor, Mrs. Muriel Forest, had already attempted a program of early identification of children with potential learning problems. Initially, Mrs. Forest met with many problems. First, the lack of consistent norms at a young enough age, the lack of systematic remedial approaches after identification, the lack of parent understanding and involvement, and the lengthy time required for full screening of all children. There was also at that time in our area a lack of further diagnostic resources and even when available, suggestions were made that were not relevant regarding remediation that could take place in a public school.

With the introduction of the Search and Teach program, these problems were minimized. In the fall of 1975, I saw each parent individually to get a birth and developmental history, to explain the program further, and to get a written release from the parents for further testing by myself and later by Dr. Silver. In this way also the teachers, by looking at the Search scores, were alerted early to special needs and they began to be supportive with the children even before further testing or intervention was undertaken. I then examined with the Wechsler scale and other testing as indicated, each child which Search identified as vulnerable. Then, early in the fall, Dr. Silver and one of his residents came and they examined each child individually with neurological and psychiatric evaluations. The biggest and most exciting part came next. Those were the case conferences in which our building team, consisting of the nurse, psychologist, the skills teachers, the principal, sat down with the classroom teachers, and met with the NYU team to discuss the findings of all the combined studies, and to plan future steps including remediation, and/or further evaluation. Following that I had parent conferences again. At this time I particularly invited both parents, and almost always both parents came with great interest, because they knew we had something to communicate. We gave them the results and the recommendations in full. It was then my job to do the follow-up, to coordinate the ongoing activities of the teachers, the language arts specialist, the outside resources and to maintain contact with the NYU team.

At the end of the year, we used the Wide Range Achievement Test as well as our other achievement tests and teacher observations, which helped to make careful placement for second grade. Some children re-

quired continuing intervention. The follow-up neurological that was required in some cases was also done by Dr. Silver, who came to our school
again.

Some of the inherent problems that I found on starting a new program were the need for me to see so many first grade children and parents
early in the school year, the rescheduling of staff to provide for intervention, and meetings with parents to explain the program. The inherent advantages that I found specifically, were that we now had norms suited to
our population, outside specialists to come to our school and help with diagnosis: they shared information and indeed gained information at our
conferences. They became familiar with the school program so that realistic recommendations could be made and implemented. There was more
early parent and teacher awareness of the needs and teaching to those
needs before multiple frustrations could ensue.

At the second parent conference, following the professional case
conference, the findings are described to the parents, and we then plan
subsequent steps together. We discuss with them the things they could do
that would be helpful and indeed at times some of the things to avoid that
may exacerbate the problem. We try to deflect some of the parents' anxiety from the classroom teacher and from the parent-child relationship.
Often the teachers feel when they identify children with problems, the
parents consider them as causative agents in the problem. Having a scanning instrument define the issue, then having the psychologist talk with
the parent, makes the parent-teacher relationship a more cooperative and
a more positive one. At the end of the year I would write up a brief report
in the form of a letter to the parents giving a summary of our findings, the
progress, and some of the things that had happened during the year.

In summary, our experience has shown that there are a variety of
problems that run the gamut of serious neurological problems to those
that are relatively minor or not neurological problems at all. We feel that
Search can be replicated in other schools with modifications necessary to
fit the specific situation. We find that a working relationship with the
teaching hospital is mutually advantageous. Some quick observations:
first, that the model is flexible; it varies each year, according to the children we have and the personnel involved, and our experiences from previous years. One change that we are initiating this year, for instance, is to
administer Search earlier in the kindergarten year, midway, rather than
waiting until the end. The second observation is that the staff reacted fa-
vorably to the team approach and they felt that they were receiving support with those youngsters most difficult to teach and support with their
parents. Third, the level of diagnosis from the combined approach was
high. In follow-up to specialists out of the program, its findings tended to

be verified. Lastly, via this program, major criticism of early identification projects we feel is overcome, namely that the diagnostic findings are usually not translated into educational processes that can help remediation and lead to greater academic success.

THE GASTONIA CONNECTION (RUTH ANGEL)

The Gaston County School System has 35,000 students. It is the fifth largest school system in the state of North Carolina. Textiles is the major industry. Great efforts have been made in the last 10 or 15 years to diversify the industry. However, for many of the students we have in our system, neither they nor their parents aspire to high levels of education. We have the third highest drop-out rate for any school system in the state of North Carolina.

We think, however, we have a wonderful school system, good leadership from the school board, our superintendent and his associates, and most parents who are very interested in what happens to their children in school.

It was not until 1969 that our State Board of Education recognized learning disability as a category. The major funding for our school programs in North Carolina comes from state sources via a state tax base. This money is used to buy what our State Board of Education and our state legislature would view as a minimum county program. The local unit is to make up the difference in regards to excellence.

In 1969, when the state recognized the category "learning disability," the state was giving us 64 teachers of exceptional children to be used in all categories of exceptional children. It was not until three years ago that our state provided the first cent to employ a school psychologist in a public school in North Carolina. To this day, we have two and three-fifth positions for school psychologists, for our system of 35,000 students. However, 15 of our staff members, who already had Masters level certification in reading and in child guidance, made a commitment to go through a training program whereby they could become certified as a level one school psychologist.

Then suddenly things began to happen. The active group in our state was the Association for Retarded Citizens. They brought a suit against our State Board of Education and State Department of Public Instruction. But what they asked for their children, they asked for all exceptional children, and we started seeing rapid changes. In the fall of 1973, certification requirements for all our teachers was mandated by the fall of 1977. About this time also, we had an active parent group in our county. For many of those who had children who were not doing well in reading, parents turned elsewhere for help, to the private sources. This group of parents became vocal, and they made dyslexia and specific learning disabilities a household word in Gaston County and other areas in the Piedmont section of North Carolina.

At that point—1972, '73, '74—we had only one or two colleges and universities in our state that offered any course work in learning disabilities. But suddenly all these children who were having problems with reading, who were having failing experiences in schools, these were Ruth Angel's kids, and there were thousands of failing children. As an initial effort to do something about them, we set up our own training programs in our county to help meet the certification deadlines. We wrote a Federal Title III project (which has since become Title IV-C) in such a manner that it would stay completely intact. Our major effort was directed towards staff development. This is where the Gastonia connection makes the New York connection. The scope of our project was far reaching. From K–12 we were going to develop a comprehensive program of services for learning disabled children. We think what we are doing here with Search and Teach has made a great difference to our system. It has, in fact, changed the structure of our kindergarten program.

We are now scanning with Search and we are picking up with remediation activities. We think we are making a difference. The data is being collected by our staff statistician bearing this out. We also are doing some longitudinal studies. Maybe the problems our system has are unique, but I can't feel that they really are, considering the rapid changes we have had in the field of exceptional children in the last four or five years.

THE GASTONIA CONNECTION II (ATTIE BELLE LILES)

When we developed our Title IV-C project in providing comprehensive services to LD children K–12 grades, we were very concerned about the kindergarten children. At this time we had no instrument to which we could turn with identifying kindergarten children. We called New York and were referred to Dr. Hagin and Dr. Silver. Dr. Hagin, Dr. Silver, and Mrs. Kreeger (Liaison Coordinator, Learning Disorders Unit, New York-Belleview Medical Center) met with us. They detailed their work with Search and Teach in some of the schools in New York. Then Mrs. Kreeger took us out to P.S. 116, where we saw the operation of Search and Teach. The more we heard about their project, the more we wanted to try to do the best we could to bring that project to Gaston County. We were lucky that we had our assistant superintendent of special services with us, because he was very much in favor of it, too. We had a commitment; one of our objectives of our Title IV-C was early identification and intervention, and here it was for us. Because we could not take all our teachers to New York City, we planned to have Dr. Hagin and Mrs. Kreeger come to Gaston County and train our teachers, so that we could implement Search and Teach. At that time, we were just thinking about our LD teachers, to get our LD teachers trained to scan the kindergarten children and then to provide intervention activities with those children who would be entering the first grade. But our plan changed as we went along and we saw the need of involving other people in our system. The first time Dr. Hagin and Mrs. Kreeger came to Gaston County, we worked with them for 3 days. We wanted to give an overview of Search and Teach, so we invited the principals to bring one of their key kindergarten and first grade teachers to hear their presentation.

Then the NYU team began training our LD teachers in the administration of Search, showing them how to test a kindergarten child, and how to plot the "VABS" (scores in each component of Search which marked the lowest one-third of the distribution of scores). At that time, we only had pilot kindergarten programs. We did not have all children entering kindergarten at that time. At our pilot school, Woodhill, we did have a kindergarten class, and our LD teachers used the kindergarten there to learn how to administer Search.

Then the first grade teachers would follow through with Teach activities. Initially, however, the LD teachers did pick up those children whose scores were very low, and worked with them. When they had many children identified as needing special help, they did get some parent volunteers, but not until those parent volunteers were trained to use the Teach activities. At that time the NYU material had not yet been published, and Mrs. Kreeger taught the teachers how to make, themselves, all the activities that they would need in implementing the Teach component of the program.

One objective of our Title IV-C project was to see that Search and Teach was implemented in at least 20 of our schools. We have 37 elementary schools. In the spring of 1975 when we screened our kindergarten children, 26 of those schools wanted to participate. Two years ago we did another survey, because then we had full implementation of the kindergarten program. We wanted to see which principals signed a commitment. During the three year period of our Title IV-C project, Dr. Hagin and Mrs. Kreeger came to us five times, in the spring of 1975, in the fall and spring of our school year 1975–76, and in the fall and spring of our school year 1976–77.

As we had full implementation of the kindergarten program in Gaston County, we realized that there was no way that LD teachers themselves could screen all the kindergarten children, and we saw the need of involving kindergarten and first grade teachers in scanning. Some of our staff development, therefore, was geared toward the kindergarten and first grade teachers. The kindergarten teachers were brought in, in the spring of 1977. We videotaped Dr. Hagin administering Search to one child of the kindergarten at Woodhill School, then Mrs. Kreeger working with the child on the Teach activities. As it turned out, there were two low areas in Search that were so visible in this child that it really amazed the kindergarten teacher.

Our governor has implemented what we call Governor Hunt's Primary Reading Program. This program, over a period of three years, will put an aide in each first, second, and third grade class in North Carolina. So we have 83 teachers and 83 aides who would be trained the summer of 1978 for the Primary Reading Program. We asked one of our LD teachers to set up a training session so that everybody who went to the Institute had a chance to hear and see how Search and Teach would be implemented in North Carolina. Then, this fall, we had some work days before school started, so we brought all of our first grade teachers together. We used the videotape that we had made, showing how Search is administered and how the Teach activities are designed to help a child who is having difficulty. We showed the videotape and discussed this with the first grade teachers, and then I had asked about 6 of our LD teachers to work with the first grade teachers so we could break down into smaller groups to help them, because the first grade teachers at that time would be the ones who would be implementing the Teach component.

After school started in the fall of 1978, the kindergarten teachers called to say they would like to scan their children in the fall of the school year so that they might begin helping their children. The NYU Learning Disorders Unit agreed with this shift, to use Search and Teach in kindergarten and that they would work out the cut-off scores for these children. We have been delighted with the success that we have had with the teachers.

Let me close by saying that in Gaston County, we believe that you just don't train one group of people, we believe that you must work with your school board, superintendent, assistant superintendent, classroom teachers for K–1, resource teachers, LD teachers, reading teachers, psychologists, speech therapists. It seemed that the more we involved, the more our system became excited, and as our workshops were planned, we also invited state department personnel. We had the director of the State Learning Disabilities Unit and also one of his consultants. He was so impressed he said that we would not have to label these children at this early age to provide services for them. We found out that children who are found to be vulnerable can be served by the LD teacher if it is severe, by classroom teachers, by aides, and by parent volunteers who are trained by someone. One of our LD teachers even had a sixth grade girl do some peer tutoring with one child who was not very severe. Educators throughout the state of North Carolina have heard the success we have had with Search and Teach and many have visited our system to see the program in operation. Gaston County was invited to present the Search and Teach program to special education program supervisors at the North Carolina State Conference on Exceptional Children. We feel that the main reason we have been successful in implementing Search and Teach is because we did involve personnel at all levels in staff development. There must be a commitment at each of these levels, and I really think that we owe Dr. Hagin, Mrs. Kreeger, and Dr. Silver for the leadership and the support that they have given us, and we know that when we meet a problem right now, all we have to do is contact them.

THE COLUMBUS CONNECTION (NORMA BARNABY)

Our project was a great deal different from the projects that have been reported. First of all, ours has been geared primarily for research, and secondly, it emanated from a medical center, from child psychiatry. There is good reason for medical schools to work in schools. First, some surveys have shown that the instance of psychiatric disturbance among school children range from 10 percent to 30 percent. One author reported that the most significant predictors of serious adult psychiatric disturbance is the necessity of repeating one or more grades in school.

In an effort to interrupt such a psychiatric-educational cycle of pathology, the researchers in Columbus, Ohio, turned to the work done in New York by Drs. Silver and Hagin. Their results warranted a trial application of their intervention in a public school setting. Our population was, perhaps, a little different from that of New York. We have basically one major ethnic group, the black population. We are also in a moderate size city. We are single home dwellers, rather than apartment dwellers. But nonetheless we found there was a similarity between learning disabilities in our city and in New York. We really felt that what we were doing was replicating the New York study in Columbus, Ohio.

With the cooperation of Drs. Silver and Hagin, and the staff in New York, we consulted with them for a day and we came back with copies of Search and their intensive language battery. Our study sought to answer the following questions:

1. Will direct stimulation of the deficient perceptual areas improve functioning in those areas?

2. Will it result in better academic achievement, specifically reading?

3. Will improved perception and better academic functioning prevent emotional decompensation?

4. Will specific perceptual stimulation show advantage over another kind of tutoring?

This study was designed as a pre-test, post-test design with comparison of improvement among (1) the specific intervention group which received a specific perceptual stimulation, (2) the Hawthorne group which received regular academic tutoring, and (3) the maturation control group which had no intervention contact of any type other than regular classroom instructions.

The sample consisted of all the children in nine first grade classes at three schools, 193 in two inner city schools and 126 in middle class neighborhood schools. The ages ranged from 65 to 99 months with a mean of approximately 77 months. We received parental consent. Four examiners, two psychologists, myself and John McManus, and two certified teachers screened the children on the Search battery. The teachers also completed the Connors teachers behavior check list, the Davis hyperkinetic rating scale, and the Quay-Patterson behavior problem check list one month after school had begun, in September, as soon as youngsters started first grade. The children passing less than five of the ten tests in the Search battery were considered vulnerable. Excluding the first grade repeaters, Search identified 34 vulnerable children in the middle class school, 52 in the inner-city school. An additional 8 children in the middle class sample with borderline Search scores appeared to be vulnerable to educational problems. We did more tests with them and decided it was worthwhile to include those children in the study. Of the 94 high risk children, 8 were lost due to moving out of the school district, thus leaving 86 for the experimental assignment. These 86 children were then given a more intensive battery of tests, including the LDU intensive perceptual battery, the language battery, a neuropsychiatric examination by a child psychiatrist, the Wechsler intelligence scale for children, and Wide Range achievement tests. The high risk children were then matched for sex, IQ, school, kind, and severity of perceptual disability, and where possible, absence or presence of specific neurological signs, and were assigned to one of three groups.

The intervention group (n = 23), received channel specific perceptual stimulation according to the Teach manual. The second group, the contact control group (n = 23) received regular academic tutoring using the Ginn series. The third group was a no-contact control group (n = 40). These youngsters remained in the classroom receiving no additional help except when parents or classroom teachers offered help. The teacher did not know that the no-contact control group had been identified as vulnerable or had been identified as high risk. If the teacher wanted to give additional help, we did not interfere. The children in group one and two were assigned in equal numbers to two tutors so that each child was tutored twice weekly for thirty minutes by the same tutor as his match mate. We tried as much as possible not to favor the time of day, day of the week, or the hour all the time. The same person tutored the matched children who were in groups one and two. Tutoring was begun November 1, 1973. We concluded the experiment in mid-May of 1974, at which time we did post-testing. Scores at pre-test and post-test on Search, the Wide Range and three behavior rating scales were obtained.

At pre-testing, there were no significant differences among the three vulnerable groups. At the end of first grade, all the vulnerable groups showed improvement from pre- to post-test. Among the three vulnerable groups, however, the only difference approaching statistical significance was between the intervention group and the control groups, suggesting that intervention using specific channel intervention did make a difference. Further, the intervention group was the only group showing change on the direction of more acceptable behavior, though this was not statistically significant.

Although the data collected and analyzed showed trends in the direction of "yes" answers to the questions posed, conclusions were postponed for the follow-up study.

The entire sample of the original study was reassessed a year after post-test, at the end of second grade. The assessment instruments were the same as those used in the original study, the Wide Range, the Wechsler Intelligence Scale, and the behavior rating scales. We also used the LDU intensive battery on the children who were left of the original study.

The intervention group showed significant improvement at follow-up on every test except the Wide Range arithmetic, while neither control group showed any improvement on achievement, behavior, or intelligence test. The control even showed significant deterioration on a few tests. Overall from pre-test to follow-up, the two control groups were not significantly different from each other on any measure. The intervention group showed improvement from pre-test to follow-up significantly greater than each control group on 12 of 16 tests, including reading, spelling, and all three behavior scales, and even on the intelligence test. The questions referred to at the beginning of the study were all answered "yes."

The data presented demonstrates that for children identified as vulnerable to reading disabilities, spontaneous improvement in growth and maturation is not accompanied by equally spontaneous improvement in behavior, reading achievement, or IQ scores. On the contrary, without specific intervention, there tends to be deterioration in all three of these areas. That channel specific perceptual remediation outline in Teach has been most effective, has been demonstrated in the main study as well as follow-up. We have become convinced by the data that this type of intervention is a powerful tool in prevention of behavior and learning problems.

RECIDIVE (MARTY WILLIAMS)

To hear a collection of individuals who have been involved in planned changes in various settings has been of great interest. I am struck with the complexities of the undertakings that these people have been engaged in, and struck with the success and wisdom that they have applied to the situations. I would like to share some of my observations, as I listened.

There are several stages in the process of bringing about the kind of complex change that a program such as a Search and Teach model introduces in a school district.

The first stage is some awareness that there is a gap between what we have now and what we would like to have. The second stage is to take a look at what those needs are and to try and understand them in some kind of consentient way among the people who are feeling the need and who are intending to do something about it. The third stage of diffusion, or stage of planned change, is to select or to choose a way of coping, a way of filling the need, a way of moving the institution forward in the direction of its goal. The selection process includes indentifying available resources, looking at those to see how they fit, going through a decision making process which varies from situation to situation, involving different people, which examines the possibilities and in some way comes up with the decision to move forward in a particular direction.

The next stage is to acquire the solution or the program, and thinking through the ways in which the program needs to be adapted to the local conditions. Then, in at least those change efforts which have been proven successful, there is often a trial phase. Some of these programs and approaches are so complex that it is difficult to make a sustained commitment at the beginning, without having some experience in it.

The last stage in the process, then, is to institutionalize the change. That includes ongoing modifications and adaptations to weave the change into the fabric of the program of the total organizational structure and program. With that list of the various stages in mind, I would like to reflect on some of the comments that I heard from speakers this morning in relating their direct experience.

Selma Thackery's situation at the Seely Place School was one that had a lot of conditions favoring change. The people were always looking for ways of improving their program. It is not fearsome to them to consider adopting new programs. Another key factor was that Selma's predecessor had already involved key people from other disciplines. A critical factor in the Seely Place replication, to me, was that early on, key people were talking about the situation, talking about the needs that were being felt, talking about the possible ways they could bring about change.

Selma Thackery mentioned that case conferences that ultimately were planned into the program included the multidisciplinary complement of people. It meant then that the people who were in the multidisciplinary team shared the responsibility for the intervention that was applied.

Another critical factor that Selma mentioned had to do with the ongoing involvement of the people from the Medical Center, as they continued to implement the program. I think this allowed for them to track the necessary adaptations and be sure that they were in keeping with the overall intent and integrity of the program.

Ruth Angel, I thought, had a great deal of insight, and I was struck at her wisdom in perceiving ways of bringing about change in a very difficult situation. Her efforts to include numerous people in the planning for the change, I think, may have been critical to its success. Early on key kindergarten teachers were involved in the training for the purpose of expanding the pool of people who could administer Search. But more importantly than that perhaps, is that those people then became involved in the overall change effort, became part of it, and cared about whether it worked or not because they had invested their time into it.

Another crucial factor to me was that adoption in that situation was staged over time. It started small; kindergarten teachers were added to the training pool as it became clear that there was a need for more people to do Search. In addition to that the school board people were involved right at the very beginning. One of the first groups she mentioned approaching was the school board, a critical group in any school district, because they can stop efforts to bring about change usually very easily. Other decision makers and ultimate eventual implementers were involved early on as well and had a chance to shape the decision. How many times have we seen programs where teachers have had imposed on them a new technique, new program, new strategies, and have at least superficially agreed to go along with it or felt that they had no choice but to go along with it, but in actual operation, if you were to observe their classrooms you would see very little change occurring. If teachers are brought in early in the process and encouraged to take part in shaping the decision and the selection, they will feel more committed to it, have invested more in it and feel more comfortable with it.

Attie Belle Liles's comments highlighted for me the importance of having leadership early on in the process. She mentioned that the school board had been approached and the situation discussed with them in the early stages. One of the key forces working for them, as she described it, was that they have a school board that does provide leadership. If we involve the key people early on when the thing is being shaped, every one has a chance to influence the outcome and has the chance to really think through for themselves what they like about it, what their reservations are, what changes they think would be important to its success.

The limited resources in the North Carolina situation, in many cases, would have just overwhelmed any efforts or any good intentions to bring about change. It sounds like what they were able to do was to modify the program in such a way that it made it possible for them to fit it into their available resources. Crucial in this is the availability for the developers to consider possible ways of modifying the program which would again retain its integrity and its effect while making it possible for it to be done on a smaller scale. It occurred to me also that probably one of the appeals of this particular program, probably one of the basis on which they selected it, was that it is cost effective and efficient.

It is important for decision makers and the planners to be clear about why the program is attractive. What are some of the other things that make it an appealing solution? In this case I imagine a crucial one was that the teachers could be trained in a day. Kindergarten teachers could do it, it did not rely entirely on specialists. The intervention strategies were ones that fit in with the ones that the school is already doing and did not require vast amounts of training or change for people that require new skills.

The collaboration with the Title III (then Title IV-C) project was an interesting dynamic to me. It pointed out the desirability of looking for ways that a new program can be tied into existing efforts other than just the regular ongoing classroom program.

Another crucial part is that of capacity building. By capacity building, I mean doing more in the system than simply adding on a new learning disabilities program. Capacity building has to do with looking at ways in which we are increasing our total capabilities as a school, using this new program as a way of building strengths in other areas. In the example that I heard in the North Carolina situation, the emphasis was on teacher training. While teachers were being trained on the surface to administer Search and Teach, in fact a lot more was going on. If teachers feel a need for something and see a program as providing a solution for situations that are causing them pain in the day to day work, there is no better incentive or motivation for teaching training. It sounds as though that was the case here and the teachers really wanted the training. One capacity building outcome that was mentioned was the influence on the entire kindergarten program. The whole structure of the kindergarten program was reconsidered and modifications were made in it.

The Ohio situation is a quite different approach to the change effort. The key for me in that situation was the importance and value of ongoing evaluation in monitoring the effect.

It is so hard to tell what is causing the success with children. What the Ohio situation has done is try to control as many variables as possible and to look at the effect of the program itself on children, compared with other possible approaches. That kind of ongoing assessment, both at the ongoing work of the New York University Medical School project as well as in some of their replication sites, is important to maintain the credibility and to examine the effects of a program.

Because of what new programs require of us, new roles, new relationships, new skills, changing our attitudes, dealing with people we did not deal with before, working in different settings, etc., fill out new reports, we have an instinctive need for support and assurance. The ongoing support aspect that I have heard mentioned in the two examples we have heard about today, tells me that those situations are likely to succeed, because they can still have contact and occasional visits from the developers, and because they have internal support. I think programs like these, handled as they have been, and replication efforts such as these, minimize the extent that it takes and the length of time for effective change to take place in the schools at the grass roots level.

5

Specific Learning Disability Demands Specific Remedial Teaching

How SPELD New Zealand, Meets this Need

Jean A. Seabrook

Pᴇʀʜᴀᴘs ᴀ sɪᴍᴘʟᴇ ᴀɴᴅ ꜰᴀᴄᴛᴜᴀʟ sᴛᴀᴛᴇᴍᴇɴᴛ that children and adults with learning difficulties of a specific nature require teaching of a special kind is self-evident and will be accepted without question. Michael Rutter and William Yule in their research, have proved the validity of *specific* reading retardation. These children *do* exist. But what is being done about it? Indications are that these children, who are intellectually able, emotionally stable, and culturally non-deprived remain in the schools failing to learn. The phenomenon is world wide.

The purpose of this paper is to show what SPELD New Zealand, is doing to help children and adults with specific learning problems. SPELD means specific learning disabilities. SPELD New Zealand, has accepted that intellectually able children, who demonstrate specific disabilities, require specialized teaching by teachers who realize the *neurological* nature of the particular difficulties exhibited. Teachers must be competent to implement individual teaching techniques directed specifically toward the improvement of the disabling deficiencies. Firstly, a clear distinction must be made between the child who is failing because of general causes and the child who is failing because of specific causes.

Learning difficulties which are attributable to general causes are irregular attendance at school, under-achieving because of wrong placement, socioeconomic and cultural deprivation, school changes, and inconsistent methods. Under the heading "specific" would be included inability to understand and/or express language, incoherent arrangement of thoughts of words, difficulty in processing words heard to words written, defective visual/auditory memory, disparity between concrete and discursive thinking, inability to sort out figure and ground.

When we look at general and specific causes, it is obvious that they are quite different. Specific disabilities involve the different cerebral systems and the input-mediating-output mental processes of the child. Specific disabilities are part of his neurological-psychological make-up. General difficulties, on the other hand, can be considered extraneous. In a way, they are imposed upon the child. They come from without, although in time their effect can so upset the learning continuum that psychologically and educationally the child fails because he is out of step. He has gaps which, without extra help, he cannot bridge. Neurologically, however, this child is intact.

In an intellectually able child with a learning difficulty of a general kind—let's suppose an inability to decode words because he was frequently absent from school during times when these particular skills were being taught—his cerebral mechanism is in order. The tabula rasa awaits the imprinting by the teacher. However, because of school absence the brain has not been subjected to the teaching, in this example, of the decoding skills; therefore the child has not acquired them. No special methods are necessary to remediate such a child, unless, of course, he has developed some bad habits. Subject him to ordinary classroom techniques, and he will acquire the necessary knowledge. Not so the child with specific disabilities. Not all his cerebral processes are at the ready. Some need developing, others need reorganizing to function in new ways. Teaching of this child requires a specialized approach—an understanding of how the brain works and what can be done to develop the functioning power of the non-working or imperfectly working part.

Although many questions remain unanswered about mental activity, there is a wealth of material to indicate the fundamental organization of the brain, the basic principles governing its work, and the role of primary, secondary, and tertiary brain systems in the organization of mental activity. An applied knowledge of perception (the basis of learning) as a cerebral system entailing the combined working of individual areas of the brain, for its complex functioning should be the right of every teacher who is required to teach children with specific difficulties. But knowledge alone is not enough. There must be an enlightened application of it in the educational methods which are used when a specific LD child presents. These methods must apply specifically to the neurological-psychological needs of the child.

If the child's individual differences are perceived and the implications understood by the teacher, then much time and effort for both teacher and child would be saved. For example, the child with disability in visual discrimination would not be given lists of sight words to learn before his basic discriminatory problem had been mastered; the child with auditory imperception would not be continually in hot water for inattention or disobedience of commands; he would be on a special program to improve his reception and understanding of language; the child with seemingly a graphic sequencing problem would not be asked to write dictated material until his difficulties in this respect had been sorted out into auditory or visual, spatial or motor, or a combination of these, and corrective training implemented. The little boy who pleads "Why me no tell" (meaning why can't I find the right word) would be recognized as a child with a nominal loss, groping for the correct word and not just a cute little chap who says the funniest things.

The teacher would know that the same low scores for reading, spelling, and arithmetic in different children can be caused by inadequate cerebral functioning, requiring quite different treatment, and that certain mental activities might be ideal to improve the skill of one child, but entirely a waste of time for another. The teacher would not be self-pressured into trying methods which she feels might help as a last resort because she would *know* the different possibilities open for that particular child to reorganize or develop the ability in question. If the education of the child with specific learning difficulties is to be improved, then the classroom teacher must be aware of what is required to make the child neurologically "tick" and the specialist teacher employed to teach these children must know what basic mental components are involved in the learning of each skill required in the acquisition of reading, writing, and arithmetic. Furthermore, the teacher must know what to do about it. This is only possible through a study of the afferent information reaching the child through the various senses—in particular the visual, auditory, tactile, and proprioceptive—its synthesis, and the essentiality of this in the performance of any motor task.

SPELD New Zealand, has accepted in its testing and teacher training scheme these principles, and I want to briefly explain the scheme. Firstly a few words about SPELD in New Zealand.

It was due to the efforts of parents to get educational help for their LD children that SPELD was founded in Christchurch by Brother Damien Keane in September 1971. The New Zealand SPELD associations are incorporated bodies set up voluntarily in different regions and constitutionally directed to promoting the educational welfare of children and adults "of adequate intelligence whose formal learning development has been less than their potential because of difficulties of a specific kind" (Constitution, SPELD New Zealand). At present there are twenty-two associations established, with others in the process of being formed.

In 1973 Christchurch started training teachers to work with children and adults within the Canterbury province, but in July 1976 a scheme was initiated, on a national basis, to train selected certified, but non-practicing teachers, who would provide a pool of specially trained teachers to work in the different regions with children and adults referred to SPELD.

The scheme is dependent upon the provision of a tester, plus a group of SPELD-trained teachers in each SPELD region. In both areas—teacher training and testing—SPELD New Zealand, has endeavored to keep a high professional standard. In some of the branches, there are a few testers, highly qualified and experienced in clinical and neuropsychology, who have given a professional lead in diagnosis and assessment. Other testers have been sought from the SPELD teacher-training course, where candidates have been found with the approved qualifications and experience required for testing. These people have been granted registration as top-level testers by the New Zealand Council for Educational Research, the body responsible for the registration of people administering tests and measurements.

Each SPELD-trained teacher is entitled, as a certified school teacher, to use certain tests and screening procedures for her own use, but it is important and objective to have one or two highly qualified testers recognized officially as the key people responsible for the assessment of people referred to the associations.

On referral, parents fill in a short case history form, which gives information on the child's medical and educational background, hobbies, interests, and attitudes. The parents are interviewed by the tester and are present at the test, which takes approximately 1½ hours. The work of the tester is to produce two types of results. From the standardized tests administered in reading, spelling, comprehension, vocabulary, and word recognition, an attainment age is obtained. The child's intellectual ability, which has been previously assessed by the school psychologist, is noted in respect to the attainment scores. Although it is recognized that these do not necessarily parallel the same degree of attainment, score depression in a child with superior intelligence might be considered to be wider than in a child of normal intelligence and the same chronological age. The standardized tests serve a very useful purpose of providing a level for an accurate estimate of the child's progress when re-tested. Children are retested at varying intervals, depending upon numerous factors, but parents, the child himself, or the SPELD teacher may request a re-test at any time. Children are keen to have follow-up tests and will ask for these of their own free will.

The other results that the tester produces through the use of a test battery, based on age norms, indicate the specific difficulties which are the fundamental factors in his failure to achieve academically. The tests are itemized on the record sheet. In addition to the test results, a skilled and experienced tester will retrieve from the investigation important clinical material.

On arrival for the test, most children and adults feel somewhat tense. They realize that they will have to face a failing situation. The presentation of the initial tests—those of laterality, coordination, spatial relationships, and copying geometric shapes—are, however, not what the child expected. These tests give the child a chance to move about the room, to disperse some of his tension. This is particularly important for the overactive child. They can be fun also and rapport is quickly established. These tests reveal not only the obvious—the controlling side of the brain, movement patterns, and eye-hand coordination, balance, spatial synthesis—but also give indications of covert difficulties in mental functioning, which will be clarified later in the other test items. Basic information is gathered and difficulties unfold as the test items proceed, and by the time the standardized tests are reached toward the end of the assessment the tester already knows the kinds of errors the child will be unable to avoid making.

However it is more important to know *why* he makes the errors, and it is this knowledge which forms the base upon which the SPELD-trained teacher will construct her program later. Confused results in the laterality tests, with non-establishment of dominance, could be a clue to the slowness of response in other performances; difficulties in spatial orientation, if severe, should lead the tester to expect difficulties in telling time, reading maps, and arithmetical calculations. Also difficulties in the understanding of grammatical structures which incorporate logical relationships, such as "The autumn before that very wet winter," would be expected to be impaired.

Although these processes appear different, they have a common factor and involve structurees in the same part of the brain. Sentences which do not involve such relationships would not be affected, since different cerebral centers are used.

The tests then move on to explore the auditory perceptual area and the child's ability to discriminate between sounds and words, sequence, reproduce sentences and numbers from memory, blend, syllabify, and recognize and produce sounds in different positions in words. An analysis of these results shows the child's strengths and weaknesses in interpreting verbal material; it points to the wisdom or otherwise of using a phonic approach in teaching this child; it highlights the items in the child's auditory perception which need to be improved before the auditory modality can be used successfully in learning; it uncovers the reasons for the particular errors which in all probability will be found in reading, spelling, and comprehension tasks later.

Because the auditory tasks are taken en bloc, children who have a number of deficiencies in this area, on occasion, as the tests proceed, become auditorily overloaded. This is noticeable in their behavior. They begin to lose concentration, become restless even to the point of hyperactivity, rock, and sometimes they cover their ears with their hands. As soon as a switch is made to the visual perceptual tasks they settle, regain their concentration, and proceed.

In one child this behavior was so evident it was suggested to the school that a quiet corner be found for the child, and ear muffs be provided, until he had built up a tolerance for verbally produced material, through the use of a graded program. Open-plan classrooms are devastating for children with this type of problem. Auditory memory loss and auditory sequencing difficulties are common problems. In one city a few years ago I tested 249 intelligent boys over the age of ten, and only three could give the months in order. Some could not remember the months out of order. It is not just remembering 12 words, but 28 syllables in sequence.

Sometimes parents complain about their child being "forgetful," but they seldom think of this as being unable to remember. They describe it as "his mind is always on something else" or "he doesn't listen" or "he's just not interested," and they are quite surprised when it is demonstrated that for his age the child has a low memory score. Parents can do much to help the improvement of memory.

The items of the visual perceptual tests are similar, and they fulfil the same purpose as the auditory in portraying the learning foundations profile of the child, but this time it is in the visual symbolic area. Children whose difficulties are mainly in visual perception are more verbal than those with auditory imperception. They get along well at school until the puzzle of mastering reading through the interpretation of visual symbols can no longer be disguised by learning it by heart. Many of these children cannot link the sound heard with the appropriate letter, and this may be for several reasons. Included may be an inability to visually discriminate due to a direction problem, a difficulty in visually organizing the spatial positions of the lines which form the letters, inadequate closure or too much closure; or it may be a visual memory impairment, or figure-ground sorting. It may be in the mental activity connecting the auditory and visual, and not in either of the modalities separately. When it comes to blending letters into words, ordering the letters into words in spelling, and arranging the words in sentences, these children are hopelessly lost. However, children with visual sequencing problems may call upon their auditory sequencing ability, if this is intact, to help the visual. They may reauditorize the sentence and work it out from there.

A warning—relying upon the strengths, without attention to building the weaknesses, will not bring lasting results. In most cases, this is what the child has been doing to get by, and not making any real progress, in his attempts. The tests go on to combine auditory and visual, then auditory, visual, and graphic. By working carefully through the results and understanding the ramifications of the mental combinations, a profile of basic processes can be produced.

It is the revelations of the test battery which tell the tester the levels at which basic programming must be pitched. It points to the correct in-road to learning for the individual, the fundamental weaknesses, which need special work to develop or improve them and what help can be expected from the stronger modalities. It can tell whether a child needs to read aloud to get auditory and proprioceptive feedback from the speech musculature; whether the child's difficulty in answering comprehension questions is due to an inability to understand only the last part of the story. It shows whether the "lack of concentration" is primary or secondary in the school situation—the child has been tested for 1½ hours with plenty of concentration.

Following the test battery items, standardized tests—Neale, Carver, Schonell—are given. Although the Carver Test is standardized for children up to the age of 8½ years, many older children fail this test. If they pass it, they do not have a problem in recognizing words visually. Speech and language disorders are referred to a speech therapist. The tester has the responsibility of reporting to the agency which referred the child, and this may be the school, educational psychologist, medical practitioner, hospital, or child health clinic.

Most referrals come directly from parents. The parents are given a summary of the results, at the assessment. Following assessment, the child is referred to a SPELD-trained teacher. The tester reports and discusses the findings with the teacher. The SPELD teachers are trained in the interpretation and application of the test results. During their training, children who manifest widely, differing clusters or deficiencies have been demonstrated. Children's assets and liabilities may differ not only in proportion, but in importance according to their time of development; their defect in one critical process can impair other processes. The demonstrations not only stimulate, but convince the teachers in training, that the brain, as a computer organizing human mental activity, must be to them of immediate concern in their understanding and working with children and adults who have specific learning difficulties. Thus their interest in and enlightened approach to the neurological, psychological aspects upon which the content of the training course is structured is strengthened. Their study of the integration of the brain mechanisms upon which speaking, reading, writing, and comprehension are based gives the teachers knowledge and skill in applying methods which will be *directly* relevant in developing the effective use of cerebral areas which are not functioning adequately in the children coming under their tutelage.

Although in the training course studies are made of the well-known instructional systems—such as Fernald, Kephart, Spalding, Frostig, Cruickshank, Barsch, and others—teachers are encouraged to use their own special skills creatively in presenting their lessons, for example, skills in music, art, drama. However, it is emphasized that each lesson must have a direct aim, in accordance with the child's neurological-psychological need, and that each must also be an integral part of the over-all plan of treatment. Lessons must be carefully and finely graded from the simple to the complex, but they start at the level which the child has reached in successful performance. The teacher must always bear in mind that what may appear to be a similar type of exercise may in fact be an entirely different one, involving another part of the brain, for example, the visual sequencing of geometric shapes by memory and the visual sequencing of letters or words. Although the shapes may bear a close resemblance to letters and the child may produce the shapes correctly, perhaps twice as many, he may fail dismally in remembering in sequence the letters of a simple word e.g., *den.*

In addition to practical demonstrations, the training course includes a study of child development and human behavior, with language development emphasized. The typical and the atypical child are contrasted. The characteristics of the emotionally disturbed, the autistic, the sight and hearing impaired, the underachiever due to lowered intelligence are studied. These children by our Constitution are not SPELD children, and they would be referred on to the appropriate authority at the initial testing. However, SPELD teachers need background information of such children, so that, if the need arises, they can advise parents about referral agencies. Also knowledge of the differences in the characteristics of these children, is useful diagnostically and in clarifying the teachers' thinking in relation to specific learning difficulties.

In training, teachers are introduced to the basic tenets of interviewing and parent counseling. It is not expected that counseling would ever be at depth and indeed, it is found in practice that the concerned and understandably anxious parents quickly lose their tensions as the children begin to improve. As for the children, their frustrations, poor self-image, and negative attitude to learning disappear within a few weeks. Their behavior is the first improvement noticed in the school.

Wherever possible, the SPELD teacher cooperates with the headmaster and class teacher. On application to SPELD, parents are advised to discuss with the school their approach to SPELD, and in cases where a child has not been seen by the school psychologist, the parent is requested to ask the headmaster to refer the child to the psychological services for an assessment of intelligence. Should it happen that the child's hearing and vision have not been tested, this is also requested, although seldom is it found that this has not been done. These are the two senses, which obviously come under scrutiny early in an educationally failing child. Children receiving help through SPELD are placed with a teacher nearest to the child's home. The majority of lessons are of one hour's duration or sometimes two half-hours, if the child is young or distractive.

Remuneration varies in the different regions, with the average rate being NZ $3-4 per hour. A maximum of NZ $5 per hour has been set.

All matters pertaining to the teachers and teacher training are the responsibility of a group of professional people within the SPELD organization. The director of the teacher training travels to any area which requests a course. The course is of 75 hours intensive study of theory and practice directed toward specific disabilities in learning. It is supported with films and tapes. Following the course, candidates are required to write assignments and participate in tutoring children and adults with specific learning difficulties who are referred to SPELD. A prerequisite reading task is also set. Short refresher courses are held periodically, and the SPELD teachers meet regularly, in their regions, for professional discussion. In summary, SPELD N.Z., Inc., has initiated a system of testing, linked with teacher training, which provides a pool of specially trained teachers to work locally with children and adults who are referred through the SPELD associations. The program for each client, revealed through the assessment by the SPELD tester, is based on the application of the principles of child development, psycholinguistics and neuropsychological needs of the child, which directly relate to his/her specific disabilities in the communication skills.

6

A Cognitive/Psycholinguistic Model for Educating Young Handicapped Children

Precise Education of Children with Handicaps (PEECH)

Merle B. Karnes

HISTORY

Precise early education of children with handicaps (PEECH)
originated in 1970 when a grant was received from the Bureau of Education for the Handicapped (BEH). As a First Chance Project, PEECH
was funded during a three-year period with the purpose of developing a
model for the education of multiply handicapped children ages 3–5. The
focus of the project for the first three-year cycle was primarily the development and refinement of the model. In addition, attention was given to
developing awareness among educators and concerned individuals of the
existence of the project.

In 1973 PEECH entered the second three-year cycle which focused
on outreach activities. At this time PEECH disseminated information
and services to all interested agencies in the state of Illinois. The number
of PEECH demonstration sites in Illinois eventually numbered 80 and included Head Start, private, and public schools. It became apparent at this
time that the PEECH model could be adapted by many different agencies
and in a variety of settings. Other PEECH dissemination activities included a quarterly newsletter, numerous awareness and training workshops, a regional and national conference, distribution of printed information, and observation of the PEECH demonstration classrooms at the
University of Illinois.

To be granted funds for the outreach phase of the model project,
BEH requires that the demonstration or service program be funded by another agency. When PEECH entered the outreach phase, in July 1973,
funding for the demonstration classes was assumed by the Joint Early
Education for the Preschool Handicapped (JEEPH) agreement between
the University of Illinois and fifteen school districts in Champaign
County. The early procedures and practices developed were revised and

adapted because the group of children identified for programming changed from the more severely handicapped to a mildly to moderately handicapped population.

In November of 1975, PEECH was selected as one of seven exemplary programs to receive BEH funding for national replication. In the first year of this third phase, ten sites were selected across the country to replicate the PEECH approach. In this replication phase, specialists trained in the PEECH approach assisted the sites in developing their programs following the PEECH model. Initial training begins with an orientation/training workshop at the university or a three-day visit at the site. For the remainder of the year, a replication specialist visits each site for two days a month to train site staff in the various components of the model. After nine months of training, it is anticipated that the site will be able to demonstrate the approach to interested parties in their region.

THEORETICAL ASSUMPTIONS AND BASIC PRINCIPLES

The PEECH model was based on the assumptions that: (1) the earlier the handicapped child and his or her family are involved in an intervention program, the greater the potential for enhancement of their subsequent development, and (2) gains (intellectual, social, and emotional) made during the early years can have a cumulatively beneficial effect in subsequent years. Since few model programs for educating preschool handicapped children existed at the time of the development of PEECH (1970) and interest in model preschool programs was increasing, the development of the PEECH model was both timely and useful.

As specific components of the PEECH model were being developed, eight principles were used as a basis for decision making. These principles were based on research findings and the experience of the PEECH Project Director, Merle B. Karnes. These principles are:

1. *A high teacher-pupil ratio is a requisite of an educational program for preschool handicapped children.* Explicit positive reinforcement obviously requires a high teacher-pupil ratio. Additional support for the high teacher-pupil ratio inheres in the fact that eight handicapped children of ten have a deficit in language, particularly oral language, and require a high level of verbal interaction with the teacher. The planning and implementation of individualized instruction requires a commitment of time that only can be achieved with a high teacher-pupil ratio. Individual programming requires that the teacher have a thorough knowledge of

each child. The PEECH Model uses the ratio of one teacher to five pupils (1:5). Customarily the ratio for nonhandicapped children is a teacher for every eight children.

2. *The services of a limited number of competent professionals can be extended through the use of paraprofessionals as teachers.* Due to the financial limitations of many programs, including PEECH, it is sometimes not feasible to maintain an adult-child ratio of 1:5 using a staff comprised entirely of professional teachers. Consequently, a high teacher-child ratio is maintained through paid paraprofessionals. Karnes (1969) has demonstrated that paraprofessional staff, under supervision, can substantially extend the services of the professional teacher. Thus, the services of highly trained staff are extended to substantial numbers of children at reasonable budgetary levels without jeopardizing program effectiveness.

3. *Instructional approaches should be highly consistent with sequences and/or stages of child development and are most effective when individualized.* The PEECH model programs for the total development of the child, e.g., language, cognitive, self-help, fine motor, gross motor, and social/emotional skills. Within the first eight weeks of the child's placement into the program an evaluation is conducted of his entry behavior in each developmental area (Glaser 1967). The next step up in each developmental area is then defined in terms of behavioral objectives (Mager 1962). Learning activities are planned so they are congruent with the child's present level of development. Thus a deliberate attempt is made to achieve the proper match (Hunt 1964). This match provides learning tasks where success is possible. As a result, the child is also more likely to develop a strong positive self-concept. When programming is designed so that the level of instruction is matched to *each* child's developmental levels, it is not only more appropriate but is also individualized.

4. *The implementation of an effective educational program must be precisely planned and evaluated.* In order for the implementation of an individualized program to be successful, each instructional activity must be precisely planned and evaluated. Based on the work of Mager (1962, 1968) the PEECH model utilizes the procedure of writing educational objectives in behavioral terms for each instructional activity. Once a behavioral objective is defined, a criterion task is established which permits the teacher to observe each child in a structured setting, and to formulate an objective evaluation of his behavior. Children who succeed in the task are scheduled for the next phase of the program while children who do not attain the specified competency receive additional instruction. Furthermore, the teacher is immediately aware of the success of her instruction and can make appropriate adaptations. The teachers also develop greater insights

into the needs of the children through this attentiveness to specific behaviors. Because this procedure provides data for evaluating program effectiveness, it is an integral part of both the instructional and evaluation components. Following are features of planning and evaluation which are essential for achieving an individualized program.

A. Initial and ongoing evaluation is made to delineate the specific curricular activities to be implemented by the teacher with the child (Kirk and McCarthy 1961).

B. A feedback system is provided for the teacher both in terms of the performance of the child on specified tasks and in terms of the evaluation of the teacher-child interaction.

C. Sufficient time is provided in the daily schedule for the teacher to prepare instructional materials. In addition, she reviews materials and consults with other program personnel to discover new ways of solving differing educational problems.

5. *An effective program carefully structures the learning environment.* The nature of teacher-child interaction is an important aspect of a program for preschool handicapped children. One study comparing programs with varying degrees of structure (Karnes 1969) demonstrated that children in the highly structured programs made greater cognitive gains.

Children will function more effectively in an environment that has established consistent expectations and limits from day to day. Many preschool handicapped children have not yet acquired the skills necessary to make decisions, solve problems, and to interact in a meaningful and growing way with the environment. Consequently, in a "structured" approach, the teacher plans activities for the children based on their needs and assists and reinforces them during the activity.

Reinforcing a child who has a short attention span during the activity is likely to encourage him to spend more time in a learning session. The structure provides a framework for the teacher to plan within and reduces the number of decisions she has to make during the actual learning period. The teacher knows what she is going to do and how she is going to do it; thus, she is free to focus on the unfolding behavior of the child in the learning situation and to provide an optimum learning experience. By planning each day's activities, the teacher can provide a balanced program based on the needs of the total child.

6.   A. *A preschool program will help a child develop his optimum potential when cognitive development, with particular emphasis on language development, is stressed (Karnes 1969).* The development of language skills provides a foundation for all areas of cognition. To be successful in school and in life, a person must be proficient in language processing skills. Acquiring new concepts and ideas, relat-

ing these concepts and ideas in new ways, and communicating them to others are skills that are essential for an individual to fully develop his potential. Similarly, certain skills must be developed to the extent that they can be performed automatically and thus free the individual's energies so he can engage in higher level thought processes. It cannot be overemphasized that acquisition of language skills is highly related to almost all facets of school success. Since language development is cumulative, attention to helping children develop language processing skills should begin at an early age. Since inadequate language development represents one of the greatest problem areas for children being served by the PEECH Project, it seemed obvious that the program include a strong language component.

   B. *An instructional model plays an important role in ensuring the success of intervention.* A model combats the teacher's use of a haphazard, hit-or-miss instructional approach. The use of a model directs the teacher's attention to various aspects of development and helps the teachers avoid overemphasis in some areas to the neglect of others. Furthermore, individualization of instruction is enhanced by calling attention to each child's level of performance in various aspects of the model. Since PEECH has a strong language component, a language model is used based on the clinical model of the Illinois Test of Psycholinguistic Abilities. This language model was derived from Osgood's theoretical model (1957) by Kirk and McCarthy in 1961 and was modified by Kirk, McCarthy, and Kirk in 1968.

   One of the advantages of this model is that the test derived from it can be used diagnostically to ascertain the assets and weaknesses of individual children or commonalities in a small group of children. Further, each subtest in the ITPA is deemed highly relevant to the development of language and reading skills. Another strength of the psycholinguistic model lies in the structure that it provides professional teachers and paraprofessional personnel. When the model has been mastered, it provides a convenient connection between diagnosis and the development and implementation of an educational program. During the evaluation process, a psychologist, teacher, or trained observer can use the model to observe and evaluate the strengths and weaknesses of each child. These data can be gathered through the formal administration of the ITPA by a psychologist or through less formal observational procedures used by the teacher. Once the initial information has been obtained, decisions and planning relative to curricular offerings are made for each child to ensure that he is provided with the appropriate experiences to correct his weaknesses and to enhance his strengths in the various language facets included in the model.

7. *Educational intervention is most effective (generalized and long lasting) when emphasis is placed on systematically involving all family members in the educational process.* Research by Karnes, Studley, Wright, and Hodgins (1968) and by Karnes and Badger (1969) revealed that parents can be taught procedures that will be reflected in the accelerated growth of their children. Interaction and involvement with parents follow the same guidelines as child-teacher involvement. Differences in families must be recognized and respected. Family members should be viewed as individuals who have their own unique set of needs, strengths, and weaknesses. The involvement of family members in the program and with their child is dependent upon appropriate assessment of and responsiveness to these needs. Objectives are set for family members and a program is developed to encourage their growth and involvement. As with the child, the teacher must be constantly aware of the development of the family as it relates to their child's educational needs.

8. *Learning may be best accomplished by the appropriate use of positive reinforcements.* Positive reinforcement coupled with explicit remarks delineating the reasons for praise was chosen as the approach to be used in the PEECH Model since it was observed that such an approach, when applied with handicapped children, would help them to internalize work-related skills and help them sustain their involvement in more difficult tasks. Mitzel's article (1970) is the latest in a series of papers which suggests that learning may be best accomplished by positive reinforcement when responsively applied to meet the needs of the learner. Thus, praise from an adult, the child's own recognition of his completion of a concrete object (such as a picture), winning in a competitive setting, or work for symbols (such as tokens that can be later exchanged for a selected reward) may have generally beneficial effects on learning. The PEECH model provides for the use of various types of positive reinforcement to ensure the best possible learning environment and to help children achieve developmentally and individually appropriate goals.

COMPONENTS OF THE MODEL

Based on the eight principles discussed in the preceding section, a series of interrelated procedures (components) were developed. These components comprise the PEECH model which is a total program for educating pre-school handicapped children. Following is a list of the procedures and a brief discussion of how they are implemented:

1. *Procedures which plan for continuing staff development.* All staff members in the PEECH Project receive preservice and ongoing in-service training. The needs of *each* staff member are assessed and an individualized program is developed to ensure continual professional growth.

2. *Procedures which involve paraprofessionals in the teaching role.* Paraprofessionals in the PEECH classrooms present lessons to small groups of children and conduct large group learning activities. They are responsible for planning (writing lesson plans) and evaluating the sessions. The paraprofessionals also are the primary contact person for several families of children in the program.

3. *Procedures for identifying children and determining eligibility for program services.* PEECH has defined procedures for identification and screening, evaluation and program placement.

4. *Staff plans a daily schedule so that individualized programming may be implemented effectively through large group, small group and one-to-one activities.* Children attend PEECH for one-half day, five days a week, nine months of the year. A typical day includes three small-group (five children) sessions which are preplanned based on the children's needs. Child accomplishments during the sessions are recorded. The small group sessions are alternated with large group sessions such as art, outdoor play, music and snack. The children also have time for independent work and play. Teachers are allowed two hours a day for planning and evaluation of the instructional program.

5. *Procedures for teacher conducted assessment of each child's cognitive, affective and motor strengths and needs.* Within the first month of school, the classroom staff systematically observes and assesses each child's developmental level in the areas of language, math, self-help, social, fine and gross motor using a procedure referred to as SCOAP (Systematic Child Observation, Assessment and Programming). From the assessment information, educational goals are established for each child in each of the developmental areas.

6. *Procedures for involving parents in the process of establishing goals for their child's individual education program.* In compliance with PL 94-142, parents participate in developing an Individual Education Plan (IEP) for their child. This process occurs after the classroom assessment. The information gained during the assessment and from the parents is the basis for writing the IEPs, which become the core of each child's instructional program.

7. *Procedures for assessing needs of family members as related to*

their interests and concerns and for planning an individualized flexible program based on assessed needs. PEECH uses a procedure for assessing the individual needs of all parents and for writing goals based on the needs. A variety of activities are used for meeting these needs resulting in an individualized and flexible family involvement program.

8. *Procedures for documenting the frequency and outcome of family contacts.* PEECH has developed a record keeping system for the family involvement component. The system includes a record of plans, outcomes and frequency of involvement activities. Parental feedback concerning satisfaction with their child's educational program and with their involvement in the program is obtained.

9. *Procedures for establishing appropriate individualized goals based on classroom assessment, parental concerns and the results obtained from formal assessment.* A list of prioritized goals, teaching strategies, and evaluation criteria are written in the six areas of language, fine motor, gross motor, social, self-help, and math. This is to ensure a comprehensive instructional program based on individual needs.

10. *Procedures which systematically develop language, applying a language model such as the ITPA as a basis for instruction.* Teachers in the PEECH classrooms use a model for systematically developing and enhancing all areas of language development (reception, process, expression).

11. *Procedures which encourage a multidisciplinary team approach for developing and implementing each child's educational program.* The educational team in the PEECH model includes the administrator/coordinator, teacher, paraprofessional, speech therapist, social worker, psychologist, and occupational therapist. These professionals work together to provide a comprehensive educational program. The expertise from each discipline is integrated throughout the child's entire educational program.

12. *Procedures which systematically use children's strengths as a model to demonstrate desirable cognitive, affective, and motor behaviors to other children.* The strengths of the children in the classroom are used as a model to demonstrate cognitive, affective, and/or motor behaviors. Both handicapped and nonhandicapped children can model behaviors that will help facilitate the growth and development of the other children in the classroom.

13. *Procedures for planning and implementing an instructional program through lessons.* Individualized lesson plans are written daily in the areas of the child's greatest needs. Each plan specifies a behavioral objective, a sequence of activities for teaching towards the objective and a criterion activity for evaluating the child's ability to obtain the objective.

14. *Procedures and techniques for presenting written lessons effec-*

tively. Effective presentation of lessons is considered as important as precise planning. A well-planned lesson is worthless if it is not presented or if it is presented in an ineffective manner. PEECH lessons are planned to be game-oriented, interesting and challenging but not frustrating. They encourage active child participation and apply a multisensory approach.

15. *Procedures that create a positive affective environment and that include appropriate behavior management techniques.* The teachers use consistent positive reinforcement in their interaction with children. They clearly state rules and model acceptance of others' feelings, tolerance, fairness and responsiveness to each child's needs and interests.

16. *Procedures for objectively documenting and reviewing each child's progress in all instructional areas.* A record-keeping system is used which includes daily documentation and review of each child's progress towards behavioral objectives and prioritized goals.

17. *Procedures for evaluating, staffing and placing children who are no longer eligible for the program.* At the end of the school year, all team members write summary reports on each child's progress and current level of functioning. A staffing is conducted, all team members share their information and the team determines the most appropriate placement for the child.

18. *Procedures for evaluating the overall effectiveness of the educational programs.* Evaluation is an important component of the PEECH Model. Needs are assessed, activities and progress are documented and a measure of satisfaction is obtained in the child, parent, and staff components. This information is used for program growth and improvement.

19. *Procedures for organizing classroom space which facilitates effective implementation of the educational program.* An optimal learning environment is created which encourages independence, creativity, exploration, and learning in all developmental areas.

20. *Procedures for expanding and encouraging language throughout the day.* Specific language lessons are developed and implemented daily. Language is encouraged during all small-group, large-group, and one-to-one activities.

IMPLEMENTATION OF THE MODEL

Following is a description of the model as it is implemented at the University of Illinois, Urbana-Champaign. The procedures or components discussed previously have been developed into a comprehensive and effective model program.

The Children

The special needs of eligible children include cognitive, speech-language, and motor delays and deficiencies; suspected learning disabilities; social and emotional problems; hearing and visual impairments; and neurological impairment. Also integrated into the program are children who evidence no special educational needs. These children serve as models for language, self-help, social, emotional, and cognitive skills. Presently, two classrooms of fifteen children each serve as demonstrations of the PEECH model.

The Staff

The classroom staff includes one certified teacher and one or two paraprofessionals depending on the number of children enrolled and their needs. In addition to planning and implementing the educational program, the teacher is responsible for coordinating the family involvement program. The paraprofessionals assist the teacher in most aspects of the classroom and family involvement program. The psychologist is responsible for the initial diagnosis of the handicapped child and is a resource to the teacher throughout the year. The speech and language therapist and occupational therapist are involved in the initial diagnosis of the child, provide ongoing therapy and serve as a consultant to teachers and to parents to help them understand the child's needs and reinforce the program they are providing. The social worker is responsible for gathering initial data from parents during the intake process, for providing services to the families of the children enrolled in the program, and for serving as liaison between the center and community agencies. This multi-disciplinary team along with the project coordinator work together to provide comprehensive services to each child and his or her family.

Classroom Assessment

Classroom assessment is the process of systematic and objective observation and analysis of a child's skills and deficits to determine a starting point for educational programming. The information obtained from this assessment along with evaluation information obtained by other professionals and parental input is the basis for decisions made when establishing annual goals and short-term objectives. The areas of greatest deficit will obviously become areas of programming. The child's strengths will be used (1) while programming in his deficit areas, and (2) as a model for other children.

Classroom assessment in the PEECH Project is conducted by the teachers and paraprofessionals. At times they will be assisted by parents and ancillary personnel (speech therapist, psychologist, and occupational therapist). The assessment begins after the children have experienced an initial adjustment period of approximately two weeks. Good classroom assessment instruments will include all developmental areas. The PEECH assessment instrument measures each child's skills in the language, motor, social, self-help and cognitive areas. The information is collected through careful observation of each child's performance in the classroom. Some skills are observed during the child's natural activities such as while he is putting on his coat (self-help) and while he is interacting with other children during free play (social). Other skills can only be observed during a situation structured by the teacher such as labeling shapes.

The advantages of conducting an assessment of each child while in the classroom are obvious. Teachers are given an opportunity to carefully observe each child at the beginning of the year which will greatly increase her knowledge and understanding of each child's needs and strengths. This knowledge is necessary for appropriate programming. The process not only helps the teacher to identify what each child can and cannot do but encourages her to explore why the child is not able to perform the tasks. She may determine that in some areas it is due to a lack of experience while in other areas the child may not have the necessary prerequisite skills such as a pincer grasp which is necessary for buttoning. In addition, assessment information may validate or question formal test results or may indicate a need for more in-depth evaluation by other professionals. Through the classroom assessment the teacher obtains the information she needs for planning an individualized program. The process helps assure that the experience and guidance she is providing is beginning in the areas of each child's greatest needs and will therefore produce the greatest benefits for each child.

Planning an Instructional Program

Designing the instructional program involves two steps. First, the teacher must design a general plan defining what she wants each child to accomplish by the end of the year. With the recent passage of PL 94-142 this plan takes the form of the IEP. The next step requires the teacher to analyze the goals and objectives specified in the IEP into a series of objectives and strategies which are appropriate to immediately teach the child. This step involves then, developing daily lesson plans which will assist the child to achieve the goals and objectives specified in the IEP.

The information included on the IEPs is based on: (1) the classroom assessment, (2) evaluations conducted by the psychologist, social worker, speech therapist, and occupational therapist, and (3) parental input concerning their goals and concerns for the child. The IEP should include: (1) a statement of present levels of educational performance, (2) annual goals, (3) short-term instructional objectives, (4) educational services to be provided, and (5) appropriate objective criteria, evaluation procedures, and schedules for determining whether short-term instructional objectives have been achieved.

In addition to complying with PL 94-142, an IEP also serves the purpose of integrating all the information that was collected during the evaluation/assessment process. It provides the teacher with a blueprint of the program she will provide the child and the goals she expects each child will achieve as a result of the program. This type of planning is certainly helpful for beginning the program and for checking its progress and appropriateness throughout the year.

The short-term instructional objectives specified on the IEPs must be task analyzed into a series of daily behavioral objectives. The behavioral objectives for each child are written so they specify: (1) who is involved, (2) what they are expected to do, (3) under what conditions will they do it, and (4) how accurately they are expected to do it. For each daily behavioral objective a strategy or lesson plan is developed. The lesson plan specifies the activity in which the child will be involved, in order to learn or practice the skill specified in the behavioral objective. Whenever possible the lesson plans are game-oriented and encourage active child participation. The activity ideas may come from published curriculum kits or activity and idea books or they may be developed by the teacher based on materials in the classroom or materials she has made. Finally, the lesson plan also includes a criterion activity which is designed to "test" whether the child achieved the objective. The individualized lesson plans are usually implemented during small group (3–5 children) instructional periods, but they may also be implemented in large group or in one-to-one situations.

The child's performance on the criterion activity determines whether the behavioral objective was achieved. Performance is recorded by a + (skill present), ± (skill emerging), or − (skill not present). Anecdotal notes that may be helpful in planning further instruction are also recorded. This data provides the teacher with information as to how the child is progressing as well as feedback on the success of materials and procedures.

Successful performance on a sequence of daily behavioral objectives should result in the attainment of a short-term instructional objective specified in the IEP. Goals are reached when each short-term objective that comprises the goal is attained. Progress toward short-term objectives and goals on the IEP are reviewed biweekly.

Child progress data provides the teacher with information regarding the success of each child's instructional program. If a child is not adequately progressing, it may indicate that the objective, procedure and/or materials are not appropriate and should be adjusted. It may also indicate that the task needs to be broken down into smaller steps or that an unidentified problem exists that is interfering with learning. If a child is progressing, the teacher is assured of the appropriateness of the objectives and teaching procedures. As objectives and goals are achieved the instructional process begins again with assessment.

Family Involvement

Family involvement has always been an essential component of the PEECH Model. The PEECH staff is keenly aware of the benefits to children, parents and staff alike when family members are involved in the educational program.

Once the family is familiar with the classroom staff and the educational program, a needs assessment procedure is used to identify the concerns of each family and of the educational team as it related to the development of the child. The goals of the parent program are individualized for each family and are often as diverse as the number of parents in the program. Individualization does not stop with the goal setting process. Family members are given activity options for working towards goals. The activity options represent a variety of social settings and methods for obtaining each goal. Records are maintained on the type and frequency of family contacts and family members are asked to provide feedback on the usefulness and their satisfaction with involvement activities.

OUTREACH

From its beginning in 1970, the PEECH Project has been involved in some form of outreach activities. Although the focus from 1970 to 1973 was development of a model program for preschool handicapped children, the classrooms were made available for observation. Educators from various schools and agencies throughout the United States observed the classrooms and received information about developing a program for young multi-handicapped children in the form of printed materials, awareness workshops and meetings with the PEECH staff.

Outreach Activities 1973–76

When PEECH entered the initial outreach phase in July 1973, funding for the demonstration classes was assumed by the Joint Early Education for the Preschool Handicapped (JEEPH) agreement between the University of Illinois and fifteen school districts in Champaign County. Eight classrooms are currently being maintained through this agreement, two of which are demonstrating the PEECH model.

During this outreach phase, the ongoing training efforts of PEECH were concentrated in the state of Illinois. Two events occurred which produced a need for extensive preservice and inservice training of teachers and ancillary personnel throughout the state. The first was state legislation that went into effect in 1973–74 which mandated the provision of educational services to preschool handicapped children. Also during this time, Head Start programs were beginning to serve handicapped children. In response to the need for training within the state, PEECH worked with a total of *192* sites, including Chicago Model Cities/CCUO Head Start. These sites represented more than *500* school districts and *20* Head Start programs. Activities included numerous visits to the sites, workshops conducted at the sites, massive distribution of printed materials, and conferences with early childhood/special education personnel.

Training and awareness activities were not limited to PEECH sites. Numerous training workshops and awareness presentations were held throughout the country and the project was interpreted to many individuals who visited the demonstration center in Champaign-Urbana. The components of the project and techniques and procedures used in their implementation were shared through printed materials, which proved to be a fairly inexpensive and effective method to disseminate information. The materials were distributed through the mail, following presentations at professional meetings, conferences, conventions, workshops and at the demonstration site in Champaign-Urbana.

PEECH sponsored several workshops and conferences. A one and one-half day regional conference on "Alternative Approaches to the Education of Young Handicapped Children" was attended by people representing *16* states and a similar conference held on a national level, was attended by people representing *45* states. Three statewide workshops focused on motor development in young children. More than *900* individuals working with preschool handicapped children were on the mailing list to receive the PEECH newsletter which was published quarterly.

National Replication 1976–79

In 1976, PEECH received funds from the Bureau of Education for the Handicapped to provide technical assistance on a national scale to those programs interested in replicating the PEECH model. Based on previous experience, an outreach model has been developed which includes plans for creating awareness, selecting sites, training site personnel for both replication and demonstration of the PEECH approach and for evaluation of all activities.

National awareness of the PEECH Project is continued through: (1) presentations at conferences and professional meetings, (2) distribution of brochures and printed materials at workshops, conferences and by mail, (3) personal contacts made by the PEECH staff, especially the director, and (4) observation of the demonstration classrooms at the University of Illinois.

When a site expresses an interest in replicating the PEECH model, a packet including an informative description of the model design, an outline of mutual responsibilities involved in replication, and a sample sequence of potential training objectives and activities is mailed.

Administrators and teachers who express continued interest are asked to complete a brief questionnaire designed to supply PEECH with information which assists in the site selection process and to submit in writing an agreement to replicate, with necessary local adaptations, the major components of the PEECH model. Each candidate site is reviewed in terms of the following considerations:

1. The potential of a site to successfully replicate (commitment and funding).

2. The potential impact of the replication site on the state (influenced legislation and improved quality of services).

3. The geographic location (outside of Illinois and distributed strategically throughout the country).

4. The potential of the site to serve as a demonstration site (continued funding, willingness to accommodate visitors, and plan for preservice /inservice training).

Table 6.1 delineates PEECH replication sites for the years 1976–77,

TABLE 6.1

PEECH Replication Sites

1976–77 Sites	1977–78 Sites	1978–79 Sites
Buffalo, WY	Providence, RI	Denver, CO
Providence, RI	Flagstaff, AZ	Osage Beach, MO
Frederick, MD	Fullerton, CA	Fairfield, IA
Sikeston, MO	Missoula, MT	Franklinton, LA
Salt Lake City, UT	Cokato, MN	Ashland, KY
St. Paul, MN	Jackson, MS	Murfreesboro, TN
Ft. Lauderdale, FL	Conway, AR	Patchogue, NY
Jacksonville, FL	Cleveland, OH	Nashua, NH
Jonesboro, GA	Rhinelander, WI	

1977–78, and 1978–79. Following the site selection, a contract is developed which states detailed, mutual responsibilities and expectations of the site and the PEECH Project.

The training of each site begins with an on-site orientation workshop. This visit is followed by a four-day workshop held in Champaign-Urbana which provides in-depth training in model components, observation of the demonstration classrooms and an opportunity for site personnel to meet with replication specialists and other professionals. Training continues through monthly two-day visits to each replication site. During these visits the classroom activities are observed, information and materials are shared and training in specific program components occurs. The focus of the training sessions is determined and agreed upon by the PEECH replication specialist and the site personnel. These sessions are specified in terms of objectives, activities, evaluation of the training and evaluation of the implementation of procedures by the site personnel. At the end of the visit, tentative objectives are specified for the following visit. Phone contacts occur between visits to gain feedback on the success of: (1) the implementation of procedures, (2) the need for follow-up activities and/or materials that may have aided in the implementation, (3) the appropriateness of the tentative objectives that were established for the upcoming visit, and (4) any adjustments or additions that may be necessary. To aid in the implementation of the procedures of the PEECH model, manuals in the areas of classroom planning and programming, administration, family involvement, and evaluation are available for staff use.

A visit is scheduled at each site during the year following replication training so the replication specialist can evaluate the quality of replication according to the components of the PEECH model. This visit also includes training and assistance in the site's efforts to demonstrate and conduct awareness workshops in the PEECH model to other educators in their community and state.

In addition to the intensive services provided the replication sites, the PEECH Project continues to provide assistance to numerous other programs and educators throughout the United States. These activities include the distribution of materials through the mail, observation of the demonstration classrooms at the University of Illinois, distribution of materials at the PEECH demonstration site and workshops which are conducted on the components of the PEECH model.

REFERENCES

Glaser, R. (1967). Some Implications of Previous Work on Learning and Individual Differences. In R. M. Gagne, ed., *Learning and Individual Differences.* Columbus, Ohio: Merrill.

Hunt, J. McV. (1964). The Psychological Basis for Using Preschool Enrichment as an Antidote for Cultural Deprivation. *Merrill-Palmer Quarterly,* 10: 209–48.

Karnes, M. B., Studley, W. M., Wright, W. R., and Hodgins, A. S. (1968). An Approach for Working with Mothers of Disadvantaged Preschool Children. *Merrill-Palmer Quarterly* 14: 174–84.

Karnes M. B. (1969). *Research and Development Program on Preschool Disadvantaged Children.* Vol. I. Final Report. Bethesda, Md.: ERIC Document Reproduction Service (ED 036-663).

Karnes, M. B., and Badger, E. (1969). Training Mothers to Instruct their Infants at Home. In M. B. Karnes, *Research and Development Program on Preschool Disadvantaged Children.* Vol. I. Final Report. Bethesda, Md.: ERIC Document Reproduction Service (ED 036-663).

Kirk, S. A., and McCarthy, J. J. (1961). *Illinois Test of Psycholinguistic Abilities, Examiner's Manual.* Urbana, Ill.: University of Illinois Press.

Kirk, S. A., McCarthy, J. J., and Kirk, W. D. (1968). *Illinois Test of Psycholinguistic Abilities, Examiner's Manual,* rev. ed. Urbana, Il.: University of Illinois Press.

Mager, R. F. (1962). *Preparing Instructional Objectives.* Belmont, Cal.: Fearon.

————. (1968). *Developing Attitudes toward Learning.* Belmont, Cal.: Fearon.

Mitzel, H. D. (1970). The Impending Instruction Revolution. *Phi Delta Kappan* 51 (8): 434–36.

Osgood, C. E. (1957). Motivational Dynamics of Language Behavior. In *Nebraska Symposium on Motivation.* Lincoln, Neb.: University of Nebraska Press.

7

A High Intensity Approach to Teaching Adolescent Learning Disabled Students

Reading Component

Charles Meisgeier and Linda Menius

INTRODUCTION

THE PROBLEM OF DESIGNING appropriate instruction for the adolescent learning disabled student is very complex. The student's poor academic performance is frequently compounded by social skill deficits. A quick glance at the literature reveals many articles describing the LD adolescent's poor self-concept, inadequate peer relationships, academic failures, and need for success (Gutknecht and Keenan 1978; Lockett 1975; White 1975). While these are accepted by nearly everyone as substantial problems for the student, few authors have proposed methods for dealing with the combined ramifications of these traits. There continue to be confusion, differences of opinion, and perplexity regarding the education of the LD adolescent.

To achieve substantial student change at this age, a program must simultaneously have an impact on a student's skill deficits and his affective problems. Meisgeier's concept of synergistic education attempts to address the need for a dual approach. Synergy is used to illustrate the concept that a combination of affective and skill interventions will create a greater effect than either intervention would produce in isolation. The synergistic concept has been operationalized through the Houston Child Service Demonstration Center's High Intensity Learning Center (HILC).

The High Intensity Learning Center is one aspect of a broader program for secondary learning disabled students. The total Synergistic Education program includes: (1) the HILC, (2) a Support Group for Parents of students enrolled in the program; (3) a Content Mastery program to support the success of the LD student in the regular classroom, and (4) an Essential Skills program to provide limited follow-up skill instruction after a student completes the HILC. The synergistic response of the total program comes from the combined emphasis on the student in regular and special classes, the parent, and the teachers. Within itself each component is also designed to achieve synergistic learning.

THE HIGH INTENSITY LEARNING EXPERIENCE

The High Intensity Learning Center provides structured instructional activities in reading and related skills and in affective instruction. The purposes of the HILC are: (1) to improve students' basic academic skills, primarily reading; (2) to make diagnostic prescriptions for the student's future education; and (3) to encourage the student's personal/social development. The instructional program is structured to give students success experiences in both academics and interpersonal relationships, creating an atmosphere of growth and achievement. The HILC operates the first twelve weeks of the school year for three consecutive hours each day. Students who have received special services in elementary school are assigned to the HILC when they enter junior high school; students who are initially placed in special programs during their junior and senior high school careers also attend the HILC at some point (see Table 7.1).

The High Intensity Learning Center (HILC) is an eclectic approach to learning. Methods and procedures proposed by a range of instructional theorists and practitioners have been incorporated into the instructional program. The combination of these approaches is another example of the synergistic concept. The unique learning program which has resulted is considered beneficial by students, teachers, and parents. The various

TABLE 7.1

HILC Structure

Curriculum Area	Instructional Arrangement	Activities	Time
Reading Program			2 hours
Oral Fluency	Learning Partner	Oral Reading Listening	25 min.
Silent Fluency	Individual	Read books w/tapes	30 min.
Skill Development	Individual	Kits, Controlled Reader, Language Master, activity sheets, etc.	50 min.

components of the High Intensity Learning Center are described in the remainder of this paper.

HILC READING PROGRAM

Rationale

The HILC academic program focuses on instruction in reading and related skills. This emphasis has been adopted because: (1) most learning disabled students perform significantly below grade level on reading tasks; (2) the ability to read textbooks, worksheets, and other materials is a skill which most regular teachers see as vital to success of the student in the regular classroom; and (3) concentrated instruction in reading skills facilitates the teacher's ability to make accurate judgements about the student's growth potential in reading.

Many students enter regular content classrooms after completing the High Intensity Learning experience. Traditionally, teachers see near or at grade level reading ability as a must for successful entry into the regular classroom. Therefore a primary aim of the HILC academic program is to boost a student's reading ability as much as possible. While pursuing this aim, the teacher is also collecting specific diagnostic information about the student's rate of improvement, the plateaus that he has reached, the areas in which he achieves most rapidly and those where growth is painfully slow. This information is invaluable in making future programmatic decisions with the student.

For most students an instructional program has been designed which stimulates achievement closing the gap between his reading ability and the abilities of his peers. In less than 20 percent of the cases students have failed to make progress with intensive reading instruction and practice. These students are frustrated by continued failure and show little potential for progress in this phase of their education. Realistic appraisal of such a situation is vital. With a background of six or more years of special intervention and faced with a limited number of remaining school years, the student must learn skills which compensate for his reading weakness and which will lead him to a productive future. Students failing to progress in reading are enrolled in an alternative curriculum or possibly the program's content mastery—regular class support program. These students will receive no further reading instruction unless reassessment warrants such intervention. All efforts are directed toward building on the student's strengths thereby compensating for the deficit areas. By removing the student from daily reading instruction, he is removed from daily failure and frustration.

Synergistic Reading Curriculum

The controversy of how-to-teach reading is well documented. Reading theorists and practitioners debate the merits of skill instruction versus language experience versus reading practice. Individualized instruction, small group instruction, precision teaching, diagnostic prescriptive teaching, have all been lauded and criticized (Allington 1977; Gutknecht and Keenan 1978; Spache 1976; Strange and Allington 1977).

The skill-oriented approach to reading assumes that reading ability consists of skills which can be isolated, ordered and taught. The analysis of these specific skills is frequently done through oral readings. Remediation tends to emphasize improvement of phonics and word recognition, although comprehension skills are also addressed. Critics claim that there is little evidence of a hierarchy of reading skills and that by teaching fragmented skills one will not reach long-range goals of reading for meaning and of nurturing positive attitudes toward reading (Gutknecht and Keenan 1978). Strange and Allington (1977) suggest that teachers frequently use the skill concept exclusively for students with reading difficulties partially from a frustration of not knowing what else to do with a student. The skill centered approach does have the advantage of breaking the reading process down so that it is not overwhelming, of identifying specific measurable reading skills, and of providing specific information about a child's acquired reading skills.

A counter approach to the skill deficit concept stresses that reading is above all an attempt to gain meaning from the written page. Instruction should involve practice in the total reading process, comprehension activities, and study skills activities. Allington (1977) reports that in most remedial and corrective reading classrooms very little actual reading is done. In most cases students read no more than 110 words in the context of a lesson despite the fact that they participate in a myriad of instructional activities and utilize a variety of materials. He states that reading is not responding to flashcards, marking vowel rules, or responding to graphemes in isolation. An argument must be made, he says, for increasing reading in remedial and corrective reading instruction for the development of the ability to read fluently requires the opportunity to read.

When one analyzes the current literature on remedial reading strategies regardless of basic theoretical orientation one can isolate certain key points. In designing remedial reading instruction authors stress that the program should: (1) be fairly structured, (2) use individual and small group arrangements, (3) provide multimodal experiences, (4) facilitate positive teacher-student interrelationships, (5) encourage students to work with each other, and (6) provide success experiences (Gilleland 1974; Gutknecht and Keenan 1978; Wolpert 1971).

The HILC Reading Program Structure

The HILC reading program operates for two hours each day. This time is divided into two major components—the fluency program and the skill development program. The fluency program builds on existing student reading skills and strengths by providing the opportunity for extended practice in oral reading and silent reading with tapes. The skill development program deals with identified student weaknesses. Emphasis is placed on comprehension skills. However, students may also be assigned activities dealing with word attack skills, written expression, spelling, or handwriting. The fluency program and as many activities as possible in the skill program are multisensory.

The use of multisensory reading procedures has been justified by several authors. Wolpert's rationale for using several sensory modalities is that each sensory experience reinforces other sensory experiences and gives the learner a better sense of what he has learned (Wolpert 1971). Ekwall (1976) reports data which indicates that students have a much better chance of retaining what they see and hear (50 percent chance) than of retaining what they read only (10 percent), what they hear only (20 percent), what they see only (30 percent). The best chance of retention (90 percent) is for something which is said and done simultaneously. Lenkowsky (1977) recommends that since the learner depends upon a combination of multi-sense information and memories, instruction must be multimodal. Research reported by Sam Ducker on methods of presentation and modalities shows that combinations of visual and auditory input tend to be more efficient than either alone, that student's immediate comprehension of information favors visual presentation while long-term comprehension favors auditory presentation, and that visual presentation favors ease of learning while retention favors oral presentation (in Ekwall 1976).

Oral Fluency

The oral fluency program is designed to increase students' oral reading rate and to develop an ease and familiarity with the oral reading process. Oral reading is frequently a very frustrating activity for students. Yet oral reading is a skill which is used in the regular classroom and in which students need to be proficient. Oral reading is a tri-modal process— the student sees, hears, and articulates. Oral reading can be helpful in building comprehension, keeping track of student progress, teaching application of word analysis skills. Oral reading is also a skill in which students can actually hear themselves making progress. Strategies such as neurological impress, choral reading, and total class individual oral reading have all been used effectively to increase student reading ability (Gilliland 1974). The HILC oral fluency program has been built on concepts which suggest that there is a need for oral reading fluency, that diagnostic information is available from oral reading, that because oral reading is multisensory it can benefit student learning, and that students need to experience and realize success and improvement in their reading skills.

The oral fluency program gives students practice in oral reading in a non-threatening setting. Students read daily to a learning partner. Several partners are reading simultaneously so attention on any one student is diffused. Each student reads for six minutes as oral reading practice. During this time the partner is charged with correcting any reading errors which he notices. This correction process is not a painful one for the reader. He is not asked to sound out the word or to figure it out for himself. The partner merely gives the correct pronounciation so that the reader has increased exposure to new words. Following this practice the students perform a one minute time sample of oral reading in context. Partners count errors during this time, but do not verbally correct them. The student charts his word-read-per-minute rate and his error rate. Following the oral reading practice and timing, students perform a short, two-minute comprehension activity with each other. During this time the reader summarizes what he has read, answers questions raised by his partner, and discusses any interesting ideas generated in the story. This activity improves not only the student's ability to summarize, but also his communication skills. After one student has gone through the read-time-chart-discuss sequence, the partner follows this same procedure. A step-by-step outline of the oral fluency process is carried in Table 7.2.

Teacher's Role in Oral Fluency

The teacher's role in the oral fluency process is primarily to monitor students as they read. Daily assessment of the student's oral reading progress also serves as a platform for teacher reinforcement of student suc-

TABLE 7.2

Oral Fluency Process

Time	Student Actions		Teacher Actions	Materials	Products
Daily min.	*Oral Fluency W/Learning Partner*				
			A.1 Teacher assigns learning partner		
6				A.6 Short reading selection on reader's appropriate level (2 copies)	
10	A.3 Reader reads orally to partner	A.4 Listener follows along, verbally correcting reader when he errs	A.2 Teachers assigns reading level		
			A.5 Teacher monitors oral reading of all students on regular basis, makes notes on each student	Space for partner work Timer	
1					
10	B.1 Reader performs one minute time sample of oral reading	B.2 Listener follows along, counting but not verbally correcting reader errors	B.3 Teacher sets student rate aims Teacher times total group of readers	B.4 marked passage in reading selection Timer or stopwatch	B.5 word per minute and error rate for reader
3					
	C.2 Reader records oral reading rate on chart	Partner assists with charting if necessary	C.1 Teacher instructs students in charting, monitors student accuracy, reads charts regularly	C.2 Oral Fluency Chart Pencil	C.2 Graph showing wpm and error rate each day
6					
10	Listener follows along, verbally correcting reader when he errs	Reader reads orally to partner		short reading selection timer	
1			as above		
10	Listener follows along, counting but not verbally correcting reader errors	Reader performs one minute time sample of oral reading		marked passage in reading selection timer or stopwatch	wpm rate
3					
	Partner assists with charting if necessary	Reader records oral reading rate on chart		oral fluency chart	graph

cess. The partner program allows students to work with each other on reading skills, and also on interpersonal and coping skills.

Short stories on a range of reading levels, student charts, and a stop watch are the materials necessary in oral fluency. Stories should be of a length which can be easily read in one or two six minutes sessions. The primary source for stories used in the HILC has been the Reader's Digest Skillbuilder Series. However, basal readers, high interest/low reading level programs, and even magazines are sources for material. Students maintain greater interest in the oral fluency program if the materials are not used in skill development as well.

Silent Fluency

The silent fluency program encourages students to read for enjoyment as well as learning. Students choose from among several books on their level and read daily for twenty five minutes. Read-along tapes are available for all books. A schedule of reading is established between teacher and student whereby the student reads a number of chapters with the tape alternating with reading chapters without the tape (see Table 7.3). In this way the student benefits from his own efforts at silent reading and from the multisensory experience of listening and reading simultaneously.

The need for silent reading practice has been documented by several authors. Oliver (1970) states that efficiency in the application of reading skills seems to be developed from about 20 percent instruction and 80 percent practice. McCracken (1971) has recommended that each student in grades K–12 be required to read silently for 30 minutes a day. The student must have sufficient practice to benefit from his teaching and he must drill himself until he becomes proficient. His claim is that LD students are overtaught and underpracticed. The Sustained Silent Reading program (McCracken 1971) and the High Intensity Practice (Oliver 1970) were both developed to meet the need for such practice. According to Oliver (1971), children who are given time to read in school, under conditions that encourage reading, will demonstrate some very remarkable and favorable behavior changes. He states that when children are actively involved with intense response to words under structured practice conditions, the learning activity is of high intensity.

The HILC silent fluency program incorporates the ideas of these two programs, but goes beyond them with the introduction of read-along tapes. Read-along tapes have become quite popular in the last five years.

TABLE 7.3

Silent Fluency Schedule

Time	Student Actions	Teacher Actions	Materials	Products
Daily 25 min.	*Silent Fluency/Individually*			
Varies	D.5 Reader listens to tape of one chapter of book, follows along in written text	D.5 Teacher assigns reading level Teacher monitors class	D.2 Student selected book at appropriate reading level D.3 Tape of book, tape	
Varies	E.1 Reader continues in book, reading one chapter without listening to tape		D.4 recorder/headset for each student	
	F.1 Reader systematically reads book by alternating reading alone and listening/reading along	F.2 Teacher establishes individual reading routine as warranted	Reading selection Reading selection	
Regularly	G.1 Reader answers comprehension questions over book (verbally and in writing)	G.2 Teacher checks written comprehension activities G.3 Teacher discusses book with each student upon completion, assigns next selection	G.4 Multiple choice questions over book chapters Discussion questions over total book	G.5 List of books read Comprehension answer sheet

A few programs such as the Listen-Read program (Schneeberg 1977) have reported increased reading ability especially in comprehension as measured by standardized tests through the use of read-along tapes. Monteith (1978) surveyed current information on read-along programs. She describes three programs which reported favorable results in using read-along tapes, but she claims there is a lack of information on how taped books are used, why they are being used, and how effective they are.

The HILC silent fluency program includes taped books for several reasons. First, students who have encountered failure at reading will seldom read voluntarily. The use of read-along tapes makes the reading experience less frustrating and encourages a willingness to read in many students. Second, read-along tapes give the student a model for proper inflection in reading, for correct pronounciation of new words, and for proper usage of words to which they have been exposed. Wolpert (1971) suggests that when a student does not give the correct vocal response to a word he has been taught, the problem may be that he does not associate the correct sound with the symbol. Instruction in this case should be directed to strengthening the association between the visual sensation of the written word and the vocalization of that word. Read-along tapes are a method of providing students with practice in visual and auditory association. Third, the use of read-along tapes allows teachers to assess a student's comprehension abilities as they relate to his ability to master concepts versus his ability to read. Through diagnostic teaching a teacher can determine whether a student is unable to comprehend the material due to the level of complexity or whether a student comprehends it if he can hear the concept or story line as he reads it rather than reading it alone.

The silent fluency program encourages students to read interesting, enjoyable books, both fiction and non-fiction. But the goal of enjoyment does not supercede the goal of comprehension. Built into the silent fluency format are regular comprehension checks. Some of these are paper and pencil activities, some are discussions with the teacher. Information gained from comprehension activities is useful in assigning subsequent fluency books and in designing a student's skill development program. For example, if in discussions with a student, a teacher finds that the student is unable to summarize the actions of the book into a main idea, but rather relates a progression of events in answer to this task, she will structure activities to be completed in the skill period which build summarizing skills.

Skill Development

The skill development program operates for one hour each day. During this period students work on a variety of activities designed to remediate skill weaknesses. Criterion-referenced tests are used as initial determiners of skill deficits. This information is supplemented by teacher observations and analysis of the student's work and by data gathered during the fluency periods.

Each student works on at least one comprehension objective. In fact, many students work on several comprehension activities. This emphasis originates with the philosophy that the ability to comprehend material, or give meaning to it, is vitally important for success in the regular classroom. Many students entering junior high school have been inundated with vocabulary development, phonics activities, and word attack instruction. A shift in the focus of instruction is necessitated by the student's earlier failure in the above approach and by a student's advancement in school. In addition to comprehension activities, a student's skill program may include activities on sentence analysis, written expression, vocabulary development, study skills, and organizational techniques.

The HILC utilizes as many methods and materials as possible. An attempt is made to match student preference and materials and if possible, student modalities and materials. Multisensory activities are encouraged through the use of kits with tapes, the controlled reader, and the language master. Students are assigned content related activities to encourage generalization of skills from interesting stories to fact filled material.

Each student in the HILC is aware of his academic program. Teachers hold regular conferences with each student to review his Individual Education Plan, to discuss the materials he is using, and to get feedback from the student on his feelings of progress in HILC. Parents are also informed of their child's program and progress through weekly parent reports and parent group meetings.

During the skill development period the HILC teacher accumulates valuable information about each student. This data is used in making diagnostic decisions about the student's future reading instruction and about the likelihood of a student's continued growth in reading skills. The teacher also gathers information during this time which is reported to regular classroom teachers to facilitate successful accommodation of the learning disabled student in their classroom. Such data as the child's inability to copy a question from book to paper, a student's extremely slow rate of handwriting, or a student's ability to dictate paragraphs but not to write them can be extremely beneficial to the classroom teacher. The diagnostic emphasis of the HILC allows the collection and utilization of this information.

Reading Program Success

The combination of skill remediation and fluency development reflects the synergistic nature of the HILC curriculum. By impacting the student in both these areas simultaneously a significant increase in reading ability in a relatively short time is anticipated. Preliminary test reports of student achievement in HILC indicate that a growth spurt approximately four times what might normally be expected does occur.

Students, teachers, and parents all give favorable recommendations to the HILC reading program. In a recent evaluation of HILC done by students currently enrolled in the program, silent and oral fluency were frequently cited as the most enjoyable part of the program and as the part which students felt benefitted them most. Parents report that for the first time their children are coming home talking about what they read in school and are beginning to read at home. Teachers are amazed that students use their breaks to get out their tape recorders and books for silent fluency. While data for final, comprehensive evaluation of the HILC reading program is still being collected, initial indications are that it is successful not only in terms of student motivation, but also in terms of student achievement.

REFERENCES

Allington, R. L. (1977). If They Don't Read Much, How They Ever Gonna Get Good? *Journal of Reading* 21 (1): 57–61

Ekwall, E. (1976). Diagnosing and Using Appropriate Teaching Techniques for the Disabled Reader. *Diagnosis and Remediation of the Disabled Reader.* Boston: Allyn and Bacon.

Gilliland, H. (1974). Oral Reading. *A Practical Guide to Remedial Reading.* Columbus, Ohio: Merrill.

Gutknecht, B., and Keenan, D. (1978). Basic Skills: Not Which, But Why, and an Enlightened How. *The Reading Teacher* 31 (6): 668–74.

Lenkowsky, R. S. (1977). Reading for the Learning Disabled Adolescent. *Academic Therapy* 13: 47–52.

Lockett, B. (1975). Self-Concept of the Learning Disabled Adolescent. In E. Ensminger and L. Smiley, eds., *Educational Considerations for the Learning Disabled Adolescent: Selected Papers.* Georgia: Georgia State University.

McCracken, R. (1971). Initiating Sustained Silent Reading. *Journal of Reading* 14: 521–24.

Monteith, M. K. (1978). Taped Books and Reading Materials. *Journal of Reading* 21 (6): 554–56.

Oliver, M. E. (1970). High Intensity Practice: The Right to Enjoy Reading. *Education* 91: 69–71.

Schneeberg, H. (1977). Listening While Reading: A Four Year Study. *The Reading Teacher* 30: 629–35.

Spache, G. D. (1976). Strategies of Remedial Reading. *Diagnosing and Correcting Reading Disabilities.* Boston: Allyn and Bacon.

Strange, M., and Allington, R. (1977). Use the Diagnostic Prescriptive Model Knowledgeably. *The Reading Teacher* 31 (3): 290–94.

White, M. M. (1975). Peer Group Effect on Adolescent Development. In E. Ensminger and L. Smiley, eds., *Educational Consideration for the Learning Disabled Adolescent: Selected Papers.* Georgia: Georgia State University.

Wolpert, E. (1971). Modality and Reading: A Perspective. *The Reading Teacher* 24: 640–43.

8

Hypoglycemia—Fact or Fiction?

Howell I. Runion

IN RECENT YEARS many of us have broadened our concerns to include disciplines and methods once thought totally foreign and apart from traditional approaches to dealing with these special children. One specific area of concern to me is the contribution of nutrition to normal brain functioning. Real or suspected neurologic deficit in the face of inappropriate nutrition is a problem we can no longer continue to ignore. Proper nutrition is as important to the learning process as a book to the reading experience.

The question of hypoglycemia and its potential contribution to direct or secondary neurologic defect is now well established; however, its clinical identification in many instances is still a problem. Like nutrition, it cannot be ignored, particularly so in the special child who already is facing some form of motor or intellectual distress. Thus, I propose to direct our attention to one variant of the problem: spontaneously occurring hypoglycemia. In many instances, the remediation of spontaneous hypoglycemia is relatively easy, *i.e.*, a change in diet consisting of the elimination or reduction of refined carbohydrates and an increase in daily protein intake, coupled with frequent feeding periods and an intensive investigation for possible food allergies.

In 1924, C. L. Harris reported the condition in man of spontaneously occurring hypoglycemia that was not associated with hyperinsulinism. Since his paper appeared, the literature has been filled with the accounts of this phenomena. Hypoglycemia leaves the patient presenting with a wide variety of untoward symptoms which on occasion can be accompanied with distressing abnormal neurologic signs. Unfortunately, hypoglycemia is generally diagnosed clinically only on documentation obtained from the standard five-hour glucose tolerance test and the label attached to the patient when his or her blood glucose levels drop to 40–45 mg per 100 ml. Surprisingly, some patients will not present any symptomology at blood glucose levels as low as 20 mg per 100 ml, while other patients demonstrate many of the recognizable signs and symptoms of insulin-evoked hypoglycemia with blood glucose levels of 60–80 mg per 100 ml. This seemingly contradictory finding perhaps explains the confusion that attends the spontaneously occurring hypoglycemia in man and gives rise to the question by both patient and physician, "Is hypoglycemia fact or fiction?" Perhaps in those cases in which blood glucose levels of 50 mg per 100 ml or higher give rise to signs or symptoms of hypoglycemia, one is really seeing what Marks *et al.* (1961, 1965) describe as neuroglycopenia. Neuroglycopenia is defined by Marks as an "inappropriate level of metabolizable carbohydrates available to neurons for normal function". Indeed, these low glucose blood levels may be quite independent of the extra-cellular blood glucose levels occurring outside the blood brain barrier as seen in the general body tissue pool as illustrated in Figure 8.1.

Decreased glucose availability at the neuron's membrane surface may be caused by a variety of factors, *e.g.,* cell membrane dynamics, hormone influences, essential vitamin deficiencies as in B_1, B_3, B_5, B_6, B_{12}, changes in glial cell physiology, local ischemia, and selected drugs such as anti-convulsants and oral hypoglycemics (Roe 1976, Figure 1). Thus, any one or all of these factors may lead to a diminished pool of intracellular glucose so necessary to normal neuronal metabolism and functioning. It must be remembered that glucose is the only energy source that the neuron can use. In addition, neurons, unlike somatic cells, cannot store glucose; thus, a constant uninterrupted supply is absolutely essential. However, concurrently, with this micro-environmental cell deficiency, the glucose blood levels seen in the general body pool may appear to be normal. However, glucose-deprived neurons tend to function inefficiently or inappropriately. Collectively large groups of glucose deprived neurons will give rise to the signs and symptoms generally associated with demonstrable insulin produced hypoglycemia.

The probable explanation for neuron dysfunction during hypoglycemia involves the eventual disruption of cell membrane potential gradients. Changes in steady state membrane potentials and the loss of the individual neuron's ability to perform integrative functions ultimately leads to the disruption of excitatory and inhibitory transmitter activity normally seen between neurons. Quite aside from the possible defects of cell membrane permeability to ions and changes in glucose transport, it is helpful to recognize other possibilities known to lead to systemic as well as neuronal glucose deprivation: for example (Figure 8.1), impaired carbohydrate uptake via the gut, reduced liver gluconeogenesis, autonomic nervous system anomalies, the overall health of the patient, and the individual's response to hormone influences. All of these factors or any single one may lead to the hypoglycemic experience and must be considered in each patient.

While the exact mechanisms involved in spontaneous hypoglycemia are still not entirely known, Buckley (1978 *a,b*) has built an attractive

FIGURE 8.1

Neuron Glucose Homeostasis: Influencing Factors

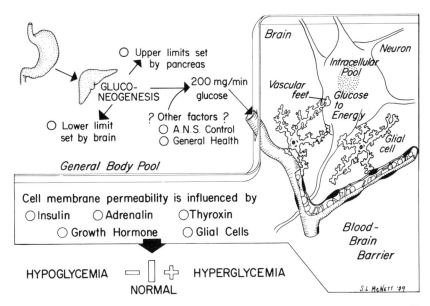

The factors involved in steady state neuron glucose homeostasis. The "normal" production of glucose by the liver in a 140 kilogram man is approximately 200 mg per minute. The availability of this glucose pool to the brain is initially limited by the blood-brain barrier. Astroglial cells associated with both the vascular bed of the brain and the neurons are equipped with tiny nodule projections known as vascular feet. The vascular feet are believed to facilitate glucose transport from the capillary beds to neurons via the cytoplasm of the astroglial cell. However, both the membranes of the glial cells and the neuron may be subject to circulating hormones which alter membrane permeability such that the transport of glucose may be facilitated or retarded. Consequently, the intercellular glucose available to a neuron may bear no direct relationship to the glucose available in the blood serum passing through the capillaries of the brain.

model for interpreting the resulting neurologic emotional consequences resulting from reduced or inadequate blood sugar levels. His model is based on the earlier studies of Gellhorn and Loofburrow (1963), Gellhorn (1967, 1968a, 1968b), and Buckley and Gellhorn (1969). His system implicates the glucose receptor centers located in the ventral medial hypothalamic nucleus. With dysfunction of the glucoreceptors, inhibitory neurons in the hypothalamus are released from active control. These inhibitory neurons project to the temporal lobe and the limbic system. Their functions are thought to modulate limbic activity, thus in the absence of inhibition normal functioning will either be modified or possibly become pathologic. The tight relationship of the glucose receptors to the limbic structures is seen in Figure 8.2. In the normal brain, Buckley's model calls for a continued level of inhibitory firing to neurons of the amygdala and hippocampus. However, if disinhibition occurs, this apparently leads to the development of "hypoglycemic symptoms." Buckley's model also provides an explanation for the patients who clinically may or may not always present with blood glucose levels of 40 mg per 100 ml or less, but nonetheless behave like a typical spontaneous hypoglycemic. He uses the term "kindling" to describe this phenomenon and suggests that small subclinical episodes of hypoglycemia or neuroglycopenia eventually lead to the development of a wide range of often baffling symptoms or periods of frank clinical hypoglycemia. Coupled with the older concept of neuroglycopenia (Marks *et al.* 1961) and the sub-acute electrical stimulation studies of the limbic system conducted by Goddard, McIntyre, and Leach

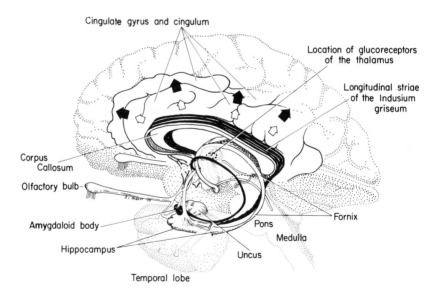

Glucoreceptors in Relation to Limbic System

FIGURE 8.2 The glucoreceptors of the thalamus and their proximity to the limbic system. See text for discussion.

(1969), this becomes an attractive model and adds validity to the concept that proven blood glucose levels may not always be required for explaining the "hypoglycemic experience" or making the diagnosis of spontaneous hypoglycemia in a patient (Buckley 1979, personal communications). The "kindling" effects are described by Buckley as frequently persisting for days following a minor fluctuation in blood glucose levels that have triggered momentary hypoglycemic events. These events may have been triggered by the patient from something as inane as missing a meal, a sudden glucose load via a candy bar, a glut of coffee, coke, or similar caffeine based drinks, or simply stress and fatigue.

The limbic system has long been recognized by neurophysiologists as a system slow to be excited and persistent in excitatory discharge once excited. The "kindling" effect can thus account for the untoward symptoms patients often report but which are not clinically verified during the glucose tolerance testing. The progressive development of symptoms leading to neurologic involvement may also flow from the "kindling" as the influence of the limbic structures ultimately affects neocortex behavior, *e.g.* (Figure 8.2), modified sensory perception, voluntary and involuntary motor activity, memory involvement and distorted vision to mention but a few of the disabling neurological events credited to prolonged neuroglycopenia or hypoglycemic episodes.

It is important at this point also to note that spontaneous hypoglycemia may have a number of underlying causes which are related to detectable organic lesions: for example, hyperinsulinism initiated by tumor or carcinoma, hypertrophy of the adrenals, hepatic disease, such as hepatitis and cirrhosis, anterior pituitary hypofunction, adrenal cortical hypofunction, and finally, autonomic disorders principally associated with the glucose receptors of the thalamus. These must all be considered in evaluation of the patient (Mark and Rose 1965; Buckley 1969a, 1978a and b). In addition, one must consider the consequences of gastric operations, the diabetic, and the puzzling psychomatic hypoglycemia occasionally seen as described by Renie and Howard in 1942. However, the vast majority of spontaneous hypoglycemia cases fall into the category of the functional variety. The literature is at this point sometimes confusing to the reader as the terms functional, reactive, and endogenous are used interchangeably by authors when describing spontaneous hypoglycemia. Under this same category, hyperinsulinism and renal glycosuria and severe muscle exercise and stress must be added to the list of potential causes to be considered. Unfortunately, detection of hypoglycemia triggered by this last group offers the clinician considerable problems in arriving at a diagnosis. More than likely, the suspected hypoglycemia will be transient and related to undetectable neuroglycopenia that precedes a clinically detectable hypoglycemic episode.

The list of signs and symptoms that have been reported with patients presenting with spontaneous or functional hypoglycemia are often as confusing and contradictory as are the presence or absence of confirming clinical blood glucose levels. A small sampling of the range of signs and symptoms reported by patients include: episodic inattentiveness, personality changes that may be abrupt or long term, unexplained excitement, hyper-irritability, drowsiness, slurred speech, loss of motor coordination, myoclonic twitching, hyperkinesia athetoid and choreiform movements, seizures, mono or hemi-paresis, sensory modality changes, aphasia, visual disturbances, brain stem involvement including diplopia, disarthria and dysphasia. In some instances, the hypoglycemia leads to extreme lethargy, stupor, and coma (Marks and Rose 1965). Other investigators have reported a clinical association of hypoglycemia to angina pectoris, peptic ulcer, hyperventilation, and unexplained alien anxiety and fatigue (Buckley 1967, 1969, 1974; Buckley and Gellhorn 1969).

Functional or spontaneous hypoglycemia probably accounts for 70 percent of the cases of hypoglycemia seen clinically. The total incidence of hypoglycemia in the general population is not known. As previously noted, the diagnosis is generally made on hard clinical data. However, when one considers the subtle implications of neuroglycopenia and the distribution of neuronal physiology that can occur following "kindling", it becomes apparent that a diagnosis of spontaneous or functional hypoglycemia in the absence of recorded blood glucose levels must often be made on the basis of the history and careful investigation of the patient's real or imagined signs or symptoms. On the other hand, too frequently the appropriate laboratory investigation might not have been made by the physician or his delegate, and as a result, the patient is not treated in the most effective way. Perhaps the most common clinical error is the use of a single blood glucose test score taken from an overall laboratory blood study or chem panel. If the value of 50 mg per 100 ml is returned in such a test, it does not necessarily confirm hypoglycemia, but it might be significant, particularly if the patient's history suggests that such a finding would be appropriate. To be sure, a full five-hour glucose tolerance test should be ordered, or if this is not feasible, the patient should be counseled as though he were a hypoglycemic. If a more thorough investigation is called for, the patient must be carefully prepared for the study. For example, if we are dealing with a child, the parents should be fully briefed on the importance of careful dietary control prior to the glucose tolerance test and the absolute necessity of a food-free fast for a 10-hour period prior to the actual glucose tolerance test. Ideally, patients should be prestressed with a carbohydrate-intensive diet 48 hours prior to the 10-hour fast and the glucose tolerance study. The 48-hour diet stressing will often evoke a reactive response to the postprandial glucose loading that otherwise might be inconclusive if only the 10 hour fast is observed.

There are a number of factors that will influence the test results; these are summarized in Table 8.1. The patient's age must be carefully considered and counseling provided appropriate for that age level. If a carbohydrate stress diet is to be used, it must be made perfectly clear to the patients or their guardians as to what to eat and why this is being done. Once the patient has arrived at the clinic, he should not be allowed to wander around during the next five hours of the procedure. Ideally, the patient should be left in a supine position over the 5-hour test. It is most important that no coexisting disease be present such as flu or colds at the time the test is scheduled. A thorough drug screen should be performed on the patient, either via history or urinalysis, and the results considered in reviewing the test results. The patient's emotional status during the test should be noted and "clinical" stress minimized, particularly where children are concerned. The imponderables, such as gastric emptying and glucose turnover rates will vary from patient to patient. While these two parameters are not measurable, their importance on the final test results must be considered. Unfortunately, the quality of the test does not simply rest with the patient's compliance, but must also involve the clinical laboratory personnel and procedure used. For example, the glucose dose and its concentration must be compounded so that it is both palatable and

TABLE 8.1

Factors Influencing Oral Glucose Tolerance Tests

Patient	Test Procedures
1. AGE/SEX	1. GLUCOSE DOSAGE
2. DIET	2. CONCENTRATION
3. ACTIVITY LEVEL BEFORE & DURING TEST	3. SAMPLE SITE — VENUS OR ARTERIAL
4. POSTURE DURING TEST	*4. SAMPLE FREQUENCY
5. CO-EXISTING DISEASE	5. BLOOD SUGAR DETECTION METHOD — color metric or hexokinase UV DETECTION METHOD
6. DRUGS	
7. EMOTIONAL STATUS	
8. RATE OF GASTRIC EMPTYING	
9. RATE OF GLUCOSE TURNOVER	

*See text for discussion

consumable by the patient in a maximum time span of five minutes. The decision to sample venous or arterial blood must be made, arterial punctures being preferable for greatest accuracy. The most important parametere is the frequency of sampling (Table 8.2). The specific sample times will be dictated by the type of test given such as oral-glucose, glucogon, leucine, or the tolbutamide challenge. Care must be exercised to reduce trauma and emotional stress during the conduct of the study.

The absolute regularity of the blood sample periods becomes significant when one is faced with findings that do not present blood glucose levels in the already accepted 40–50 mg level for the diagnosis of hypoglycemia. Indeed, the sudden precipitous drops in blood glucose level of 50–70 mg in a 30-minute period may be of more significance than final blood glucose levels of 30 or 40 mg per 100 ml. These sudden drops are frequently not seen until the third or fourth hour of the 5 hour test, although in gastrotomy patients it may appear within the first hour (Figure 8.3).

The similarities between blood glucose tolerance test in functional hypoglycemia, mild diabetics and post-gastroenterostomy patients and normals are presented in Figure 8.3. Examination of these data along with interpretive test data of Table 8.3 provides an explanation as to why the standard blood panel with a single glucose level is inadequate in making the diagnosis of spontaneous or functional hypoglycemia. Examination of Figure 8.3 reveals that the typical lows for functional or spontaneous hypoglycemia occur at the third hour post-administration of the glucose drink. Should the 5-hour glucose investigation be nonconclusive, it is important to re-examine the history given by the patient and confirm with members of the family the symptoms the patient reports. Whether one wishes ultimately to label the patient whose records cannot be verified

TABLE 8.2

Hypoglycemia Tests

Test	Route	Child-Dose	Adult	Sample Period
Oral Glucose	P.O.	1.75 gm/kw	100 gm	0-30-60-120 ETC. to 300 minutes
Glucogon	I.V.	0.03 mg/kg IV Push	1.0 mg	0-2-5-15-30-45-60 every 30 min. to 180.
Leucine	P.O.	150 mg/kg	150 mg/kg	0-15-30-45-60 every 30 min. to 180.
Tolbutamide	I.V.	205 mg/kg over 2 min.	1.0 gm	0-15-30-45-60 every 30 min. to 180.

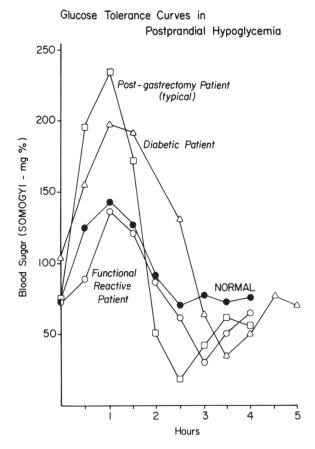

Glucose Tolerance Curves in
Postprandial Hypoglycemia

FIGURE 8.3 Composites of typical glucose tolerance curves obtained from postprandial hypoglycemia patients with predisposing conditions of gastrectomy, diabetes, or function reactive/spontaneous hypoglycemia. The values may be compared with those seen in "normal" individuals subjected to a 5-hour blood glucose study. Data point are for blood samples each 30 minutes post administration of a standard 100 gram glucose dose.

clinically as being a functional hypoglycemic in my opinion is unimportant. But rather, on the basis of the history, I would address my attention to the daily dietary habits of the individual with an eye to improving both his intellectual and motor functions with improved nutrition. Perhaps this would correct undetectable neuroglycopenia.

TABLE 8.3

Postprandial Hypoglycemia

Whole Blood 5 Hr. Glucose Test, Somogyi-Nelson, Glucose-Oxidase or
Ferricyanide Auto Analyzer if Plasma or Serum, Values are 15% Higher

Cause	Fasting	Glucose Loading Initial Findings	Final Levels
Functional or Spontaneous	Normal 60–100 MG%	First 2 Hr. Normal 160 MG% Max. 2nd Hr. Level Below 110 MG% A Drop of 40–50 MG% is potentially significant	Below 45 MG% Between 2nd and 4th Hr.
Mild Diabetes	Normal Not Above 110 MG%	1st Hr. 160 MG% 2nd Hr. 120 MG% significant 30–40 MG% shift	Below 45 MG% 3rd–5th Hr.
Post Gastroenter- ostomy	Normal	200–300 1st Hr.	Below 45 MG% 2nd–4th Hr.

While it is not the main function of this paper to discuss treatment, it is, however, necessary to make the notation that treatment of patients with confirmed or suspected neuroglycopenia/hypoglycemia is really a rather straightforward process. Essentially, it revolves around the removal of refined carbohydrates from the daily diet, supplementation with increased amounts of protein preferably accompanied by regular, frequent feeding periods. Naturally, there must be a concern for total caloric intake in prescribing such a diet so as to avoid obesity. This, however, can be easily accomplished by determining the caloric needs of the individual so that he or she maintains a fixed body weight commensurate with age, sex, and body structure, while simultaneously keeping in mind the patient's daily exercise levels and environmental stress. For example, a child age 7–10 might require 1,900 calories on the low side to 2,400 calories on the high side. Protein intake for the child 7–10 who is a suspected or confirmed hypoglycemic patient should be elevated to approximately 50 gms per day. The daily diet of these children should be spread out over six feedings. The six feedings could be organized with caloric density of 316 calories on the low side, 400 calories on the high side per feeding period.

In most cases, however, it is desirable for the patient to invest 400 of his daily caloric units at the start of the day and up to 700 with the evening meal while dividing the rest over other feeding periods by using 100–180 calories per interim main meals. For those who have worked with spontaneous or hypoglycemic individuals in establishing a diet, you will recall that it usually takes 10–15 days on beginning such a diet for the patients themselves to report they are feeling better. However, they are generally capable of reporting within hours following a carbohydrate feeding or the missing of a feeding period that adverse symptoms have returned. Thus, in counseling the patient, it is essential that he or she understand the consequences of deviation from the new diet and the choices that must be made if the patient is to be free from the untoward symptoms of his metabolic condition.

In the present context of knowledge and the technological limits that now prevent clinical verification of neuroglycopenia or subliminal hypoglycemic episodes, we do have enough clinical experience to recognize that nutrition has a profound effect on the emotional outlook, motor performance, intellectual abilities, and memory to suspect a more than casual relationship between food and homeostasis. While for some of us hypoglycemia may still remain a fictional story, for others it is a stark reality. Be it fiction or reality, improved nutrition as a part of the life style of neurologically handicapped children or "normal" individuals can only lead to positive results. It is worthy of our time and effort to instruct parents, children, and adults in the importance of nutrition and its relationship to neuronal functions whether we suspect hypoglycemia or not in order for us to achieve maximum efficiency from our magnificent brains.

REFERENCES

Buckley, R. E. (1967). Induction of Hypoglycemia As Treatment For Peptic Ulcers. *The Lancet* Sept. 2: 497.

_____ (1969). Hypoglycemic Symptoms and the Hypoglycemic Experience. *Psychosomatics* 10: 7.

Buckley, R. E., and Gellhorn, E. (1969). Neurophysiological Mechanisms Underlying the Action of Hypo- and Hyperglycemia in Some Clinical Conditions. *Confina Neurologica* 31: 247.

Buckley, R. E. (1974). Diabetes, Duodenal Ulcers and Hypothalamic Tuning. *International Acad. Metabiology* 3: 109.

_____ (1978a). Hypoglycemic Kindling of Limbic System Disorders. *J. of Orthomolecular Psych* 7 (2): 118.

_____ (1978b). Limbic Systems Kindling Hypothalamic Tuning and Psychosis or Time: The Fourth Dimension of Physiology. Presented to the California Orthomolecular Society, San Diego, Cal., Sept. 17.

_____ (1979). Personal Communications, Levine Hospital, Hayward, Cal. 94541.

Gellhorn, E., and Loofbourrow, G. (1963). *Emotions and Emotional Disorders: A Neurophysiological Study.* New York: Harper and Row.

Gellhorn, E. (1968a). Neurophysiologic Basis of Homeostasis. *Confina Neurologlica* 30: 217.

_____ (1968b). The Neurophysiological Basis of Anxiety: A Hypothesis. *Perspect. Biol. Med.* 8: 488.

_____ (1976). The Tuning of the Nervous System: Physiological Foundation and Implications for Behaviour. *Perspect. Biol. Med.* 10: 559.

Goddard, G. V., McIntyre, D. C., and Leech, C. K. (1969). A Permanent Change in Brain Function Resulting From Daily Electrical Stimulation. *Exp. Neurol.* 25: 295.

Harris, S. (1924). Hyperinsulinism and Dysinsulinism. *JAMA* 83: 729.1.

Marks, V., Marrack, D., and Rose, F. C. (1961). Hyperinsulinism in The Pathogenesis of Neuroglycopenia Syndrome. *Proc. R. Soc. Med.* 54: 747.

Marks, V., Rose, F. C. (1965). *Hypoglycemia.* Oxford: Blackwell.

Rennie, T. A. C., and Howard, J. E. (1942). Hypoglycemia and Tension-Depression. *Psychosomatic Med.* 4: 273.

Roe, D. (1976). *Drug Induced Nutritional Deficiencies.* Westport, Ct.: AVI.

9

A Study of Prolonged Administration of Methylphenidate in Childhood Hyperactivity

Linda Charles, Richard Schain, and Donald Guthrie

Despite numerous empirical studies which have demonstrated positive short-term effects of stimulant medications on the behavior and, less frequently, academic performance of hyperactive children, few studies have investigated the long-term effectiveness of these drugs. This lack is cited with increasing frequency as a deficiency in the pediatric psychopharmacology literature (Sroufe 1975; Kolata 1978). Information on long-term effects is necessary for clinical decisions as to how long drug therapy, if initially effective, should be continued. Since short-term effectiveness is well documented, assumptions are often made that long-term treatment is appropriate unless adverse effects appear during the course of treatment. Further, since withdrawal of stimulant drugs is often immediately followed by behavioral disturbance, there are strong pressures to maintain stimulant drug therapy.

A available research evidence, although limited, has cast doubt on the value of long-term stimulant drug therapy. In a study of age-related effects, Safer and Allen (1975) found no significant difference in therapeutic response to drugs for age groups compared. They did, however, find that positive drug effects were substantially greater in the first year of treatment than in the second year for all age groups. Two other studies deal directly with long-term effectiveness of stimulants with evaluations based on data collected at least two weeks after the discontinuation of drugs (Weiss, Kruger, Danielson, and Elman 1975; Riddle and Rapoport 1976). Weiss *et al.* (1975) found no significant differences between children who had been treated with methylphenidate for 3 to 5 years and hyperactive children who had never received medication. Measures used included psychiatric variables, psychometric measures (Bender Gestalt and WISC), and academic performance as measured by grades passed. Riddle and Rapoport (1976) reported continuing social and academic

This work was supported in part by CIBA-Geigy Corporation, NIH Special Resources Research Grant No. RR-3, and NICHD Grant No. HD-04612.

problems for hyperactive boys at a two-year follow up whether they had continued on medications until three weeks prior to evaluation or had discontinued previously. These studies all question the long-term benefits of stimulant therapy.

Finally, it is sometimes presumed that the continuing need for, and benefit from, medications is demonstrated by the deterioration of behavior reported by parents and teachers when a child misses a pill or discontinues medications (Oettinger 1972; Weiss *et al.* 1975). This clinical effect clearly exists for many children; however, this may be a temporary rebound effect, and there is no evidence which indicates that behavioral decrements persist over time. Supporting the rebound hypothesis, it was recently reported that 10 of 12 non-hyperactive, prepubertal boys exhibited behavioral overactivity approximately 5 hours after an acute administration of 5 mg. of dextroamphetamine (Rapoport, Buchsbaum, Zahn, Weingartner, Ludlow, and Mikkelsen 1978).

The purpose of the present study was to investigate the long-term effects of methylphenidate on the behavior and academic functioning of hyperactive children. To evaluate long-term effects, the investigators analyzed both the degree to which initial beneficial effects sustained over time and the effects of discontinuation of medication on the behavior and academic functioning of hyperactive children. This study differs from previous studies cited (Riddle and Rapoport 1976; Weiss *et al.* 1975) in that behavior and performance were evaluated before children discontinued medications.

METHODS

Subjects

Children from 6 to 12 years of age were referred by school psychologists and nurses, pediatricians, and the UCLA Pediatric Clinic for symptoms of hyperactivity, including restlessness, impulsivity, short attention span, and distractibility. Ninety-eight children whose symptoms were judged to be significantly interfering with their school performance were entered into a 16-week methylphenidate-placebo study. The results of this study have been reported previously (Schain and Reynard 1975). Of the children judged to have a positive response to methylphenidate, 36 were entered into a three-year study of the long-term effects.

Study participants included 31 boys and 5 girls from 6 years 1 month to 11 years 5 months (mean age: 8 years). Thirty-three were white and 3 were black. The original reasons for referral were both behavior and academic problems for 23, behavior only for 8, and academic only for 5. Eight had repeated grades, and an additional 6 were in special classroom settings at the time of their initial visit. According to their parents, all exhibited attentional disorders, 32 were described as hyperactive, 28 as impulsive, and 26 demonstrated emotional lability. Further, parents judged 22 of their children to have specific learning disabilities, 16 to have coordination defects, and 16 perceptual-motor problems. Full-scale IQ scores on the WISC ranged from 78 to 128 with a mean of 102 and a standard deviation of 12.3. Performance and verbal IQ scores did not differ significantly in range or means.

Procedures

Initial tests scores and ratings were collected at the child's first visit and reflect performance and behavior off medication. At this time, each child had a psychometric evaluation, including the Wechsler Intelligence Scale for Children (WISC) and the Bender Visual-Motor Gestalt. Parent and teacher rating scales (Conners) were completed at this time and at 3-to 6-month intervals. Following stabilization on methylphenidate, children were seen at 3-month intervals for the first year and at 6-month intervals thereafter.

During the period of the study, 13 of the 36 children were judged by their parents to be able to discontinue medication. These children were tested off medication after 6 months and, in most cases, again after one year. Mean duration in the study for the 23 children who remained on medication throughout the study (drug continuers) was 35 months. Mean duration in the study for the children who were taken off medication during the study (drug terminators) was 30 months, and duration of active medication for this group averaged 20 months. There were no significant differences between these groups in age, original ratings or initial response to drug, or stabilized dosage level. The children who were to become drug terminators had significantly lower WISC performance IQ scores at entry and these contributed to initial full-scale differences.

Data Analysis

Data were analyzed at four visits. The *initial* visit constituted baseline, off-drug testing. The *stabilized on-drug* data were taken four months later after dosages had been titrated and positive response established. The *both on-drug* data were taken at the last visit in which testing was done while the drug terminators were still on medication, and at a visit comparable in time for drug continuers. The mean time between the initial visit, when children began taking medication, and this mid-study visit was 20.4 months for the drug terminators and 21.5 months for the drug continuers. Discontinuation of medication was not effected at the same visit for every child. It was the intention of the investigators to evaluate on-drug performance after the longest possible duration and compare it with data for continuers. Finally, data were analyzed for the *last visit* of each child.

An analysis of variance was computed for each variable. Group differences were evaluated by examining differences among subject average scores to test for group main effects and differences. Differences among visits were used to test for visit main effects and for group by visit interactions. The t-tests in Table 9.1 are based on pooled error estimates for the analysis of variance. To compensate for basing multiple tests on the same data, critical values were computed by the Bonferroni method (Miller 1966).

Titration of Medication

Medication was titrated based on (1) evidence of negative physical or personality effects, (2) evidence that a reduced dose would be equally effective, or (3) evidence than an increased dose was required. Children were maintained at a level deemed clinically optimal. Mean dosage for the two groups did not differ significantly at any visit reported other than the last, when the drug terminators were not receiving medication. The mean dosage at the 4-month, stabilized on-drug visit was 1.2 mg/kg/day for drug terminators and 1.3 mg/kg/day for drug continuers. Dosage at the both on-drug visit was 0.7 mg/kg/day for terminators and 0.9 mg/kg/day for drug continuers. At the final visit, drug continuers were receiving 0.6 mg/kg/day.

The data described in this paper were collected as a part of the long-term clinical treatment of hyperactive children. Judgments as to titration of medication were based primarily on reports by parents and clinical observations of drug effectiveness. Decisions to reduce or discontinue methylphenidate were not, therefore, controlled specifically for research purposes. The results reported in this paper represent the objective and systematic description of this clinical experience, but lack the methodological advantages of random assignment of drug schedules.

FINDINGS

Performance on the WISC

The WISC is an individually administered intelligence test which yields a verbal score (VIQ), a performance score (PIQ) and the combined full-scale score (FSIQ). Each score has a mean of 100 and a standard deviation of 15. Scores were compared between each visit for each group separately, as were entry and final scores. The greatest improvement during the period of active medication was reflected in the PIQ. Both groups improved their performance scores significantly during this time, both had nonsignificant decrements at the final visit, and both remained significantly improved over entry levels. Both groups improved their verbal scores slightly to the both on-drug visit, and both had slightly lower verbal scores at the final visit, although none of these changes approached significance.

Although the drug terminators had lower entry scores and slightly larger decrements at the final visit, the patterns of performance and the degree of improvement during the study were not significantly different for the two groups. Repeated measures analysis of variance revealed no group by time interactions. In some cases, the terminators failed to reach the significance levels of the continuers. This was due, in part, to the smaller number in the terminator group. Absolute differences in mean change between groups were very small, although entry to final improvement on PIQ and FSIQ was slightly less for the terminators (Table 9.1; Figure 9.1).

To insure that mean score data were not masking dramatic individual differences, a frequency count of change scores from pre-drug levels was done. We were especially interested in determining whether some drug terminators suffered severe deterioration of performance when stimulants were discontinued. This does not appear to be the case, as only one terminator had a decrement of over 5 points on FSIQ, and two drug continuers showed similar decreases. In addition, there were a decreased number of drug continuers who remained improved over entry levels at the final visit (Table 9.2).

Behavior Ratings

Parents and teachers rated children on two independent measures. On the first, the Conners rating scale, the rater is required to score ten characteristics of each child as "not at all" (score of 0), "just a little,"

TABLE 9.1

Mean Scores and Significant Differences on WISC and Ratings
Comparison of Adjacent Visits

	Initial Visit (Pre-drug)		Stabilized On Drug (4 Months)		Both On Drug (Mean = 20 mos.)		Final Visit‖ (Mean = 33 mos.)		Initial vs. Final
Continuers (N = 23)									
WISC	*Mean*	*S.D.*	*Mean*	*S.D.*	*Mean*	*S.D.*	*Mean*	*S.D.*	
Performance	106.3	13.0	111.3	14.0	117.4*	14.2	116.4	14.6	‡
Verbal	101.0	14.5	103.8	14.4	107.3	14.0	103.1	14.0	
Full-Scale	103.7	12.6	108.1	13.6	113.1*	13.5	110.3	13.8	‡
Ratings									
Parents' Connors	19.2	6.9	7.5‡	6.6	10.1	6.1	10.6	7.1	‡
Teachers' Connors	16.3	6.5	6.0‡	5.4	12.9‡	6.5	11.0	5.2	†
Parents' Overall	2.0	.6	2.8‡	.6	2.6	.6	2.6	.5	‡
Teachers' Overall	1.8	.9	2.9‡	.7	2.2‡	.7	2.3	.5	
Terminators (N = 13)									
WISC									
Performance	99.1	13.5	107.4*	14.0	114.4	15.6	107.8	14.1	*
Verbal	96.8	12.9	99.6	14.7	101.0	14.4	97.5	13.7	
Full-Scale	97.6	12.0	103.6	13.5	108.0	15.1	102.6	13.3	
Ratings									
Parents' Connors	21.0	4.7	12.6‡	5.3	12.8	5.2	11.4	5.7	‡
Teachers' Connors	14.7	5.6	5.9‡	4.1	13.2‡	5.9	11.8	5.1	
Parents' Overall	2.1	.6	2.5	.5	2.6	.5	2.8	.4	†
Teachers' Overall	1.7	.6	2.8‡	.6	2.3	.6	2.2	.6	

2-tailed test of significance

* = p. < .05
† = p. < .01
‡ = p. < .001
‖Continuers on drug
Terminators off drug

"pretty much," or "very much" (score of 3). The items included are: restless or overactive; excitable, impulsive; disturbs other children; fails to finish things he starts—short attention span; constantly fidgeting; inattentive, distractible; demands must be met immediately—easily frustrated; cries often and easily; mood changes quickly and drastically; temper outbursts, explosive and unpredictable behavior. A low score is desirable on this measure.

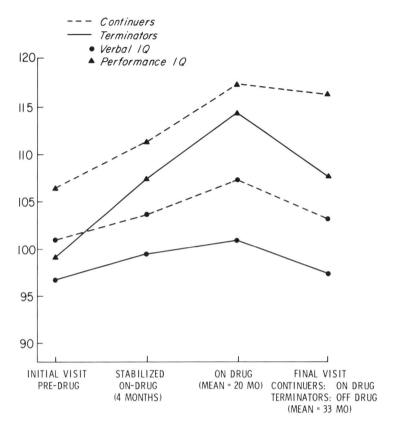

FIGURE 9.1 Mean scores on WISC verbal and performance IQ

Normative data for the teacher's scale indicate that the mean score of this measure is 4.3 with a standard deviation of 5.2 (Sprague, Cohen, and Eichlseder 1977). In a number of studies, children with scores of 15 or more—approximately 2 standard deviations above the mean—are judged hyperactive (Charles, Zelniker, Schain, and Guthrie 1979; Sleator and von Neumann 1974; Sleator, von Neumann, and Sprague 1974). In this study, the majority of children were initially rated hyperactive by this criterion both by parents and teachers. These frequencies were dramatically reduced at the stabilized on-drug visit, but showed some rebound while children were still on medications (Table 9.3).

In terms of mean score data, both parents and teachers initially rated their children near or above 15, indicating a hyperactive level. Be-

TABLE 9.2

Frequencies of Change in WISC FSIQ from Pre-Drug Levels

	Much Improved (11 + pts)	Some Improved (6 to 10)	Little Change (– 5 to 5)	Some Worse (– 6 to – 10)	Much Worse (– 11 + pts)	Total N
Continuers						
Stabilized	3 (13%)	8 (35%)	11 (48%)	1 (4%)	0	23
Both On	12 (52%)	5 (22%)	5 (22%)	0	1 (4%)	23
Final	9 (39%)	3 (13%)	9 (39%)	2 (9%)	0	23
Terminators						
Stabilized	3 (23%)	3 (23%)	7 (54%)	0	0	13
Both On	3 (33%)	1 (11%)	5 (56%)	0	0	9
Final	3 (25%)	1 (8%)	7 (58%)	1 (8%)	0	12

TABLE 9.3

Percentage of Scores of 15 or More (HA Level) on Conners' Rating Scale

	Initial Visit (Pre-Drug)	Stabilized On Drug (4 mos.)	Both On Drug (Mean = 20 mos.)	Final Visit (Mean = 33 mos.)
Continuers				
Parents	73.9	13.0	21.7	21.7
Teachers	56.5	8.7	34.8	30.4
Terminators				
Parents	84.6	30.8	23.1	30.8
Teachers	38.5	0	30.8	38.5

havior of both groups was rated much improved by both teachers and parents at the 4-month stabilized visit. Behavioral improvement as rated by teachers did not, however, sustain for the period of active medication. Both groups received significantly poorer teacher ratings while still on stimulants—although these were not quite to pre-drug levels. Parents' ratings reflected a different pattern. Essentially, behavioral ratings were stable after initial improvement for the period of the study, regardless of whether the children remained on medication or not. The patterns of change in ratings were highly similar for both groups (Table 9.1; Figure 9.2).

Frequency counts of changed ratings were also calculated with 0–4 points judged as little or no change, 5–9 points as some change, and 10 or more points as much change. All ratings were compared with initial, pre-drug scores to eliminate confusing between-visit variation with improvement over entry levels. On the parent ratings, only one child was rated worse and none much worse when taken off drug. Ten (77 percent) were rated as better or much better. For the drug continuers, one was rated worse, and 16 (70 percent) were rated better. The teachers rated 1 child as worse when taken off drugs, and 6 (46 percent) remained improved over entry levels. Of the drug continuers, 3 (14 percent) were rated worse and 13 (59 percent) improved (Table 9.4).

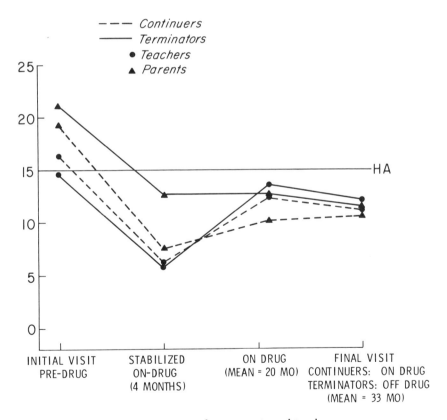

FIGURE 9.2 Conners mean scores from parents and teachers

TABLE 9.4

Conners' Ratings: Change Score Frequencies from Pre-Drug Visit

	Much Improved −10+ points		Some Improved −5 to −9 pts.		Little Change −4 to +4 pts.		Some Worse +5 to 9 pts.		Much Worse 10+ points	
	N	%	N	%	N	%	N	%	N	%
Parents										
Continuers										
Stabilized	14	60.9	6	26.1	3	13.0				
Both On drug	12	52.2	4	17.4	6	26.1	1	4.3		
Final visit	11	47.8	5	21.7	6	26.1	1	4.3		
Terminators										
Stabilized	6	46.2	2	15.4	5	38.5				
Both On drug	7	53.8	2	15.4	4	30.8				
Final visit	9	69.2	1	7.7	2	15.4	1	7.7		
Teachers										
*Continuers**										
Stabilized	12	54.5	6	27.3	4	18.2				
Both On drug	6	27.3	3	13.6	11	50.0	2	9.1		
Final visit	7	31.8	6	27.3	6	27.3	3	13.6		
Terminators										
Stabilized*	4	33.3	4	33.3	4	33.3				
Both On drug	2	15.4	2	15.4	6	46.2	3	23.1		
Final visit			6	46.2	6	46.2	1	7.7		

*Data missing for one child

Teachers and parents were also asked for global evaluations of overall functioning of their children in school and at home: excellent = 4; good = 3; fair = 2; poor = 1. Patterns of response to this question paralleled those on the Conners scales. Both groups were reported improved at the stabilized on-drug visit by both teachers and parents. Teachers rated both groups worse at the both on-drug visit, with no further deterioration for drug terminators when they discontinued methylphenidate. Overall functioning was rated significantly improved at the final visit over entry levels by parents, but not by teachers. Again, these changes were statistically equivalent whether or not children remained on medication. Interestingly, although group differences were not significant, the parent ratings of drug terminators showed increased improvement over time, even after these children discontinued medication. In contrast, the teachers of terminators, as well as both parents and teachers of the drug continuers, reported slight deterioration in overall functioning after the initial improvement (Table 9.1; Figure 9.3).

The Bender Visual-Motor Gestalt

Bender scores may be interpreted in several ways. The scoring system used in this study was developed by Koppetz based on developmental norms of performance. The child is instructed to view and copy each of nine designs exactly as he/she sees them. Designs are scored if they devi-

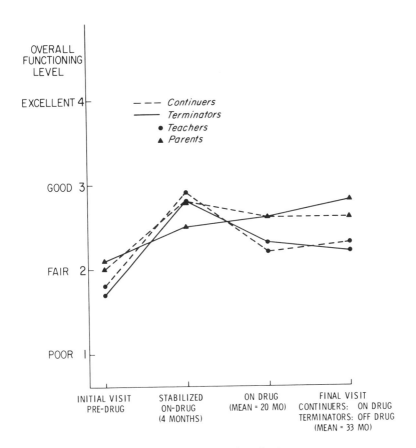

FIGURE 9.3 Mean global ratings of overall functioning

ate from the model in terms of distortion of shape, rotation, integration, and perseveration. The ability to accurately copy these designs increases with age (Bender 1946; Koppetz 1964). As errors are scored, a low score is desirable on this measure.

Koppetz scores on the Bender were analyzed in terms of their deviation from the chronological age expectancy at the time of test administration. Initially, 54 percent of the drug terminators and 30 percent of the continuers were developmentally delayed on this task. Some children in both groups improved their scores in the early months of drug administration. Typically, however, this improvement either (1) did not sustain throughout the total period of drug therapy, or (2) maintained even when medications were discontinued. Patterns over time for the two groups did not differ, and, at the end of the study, a slightly higher percentage of children from both groups were impaired than had been prior to drug administration (Table 9.5).

DISCUSSION

Two aspects of these findings are of clinical interest—response patterns for all children over time and the similarity of response patterns between groups, regardless of drug schedules. Response patterns over time indicated substantial initial improvement. This was true in varying degrees for all measures reported. Short-term improvement is consonant with the findings of many prior studies (Whalen and Henker 1976). Often, however, the assumption is made that improvement maintains for the duration of stimulant therapy. The data presented in this paper do not support this assumption. Initial improved performance was not maintained, although, for the most part, scores did not return to entry levels.

These data indicate habituation to drug. As noted, the mg/kg/day

TABLE 9.5

Frequencies of High Errors on The Bender

	Initial Visit (Pre-Drug)	Stabilized On-Drug (4 mos.)	Both On-Drug (Mean = 20 mos.)	Final Visit (Mean = 33 mos.)
Continuers	7 (30%)	4 (17%)	6 (26%)	8 (35%)
Terminators	7 (54%)	4 (31%)	6 (46%)	8 (62%)

dosage used in this study decreased over time. This was due both to the increasing weight of the children over the 3-year period and individual reductions in absolute dosages. Titration of medication was done individually and was based on clinical judgments that behavior and attention were not negatively affected by these reductions.

In light of the mg/kg decreases, one could speculate that maintaining or increasing the mg/kg dosage would have resulted in maintained improvement. The data from this study do not rule out such a possibility. However, the lack of significant differences between the two groups when the terminators discontinued medications indicates that dosages do not have a one-to-one correspondence to performance. Further, findings from other studies have indicated that high dosages may actually depress learning. Sprague and Sleator (1977) found that dosages as low as .3 mg/kg were optimal for performance on a learning task and that performance at higher dosages dropped below placebo levels. In this study, the lowest mean dosage was .6 mg/kg.

The second striking finding of this study is the lack of significant differences between children who remained on medication and those who discontinued after a period of successful treatment. For the most part, decisions to discontinue were made after a drug holiday in which the child appeared to be doing well at home and school. Typically, parents were the strongest influence for discontinuation, and their attitudes were based on beliefs that medications were no longer effective or that their children had outgrown the need for them. In two cases, teachers advocated an off-drug period during the school year, and one child strongly preferred being off medications. As drug schedules were not randomly assigned, over-interpretation of this data should be avoided. The evidence does suggest, however, that, with parental support, discontinuation of stimulants may be effected without disastrous results.

This is the first report of the performance of children after several years of drug therapy in which final testing was done while the children were still using stimulants. Two conclusions emerged from the analysis of this data. First, this study provided no evidence that initial drug improvement sustains during a long period of active drug treatment, and, second, there was no evidence that discontinuation of medication results in a return to pre-drug behavior or psychometric performance.

These findings are somewhat surprising. Most physicians continue medications because they believe they are useful, and most have seen children who seem to "fall apart" when they discontinue stimulants. It is important to remember that the belief in long-term usefulness of drugs may be influenced by many factors other than drug effects. The literature suggests that, as children grow older, many of their more overt symptoms diminish (Dubey and Kaufman 1978; Whalen and Henker 1976). Further, the effects of simply being in a study where performance is monitored and where advice and counsel are available may cause parents and children to view problems as under control. When this occurs in conjunction with the administration of medications, the drugs themselves may be assumed to be primarily responsible. Finally, the child who suffers extreme attentional and behavioral deterioration when medications are withdrawn may be demonstrating a temporary rebound effect, rather than a simple return to pre-drug levels. The fact that none of our discontinuers experienced this deterioration may be explained in part by the timing of our final measures—six months to a year after discontinuation—when withdrawal effects would presumably have dissipated.

In summary, these findings cast doubt on the long-term usefulness of medication in childhood hyperactivity. Implications for the physician and clinician are that drug therapy should be perhaps viewed as a short-term intervention—a respite period in which more positive social and school behaviors may be established (Schain 1977). The justification for long-term stimulant medication for hyperactive children remains to be established.

REFERENCES

Bender, L. (1946). *Instruction for the use of Visual Motor Gestalt Test.* New York: American Orthopsychiatric Assn.

Charles, L., Zelniker, T., Schain, R., and Guthrie, D. (1979). Effects of Methylphenidate on Hyperactive Children's Ability to Sustain Attention. *Pediatrics.* 64: 412–18.

Dubey, D. R., and Kaufmann, K. F. (1978). Home Management of Hyperkinetic Children. *Journal of Pediatrics* 93: 141–46.

Kolata, G. B. (1976). Childhood Hyperactivity: A New Look at Treatments and Causes. *Science* 199: 515–17.

Koppetz, E. M. (1964). *The Bender Gestalt Test for Young Children.* New York: Grune & Stratton.

Miller, R. G., Jr. (1966). *Simultaneous Statistical Inference.* New York: McGraw Hill.

Oettinger, L. (1972). *Workshop on the Evaluation of Long-term Effects of Stimulant Drugs.* From the meeting of the Psychopharmacology Research Branch, National Institute of Mental Health, Dept. of Health, Education, and Welfare, Chevy Chase, Md.

Rapoport, J. L., Buchsbaum, M. S., Zahn, T. P., Weingartner, H., Ludlow, C., and Mikkelsen, E. J. (1978). Dextroamphetamine: Cognitive and Behavior Effects in Normal Prepubertal Boys. *Science* 199: 560–63.

Riddle, K. D., and Rapoport, J. L. (1976). A 2-year Follow-up of 72 Hyperactive Boys: Classroom Behavior and Peer Acceptance. *Journal of Nervous and Mental Disease* 162: 126–34.

Safer, D. J., and Allen, R. P. (1975). Stimulant Drug Treatment of Hyperactive Adolescents. *Diseases of the Nervous System* 36: 454–57.

Schain, R. J. (1977). *Neurology of Childhood Learning Disorders,* 2nd ed. Baltimore: Williams & Wilkins.

Schain, R. J., and Reynard, C. L. (1975). Observations on Effects of a Central Stimulant Drug (Methylphenidate) in Children with Hyperactive Behavior. *Pediatrics* 55: 709–16.

Sleator, E. K., and von Neumann, A. W. (1974). Methylphenidate in the Treatment of Hyperkinetic Children. *Clinical Pediatrics* 13: 19–24.

Sleator, E. K., von Neumann, A. W., and Sprague, R. L. (1974). Hyperactive Children: A Continuous Long-term Placebo-controlled Follow-up. *JAMA* 299: 316–17.

Sprague, R. L., Cohen, M. N., and Eichlseder, W. (1977). Are There Hyperactive Children in Europe and the South Pacific? In R. Halliday (Chair), The Hyperactive Child: Fact, Fiction, and Fantasy. Symposium presented at the meeting of the American Psychological Association, San Francisco.

Sprague, R. L., and Sleator, E. K. (1977). Methylphenidate in Hyperkinetic Children. Differences in Dose Effects on Learning and Social Behavior. *Science* 198: 1274–76.

Sroufe, L. A. (1975). Drug Treatment of Children with Behavior Problems. In F. D. Horowitz, ed., *Review of Child Development Research,* Vol. 4. Chicago: University of Chicago Press.

Weiss, G., Kruger, E., Danielson, V., and Elman, M. (1975). Effects of Long-term Treatment of Hyperactive Children with Methylphenidate *Canadian Medical Association Journal* 159–65.

Whalen, C. K., and Henker, B. (1976). Psychostimulants and Children: A Review and Analysis. *Psychological Bulletin* 83:1113–30.

10

Individual Differences in Cerebral Lateralization
Are They Relevant to Learning Disability?

Merrill Hiscock and Marcel Kinsbourne

LONG BEFORE IT BECAME FASHIONABLE to talk about the right and left halves of the brain, North American education was indoctrinated in the notion that at least some kinds of learning disabilities are attributable to a defect of cerebral dominance (Orton 1925, 1937). This notion was supported by observations that learning disabled children frequently show weak or inconsistent preference for one side of the body relative to the other. The cerebral dominance hypothesis has proved to be an attractive one. It gained widespread popularity and even led to remedial schemes intended to enhance the influence of the left, or master, hemisphere. Unfortunately, the enthusiasm of its proponents never was justified by its empirical basis. After 50 years of research, empirical support for Orton's hypothesis is unconvincing. Benton (1975) summarized the situation with respect to reading disability in a succinct statement: "The vast literature on laterality characteristics and reading skill does not lead to any simple generalization" (p. 24). Other reviewers have expressed similar conclusions (Critchley 1970; Satz 1976; Vernon 1957, 1971; Zangwill 1962.)

Despite a heritage of inconclusive and generally discouraging results from a vast research literature, the issue of cerebral lateralization and its relevance to education seems to be surfacing again as a major topic of current interest (cf. Bakker in press; Knights and Bakker 1976; Witelson 1978). Presumably, renewed interest in this topic within education stems from the remarkable popularity of current research into the functions of the cerebral hemispheres. During the past two decades, patients with surgically disconnected hemispheres have been studied and the results of those studies have been reported to a wide audience. Other neurosurgical patients have been observed as one and then the other cerebral hemisphere is incapacitated temporarily by an injected barbituate. Research-

Preparation of this chapter was supported, in part, by a grant to the first author from the Medical Research Council, Ottawa.

ers now are able to measure changes in blood flow within the left and right hemispheres as patients engage in different activities. Noninvasive techniques for studying cerebral asymmetries also have been developed and refined. Hundreds of experiments have employed safe and relatively simple techniques to demonstrate hemispheric specialization for visual and auditory perception in normal children and adults. The development of powerful laboratory computers has facilitated the study of electrical activity in the left and right hemispheres. In view of the unprecedented research activity devoted to the study of cerebral lateralization, it is not surprising that hypotheses similar to Orton's once again are attracting the attention of educators.

If recent findings from medicine, psychology, and the neurosciences are responsible for renewed interest in the question of cerebral lateralization in learning-disabled children, then perhaps an analysis of those findings can help resolve this persistent question. The primary objective of the present chapter is to examine lateralization explanations for learning disability in light of recent research findings. It may be impossible to explain why belief in such explanations has persisted without a sound empirical basis; however, perhaps we can understand why the empirical basis itself has been so disappointing.

We shall begin by discussing studies dealing with handedness, crossed dominance, and perceptual asymmetries, respectively. Methodological and conceptual issues arising from each of these lines of study will be addressed. Subsequently, we shall discuss some general conceptual issues that pertain to all attempts to link learning disabilities and anomalous lateralization, regardless of the method used to measure lateralization. This analysis will lead us to conclusions that run counter to many traditional claims. Specifically, we shall conclude that there is little association between strength of "sidedness" and degree of language lateralization; that there is no validated noninvasive measure of individual differences in cerebral lateralization; that anomalous lateralization *per se* does not imply cognitive deficiency; and that cerebral lateralization of language does not emerge during childhood, as its precursors are present from the time of birth if not earlier.

HANDEDNESS

Handedness and Learning Disability

In the words of Vernon (1971), "No other symptom associated with dyslexia has attracted more attention than has defective *lateralization*; that is to say, the apparent failure to establish superior skill in one or the other hand, or to show strong preference for using one hand rather than the other in performing skilled tasks" (p. 138). Nevertheless, investigations of handedness as a correlate of learning ability have failed to yield consistent results (see Benton 1975; Critchley 1970; Vernon 1957, 1971; Zangwill 1962). A number of investigators have reported that children with learning disabilities tend to deviate from the norm of firmly established right-handedness. In other words, these investigators found a high incidence of left-handedness and mixed-handedness (ambidexterity) among learning-disabled children. The reported incidence of "deviant" handedness, however, varies so widely among different reports (see Critchley 1970) that sampling error of substantial magnitude must be suspected. Even if the positive findings are too numerous to be entirely the result of chance, their relative frequency may have been augmented by a systematic reporting bias. That is, positive findings are much more likely to be published than are negative findings, many of which may go unreported simply because the investigator did not consider them worth reporting. In any event, the majority of recent studies do not show any relationship between deviant handedness and academic achievement (*e.g.*, Balow 1963; Belmont and Birch 1965; Clark 1970; de Hirsch, Jansky, and Langford 1966; Guyer and Friedman 1975; Lyle 1969; Malmquist 1958; Rutter, Tizard, and Whitmore 1970). Yule and Rutter (1976) point out that the evidence concerning handedness and reading ability varies according to the way in which children are selected. Reports of an association between deviant handedness and dyslexia stem from studies of children in clinical settings (see Vernon 1971). In contrast, four studies of entire populations of children (Belmont and Birch 1965; Malmquist 1958; Clark, 1970; Rutter *et al.* 1970) have found no association between handedness and reading skill.

The Definition and Measurement of Handedness

In any attempt to relate handedness to some other individual characteristics, the investigator must resolve the ostensibly trivial matter of defining and measuring handedness. This matter is far less trivial and straightforward than it may seem. Handedness may be defined as the degree of preference for one hand *vis à vis* the other, or it may be defined as the degree to which the two hands differ in performance. Although the two dimensions of handedness—preference and skill—are not independent of each other, they clearly are not perfectly related (Annett 1970, 1976; Benton, Meyers, and Polder 1962; Johnson and King 1942; Lake and Bryden 1976; Satz, Achenbach, and Fennell 1967). The shape of the frequency distribution for handedness depends on whether preference or skill is being measured. Preference measures yield markedly skewed or J-shaped distributions with a high concentration of scores near the pole representing strong right-handedness and a relatively small number of scores at each of the other points (Johnson and Duke 1940; Johnson and King 1942; Oldfield 1971). In contrast, differences between the hands on performance measures such as speed and strength are distributed in the form of unimodal, bell-shaped curves with a mean score displaced from zero in the direction reflecting right-hand superiority (Annett 1972; Woo and Pearson 1927). Obviously, from the disparity between distributions, people who indicate a strong preference for the right hand are not necessarily as strongly asymmetrical in terms of skill. The disparity between preference and skill seems to be even greater in left-handers (Benton *et al.* 1962; Lake and Bryden 1976; Satz *et al.* 1967).

Most researchers who have studied handedness in learning disabled children have defined handedness in terms of hand preference. If, however, classifications are based on the number of activities for which the dominant hand is preferred, then the results may depend largely on the choice of activities to be observed or reported. Compiling an inventory requires that some difficult choices be made. Of the population of manual activities, which activities are the most meaningful indicators of hand preference? Should different items be weighted equally: Are writing and opening a box equally significant activities for the determination of handedness? Does one consider the degree of skill required for the performance of a task? Should one's definition of hand preference emphasize preferences that are likely to be influenced by cultural shaping (*e.g.,* writing and eating) or by the nature of an instrument (*e.g.,* scissors), or should it emphasize preferences that tend to be culture-free (see Teng, Lee, Yang, and Chang 1976)? The commonly used handedness inventories fail to account for these variables in any systematic fashion. Moreover, the predictive validity of some items from various inventories is surprisingly poor (Raczkowski, Kalat, and Nebes 1974), and factor analysis indicates that some items tap something other than a primary dimension of hand preference (Bryden 1977).

If handedness is defined in terms of asymmetrical performance rather than preference, many of the shortcomings of handedness inventories can be avoided but there are equally difficult problems to be solved. The first is retest reliability (Provins and Cunliffe 1972). Even in adults, skill differences between the hands frequently are unreliable. Right-hand and left-hand performance may be highly reliable, but performance differences between the two hands tend to be much less stable (Annett, Hudson, and Turner 1974; Provins and Cunliffe 1972; Shankweiler and Studdert-Kennedy 1975). A second problem is differential experience with the two hands. Even in the case of novel laboratory tasks, the dominant hand may benefit from its experience in performing everyday tasks with similar requirements. A third problem is that rather subtle task factors may influence the magnitude and stability of manual asymmetries (Hicks and Kinsbourne 1978). The amount of practice afforded, the order in which the hands are tested, and the complexity of the task are among the variables likely to affect performance differences between the two hands. Perhaps the most serious problem is that hand skill is not a unitary dimension. Motor and perceptual-motor performance comprise several independent dimensions (Fleishman 1972), and it is not known which, if any, of these dimensions are relevant to individual differences in cerebral organization.

Handedness and Cerebral Lateralization

The difficulty of measuring individual differences in handedness probably accounts for some of the inconsistent findings in the learning-disabilities literature. However, there is no guarantee that a consistent association between anomalous handedness and learning disability would be established even if an ideal measure of handedness were available. Such an expectation assumes that individual differences in handedness bear a direct relationship to individual differences in language lateralization; and clinical research now has provided a basis for evaluating that assumption.

There are two relatively direct methods of ascertaining language lateralization. The traditional method is the study of neurological patients who have sustained injury to one cerebral hemisphere or the other. The incidence of aphasia (disruption of language) can be computed as a function of the patient's handedness and the side of the brain injury (*e.g.,* Annett 1975; Gloning, Gloning, Haub, and Quatember 1969; Hecaen and Sauget 1971; Luria 1970; Roberts 1969; Zangwill 1967). More recently, a second technique—the sodium amytal or Wada technique (Wada and Rasmussen 1960)—has been applied to a large number of neurosurgical patients. Injection of a barbituate into the arterial system supplying one side of the brain incapacitates one cerebral hemisphere for a few minutes. The test subsequently is repeated on the other side and aspects of the patient's linguistic functioning are tested during both administrations of the drug (Rasmussen and Milner 1975; Rossi and Rosadini 1967). Fortunately, the aphasia case studies and the sodium amytal studies have yielded remarkably comparable results with regard to the relationship between handedness and the lateralization of language. Of those patients with a preference for the right hand, more than 95 percent have language represented primarily in the left hemisphere. Left-handers and ambidextrous patients seem to be more heterogeneous in cerebral representation of language. The majority of non-right-handers (about two-thirds) have left lateralized language, but the remainder of these patients appear to have language represented primarily in the right hemisphere or to have substantial linguistic capability in both hemispheres.

The clinical evidence outlined above is not infallible. Evidence from brain-damaged populations is subject to incalculable sampling error, and the determination of language impairment may be biased by an emphasis on expressive language simply because expressive functions are easier to assess than are receptive functions. Even right-handers may have a fairly well-developed right-hemispheric capacity for speech perception (Searleman 1977). Nevertheless, the aphasia case studies and the sodium amytal studies present strong evidence that nearly all right-handed adults depend primarily on the left cerebral hemisphere for their linguistic competency. Similarly, the majority of non-right-handers have language represented primarily in the left hemisphere. Only a minority of left-handed and ambidextrous people show anomalous lateralization of language. Consequently, handedness can be used to predict brain organization only in a very limited sense. A given right-hander is almost certain to have left lateralized language, but a left-hander has a one-in-three chance of having a substantial degree of language capacity in the right hemisphere. In addition, non-right-handers frequently seem to have language represented in a more diffuse manner than do right-handers. It remains to be established that, within a group of right-handers or within a group of non-right-handers, the degree of cerebral lateralization varies with the degree of handedness.

Conclusions

If there is an association between handedness and learning disability, that association may be obscured by ambiguities in the definition and measurement of handedness. The critical issue, however, is the validity of the implicit assumption that degree of handedness is an index of individual differences in degree of cerebral lateralization. The most direct measures of language lateralization suggest only that the chances of anomalous lateralization are greater in non-right-handers than in right-handers. For right-handed adults, at least, speech lateralization seems to be complete, irrespective of strength of handedness.

EYEDNESS AND CROSSED DOMINANCE

Crossed Dominance and Learning Disability

We have used the terms, deviant handedness and non-right handedness, to denote the handedness characteristics of left-handers and ambidextrous people. There are good reasons for treating these two groups as one. For instance, they do not seem to differ in language lateralization, as measured by sodium amytal testing (Rasmussen and Milner 1975). Moreover, left-handers tend to be more ambidextrous than do right-handers. Either left-handers are innately more bilateral than right-handers or else environmental influences tend to force left-handers to become ambilateral (Hardyck and Petrinovich 1977). Consequently, one may doubt the advisability of trying to distinguish between left-handedness and ambidexterity. Nonetheless, it is not left-handedness but incomplete or inconsistent laterality that has been linked most frequently to learning disabilities (Zangwill 1962). In Orton's (1937) words, "There is reason to believe that a high degree of specialization in either hemisphere makes for superiority and that the good left-hander is therefore not only not abnormal but is apt to be better equipped than is the indifferent right-hander" (p. 50). Orton recognized many of the difficulties encountered in assessing degrees of handedness and he chose to define laterality in terms of a person's consistency in hand preference, eye (sighting) preference and foot preference. The children thought to be at risk for specific language disabilities were those who were right-handed and left-eyed, left-handed and right-eyed, or inconsistent in their preference for one eye or one hand. Foot preferences were considered, but were thought to be of lesser importance.

Several studies have reported that deviation from consistent right-eyedness is associated with learning difficulties, and other studies have reported that incongruence of handedness and eyedness (*i.e.,* crossed dominance) is related to some form of learning deficit (see reviews by Benton 1975; Critchley 1970; Porac and Coren 1976; Vernon 1957, 1971; Zangwill 1962). However, as was the case in regard to handedness, the claims are counterbalanced by a number of negative findings (*e.g.,* Balow 1963; Belmont and Birch 1965; Coleman and Deutch 1964; Harris 1957).

Crossed hand-eye dominance is common in normal readers (Benton 1975). Porac and Coren (1976) cite several studies of children and adults which suggest that only 65 percent of the general population sight consistently with the right eye. About 32 percent sight with the left eye, and the remaining 3 percent are inconsistent. In contrast, the incidence of left-handedness is 8 – 10 percent of the population (Hardyck and Petrinovich 1977). If 32 percent of the general population are left-eyed but only 8–10 percent are left-handed, there must be a substantial proportion of the population that is right-handed and left-eyed. Some of these "poorly lateralized" people do have learning difficulties but the great majority do not (Zangwill 1962). In fact, crossed dominance seems to be as common in university students as in children attending public schools (Buffery 1976; Teng, Lee, Yang, and Chang 1979).

Measurement Problems

The assessment of a child's "dominance," as defined by Orton and many others, raises two new measurement issues in addition to those issues discussed in connection with handedness. The more general issue concerns the best way of deriving a single sidedness index from measures of eyedness, handedness and footedness. The more specific issue concerns difficulties inherent in the definition and measurement of eyedness.

Defining sidedness in terms of congruence of eye, hand and foot preference is problematical simply because it offers the investigator so many degrees of freedom. Besides having to choose the most appropriate activities to include in the inventory or behavioral test battery, the investigator must make an arbitrary decision regarding the proper weighting of eyedness, handedness and footedness scores. A child can be assigned a "right" or "left" score for each of the three aspects of sidedness and these binary scores can be combined to yield an overall dominance index. The use of such a procedure implies that eyedness, handedness and footedness are equal in importance. Alternatively, the different aspects may be differentially weighted and gradations in degree of sidedness may be considered. For instance, a large right-handedness score might be neutralized by strong left-eyedness but not by weak left-eyedness or by strong or weak left-footedness. The possibilities are almost unlimited, and there is little reason to favor one approach or set of weights over another.

Eyedness itself is a multifaceted variable. Porac and Coren (1976) point out that "investigators have not reached a consensus as to what measures or behaviors distinguish the dominant eye from its contralateral partner" (p. 881). The several available tests often produce dissimilar results. Some sighting tasks are confounded with experiential factors or hand preference. Correlations between eye-dominance scores and other variables may differ depending on whether strength of eye dominance as well as direction of dominance is considered (Coren and Kaplan 1973). The importance of small asymmetries in visual acuity is unclear (Porac and Coren 1976). However, in the presence of ocular or oculomotor pathology such as marked acuity imbalance between the eyes or strabismus, a child's sighting dominance may depend largely on the nature of the visual pathology.

Crossed Dominance and Cerebral Lateralization

Methodological problems probably are sufficient to account for the failure to link crossed dominance to learning disability in a consistent manner. Nevertheless, the methodological problems are no more serious than the conceptual problems inherent in attempts to explain crossed dominance in terms of cerebral lateralization. In other words, there is little reason to believe that incongruent hand, eye, and foot dominance has any relationship to degree of cerebral dominance. The assessment of eye dominance, in particular, contributes little or nothing to the understanding of an individual child's cerebral organization.

There are two fundamental reasons for doubting the significance of eye dominance as an index of cerebral lateralization. One reason is physiological: input from each eye is conducted to both cerebral hemispheres. The attempt to establish handedness and footedness as indices of cerebral dominance is justified, superficially at least, by the fact that the perceptual and motor functions of each limb are represented primarily in the contralateral hemisphere. The visual system, however, is organized quite differently. The optic tract is only partially crossed, or semidecussated, so that half the fibers from each eye project to the right hemisphere and half project to the left hemisphere. Visual stimulation from the right side of fixation elicits a response in the visual reception area of the left hemisphere and stimulation from the left side of fixation elicits a response in the right hemisphere. Since both retinas project equally to both hemispheres, neither eye enjoys an exclusive or preferential relationship with either cerebral hemisphere. A preference for the use of one eye thus does not imply that the contralateral hemisphere is dominant.

The second reason for rejecting eye dominance as a measure of cerebral lateralization is that individual differences in eye dominance do not fit a pattern of generalized sidedness. If eye dominance is part of a general characteristic of sidedness and if degree of sidedness is related to degree of cerebral dominance, then (a) the incidence of anomalous eye dominance should be consonant with the incidence of anomalous lateralization as inferred from other measures and (b) individuals should show an association between eye dominance and other characteristics such as handedness. In fact, the incidence of anomalous eye dominance (35 percent) greatly exceeds the estimated incidence of deviant language lateralization. Moreover, it has not been established that degree of eyedness is related to degree of handedness. Of twenty investigations cited by Porac and Coren (1976), nine reported associations between eyedness and handedness and eleven did not. Porac and Coren suggest that the positive findings may be partly artifactual. Because most people are right-handed and right-eyed, there may be an apparent association between handedness and eyedness even if the two dimensions are independent. Since this artifact can be attenuated by the use of graded ratings of handedness and eyedness rather than dichotomous or trichotomous classifications, it is interesting to note that studies using graded numerical ratings have failed to yield significant correlations between eyedness and handedness (Coren and Kaplan 1973; Porac and Coren 1975).

Conclusions

The diagnostic significance of crossed dominance is dubious. Even if it were possible to specify the optimal manner of obtaining and combining measures of handedness, eyedness and footedness, there is little reason to believe that crossed dominance implies anomalous or incomplete cerebral lateralization.

PERCEPTUAL ASYMMETRIES

Perceptual Asymmetries and Learning Disability

In recent years, perceptual tasks have become popular techniques for studying cerebral lateralization. On the basis of visual, auditory, or tactual asymmetries, investigators have made inferences about the presence or absence of hemispheric specialization for various perceptual processes.

The dichotic listening technique is especially popular. In dichotic listening, competing sounds are presented via stereophonic headphones so that one sound arrives at the left ear at the same instant that a different sound arrives at the right ear. When the stimuli are linguistic in nature, *e.g.*, words, nonsense syllables, or digit names, normal adults and children usually report slightly more material from the right ear than from the left. This phenomenon is referred to as the right-ear advantage. Non-linguistic sounds such as musical chords or environmental noises usually fail to produce a right-ear advantage and may even yield a left-ear advantage (Curry 1967); Kimura 1964). A similar asymmetry can be observed in the visual modality. If a stimulus is flashed briefly to one side of fixation, the resulting signal will be conducted more directly to the contralateral hemisphere than to the ipsilateral hemisphere. (If the stimulation persists beyond about one-fifth of a second, the eyes may have time to fixate on the stimulus; in that case, the signal will be transmitted directly to both hemispheres). Verbal stimuli (*e.g.*, words or letters) are more likely to be perceived when they are flashed in the right half-field (Bryden 1965; Heron 1957). Nonverbal stimuli such as geometric designs, lines, and dot patterns may yield symmetrical performance or a left half-field advantage depending on the task (Kimura 1966, Kimura and Durnford 1974). Since tactual input from the hands reaches the cerebrum largely via crossed pathways, tactual tasks also have served as a basis for inferences about cerebral specialization.

Unfortunately, the application of perceptual tasks to learning disabled children has failed to yield consistent and unambiguous results. Satz (1976) reviewed nineteen studies in which children with reading disabilities were tested for auditory or visual half-field asymmetries. In most cases, children with reading disabilities and normal controls showed a right-ear or right visual half-field advantage; and only a few of these studies suggested a reduced magnitude or incidence of asymmetry in learning-disabled children at one or more age levels. In a few cases, neither group showed a right-side advantage and one study actually reported a larger right visual half-field advantage in poor readers than in normal readers. Thus, the results include every logically possible outcome. Satz concluded that the contribution of these studies to our understanding of the role of cerebral lateralization in learning disability is "unclear" if not "obscure."

Most investigators have considered only linguistic processes and whether these processes are normally lateralized or otherwise represented in the brains of children with learning disabilities. One investigator, however (Witelson 1974, 1976*a*, 1976*b*, 1977), has focused much of her effort on tactile-spatial perception, which is assumed to be a function for which the right hemisphere normally is specialized. She has found that dyslexic boys fail to show the left-hand advantage that presumably reflects right-hemispheric specialization for her non-verbal "dichhaptic" task. Witelson's results with normal and dyslexic boys have led her to speculate that dyslexics have normal left lateralization of language but that spatial functions tend to be represented in both hemispheres. Witelson (1977) suggests that left-hemispheric representation of nonlinguistic functions may interfere with the linguistic, sequential, and analytic processing for which the left hemisphere is specialized (cf. Levy 1969). However, insofar as normal girls below the age of thirteen years also fail to perform asymmetrically on the dichhaptic task (Witelson 1976b), the performance characteristics of the dyslexic boys may not be related directly either to their reading difficulties or to their cerebral organization. If the dyslexics' symmetric performance is related to their reading disability, the relationship may be mediated by strategy or cognitive style variables (cf. Webster and Thurber 1978). In a recent study (which also failed to find any difference with respect to dichotic asymmetries between learning disabled and normal children), Caplan and Kinsbourne (submitted) showed that a measure of cognitive style did differentiate the groups—the learning disabled children being characterized by a less verbal style. It now remains to be determined whether the style difference is a cause or an effect of the reading problem.

Methodological Issues

In studies of perceptual asymmetries in children, it is not only learning-disabled children whose asymmetry scores vary from one study to the next. Control subjects, as well, have demonstrated significant right-ear or right half-field advantages in some studies but not in others (Satz 1976). Consequently, there is reason to suspect that various methodological differences among the studies are responsible to some degree for the heterogeneous results.

The most fundamental variables in dichotic listening are physical (i.e., acoustic) variables such as intensity level, bandwidth, signal-to-noise ratio, and degree of asynchrony between competing stimuli. Berlin and his colleagues (e.g., Berlin and Cullen 1977; Berlin and McNeill 1976; Cullen, Thompson, Hughes, Berlin, and Samson 1974) have shown that acoustic differences between the two channels can enhance or diminish the right-ear advantage. Phonetic variables similarly can affect listening asymmetry (Studdert-Kennedy and Shankweiler 1970). For instance, un-

voiced stop consonants tend to override voiced stop consonants in dichotic competition (Lowe, Cullen, Berlin, Thompson, and Willett 1970;
Berlin, Lowe-Bell, Cullen, Thompson and Loovis 1973). Although
acoustic and phonetic differences between channels can be cancelled by
counterbalancing stimuli and reversing headphones for half the trials, it is
impossible to compare the results of different studies when technical
specifications are either dissimilar or unreported.

The ear asymmetry for a subject or a group of subjects depends on
the kind of stimulus material used. For instance, consonant-vowel nonsense syllables and strings of digit names have produced conflicting results in young children (Porter and Berlin 1975).

Procedural variables also exert considerable influence on ear asymmetry. In most dichotic listening studies, investigators have chosen to use
a free-report procedure in which the subject is allowed to report stimuli in
any order. This procedure confounds perceptual asymmetry with order-
of-report factors (Bryden 1967; Bryden and Allard 1978; Inglis and Sykes
1967). In fact, the influence of response factors may be so great that the
task becomes a poor measure of perceptual asymmetry (Freides 1977).
Order of report is a particularly troublesome problem when the amount
of material presented during each trial approaches or exceeds the
subject's memory span. Moreover, report strategies change as the presentation rate of stimuli is varied (Bryden 1962; Witelson and Rabinovitch
1971). Alternative response measures, such as selective report (Hiscock
and Kinsbourne 1977; Kimura 1967; Kirstein and Shankweiler 1969) or
forced-choice response (e.g., Kinsbourne, Hotch, and Sessions, cited in
Kinsbourne and Hiscock 1977) may be necessary to avoid order-of-report
artifacts.

Visual half-field tasks similarly are replete with methodological
problems and controversies (cf. Hines 1972; Krueger 1976; White 1969).
For example, there is considerable disagreement over the relative importance of cerebral lateralization and scanning habits in producing asymmetric performance under conditions of unilateral and bilateral stimulation. Asymmetries in normal adults frequently are difficult to interpret,
and results obtained from children with reading difficulties are likely to
be even more problematical.

Interpretation of perceptual asymmetries is complicated further by
statistical problems. If two groups of children differ in overall performance on a perceptual task, it may be virtually impossible to determine
which group is more asymmetrical. In some cases, floor effects or ceiling
effects may reduce the degree of asymmetry. Even if there is no obvious
floor or ceiling effect, the results may depend on whether absolute or relative asymmetry scores are used. Some investigators prefer to work with

raw scores for each ear or visual half-field and others prefer to transform their data into one of a number of "laterality indices" (Harshman and Krashen 1972; Kuhn 1973; Marshall, Caplan, and Holmes 1975; Studdert-Kennedy and Shankweiler 1970). Any choice implies certain un-proven assumptions about the actual relationship between degree of asymmetry and overall performance (Richardson 1976), but the only al-ternative is to use frequency counts or rank-order data. Unfortunately, different statistical choices sometimes lead to divergent conclusions (Sparrow and Satz 1970).

Perceptual Asymmetries and Cerebral Lateralization

We have argued previously that handedness bears only a limited re-lationship to cerebral lateralization and that eye dominance is not related at all. The situation with respect to perceptual asymmetries is different. There is general agreement among researchers that functional specializa-tion of the cerebral hemispheres constitutes the basis for many of the per-ceptual asymmetries that have been reported (Kimura 1961a, 1961b; Studdert-Kennedy 1975). The critical issue is the degree to which individ-ual differences in perceptual asymmetry reflect individual differences in cerebral lateralization. Is there a one-to-one relationship between percep-tual asymmetry and degree of lateralization? Our consideration of meth-odological factors provides a partial answer. Insofar as asymmetries are influenced by fairly subtle changes in methodology, any given perceptual task is unlikely to provide a pure measure of lateralization. All together, there are at least four arguments against the assumption of isomorphism between perceptual asymmetry and cerebral asymmetry.

Firstly, perceptual tasks consistently underestimate the incidence of left lateralization of language (Blumstein, Goodglass, and Tartter 1975; Satz 1976). There is substantial disparity between the typical 80 percent incidence of right-ear advantage among normal right-handed adults (Ber-lin and McNeil 1976; Blumstein *et al.* 1975; Bryden and Allard 1978) and the 95–99 percent incidence of left lateralized language as reported in the aphasia and sodium amytal studies (Rasmussen and Milner 1975; Rossi and Rosadini 1967; Zangwill 1967). If the clinical data accurately reflect the population incidence of left lateralization of language, then the per-ceptual data, when applied to individual subjects, will lead to erroneous conclusions. Satz (1976) has used a Baysean analysis to demonstrate this point dramatically. He considered a situation in which 95 percent of the population actually have language represented in the left hemisphere, but only 70 percent of a given sample show a right-ear advantage. In this case, the probability of left lateralized language is .97 for subjects who show a right-ear advantage *and .90 for those who do not.* Clearly, under those circumstances, a subject's failure to show a right-ear advantage does not imply anomalous cerebral lateralization.

Secondly, perceptual asymmetry tends not to be a stable characteristic of individuals (Bakker, Van der Vlugt, and Claushuis 1978; Blumstein *et al.* 1975; Pizzamiglio, De Pascalis, and Vignati 1974). Using dichotic listening with normal adults, Blumstein *et al.* found that retest reliability coefficients for asymmetry scores ranged from .21 for vowels and .46 for music to .74 for consonants. About one-third of the subjects showed reversed asymmetries on the second administration of the consonant and vowel tasks. Visual asymmetries may be less reliable, for even the split-half reliability of visual half-field asymmetries has been reported to fall below .50. Unfortunately, the reliability of perceptual asymmetry scores is limited by a tendency for left-ear (or left half-field) performance to be correlated with right-ear (or right half-field) performance. Whenever two scores are highly correlated, the difference between them tends to be unreliable (Hines and Satz 1974).

Thirdly, certain situational and experiential factors can alter perceptual asymmetries. A concurrent verbal memory task tends to bias visual perception to the right (Hellige and Cox 1976; Kinsbourne 1970, 1973). It has been reported that listening asymmetries are altered as the subject's visual field is shifted laterally by displacing prisms (Goldstein and Lackner 1974) and as the apparent location of the sound source is changed (Morais 1975; Morais and Bertelson 1975). Ear asymmetries vary as attention is shifted from one aspect of the stimulus material to another (Bartholomeus 1974; Haggard and Parkinson 1971) and as the context of the experiment is changed (Spellacy and Blumstein 1970). Spellacy and Blumstein reported that vowels yielded a significant right-ear advantage when presented in a linguistic context; when the same vowels were presented in a non-linguistic context, they yielded a significant left-ear advantage. Subjects' familiarity with the stimulus material seems to have an important effect on their asymmetry of perception. Musicians show a right-ear advantage for music but non-musicians do not (Bever and Chiarello 1974; Johnson 1977); Morse Code operators show a right-ear advantage for Morse Code but naive subjects do not (Papcun, Krashen, Terbeek, Remington, and Harshman 1974); Thai speakers show a right-ear advantage for intoned Thai words but English speakers do not (Van Lancker and Fromkin 1973).

Fourthly, the typically small magnitude of perceptual asymmetries seems inconsistent with the marked language lateralization suggested by aphasia cases and by sodium amytal tests. The average right-ear performance in normal subjects seldom exceeds the average left-ear performance by more than a few percentage points (Berlin and McNeil 1976; Blumstein *et al.* 1975). In contrast, the more direct clinical evidence suggests that language lateralization in right-handers is marked and unambiguous. For example, unilateral injection of sodium amytal in right-handed patients almost invariably brings about either complete cessation of speech or no change in speech, depending on the side of injection (Rasmussen and Milner 1975). Some partial explanations for this discrepancy can be offered. As noted previously, there is evidence that the right hemisphere does in fact play a greater role in receptive language than in expressive language (Searleman 1977). The clinical evidence—especially the sodium amytal evidence—tends to reflect the patient's expressive rather than receptive impairment (Kinsbourne 1974). Moreover, the clinical evidence may be biased by inclusion of patients whose pattern of lateralization has been modified as a result of previous damage to the right hemisphere (Levy 1974). Despite these qualifications, the discrepancy between perceptual data and clinical evidence casts doubt on the validity of perceptual asymmetries as measures of cerebral lateralization.

Conclusions

Measures of perceptual asymmetry have failed to clarify the relationship between cerebral lateralization and learning disability. Investigators have assumed that auditory and visual tasks provide a relatively direct estimate of cerebral specialization but critical analysis of the literature shows that perceptual asymmetries are susceptible to a number of influences other than cerebral lateralization. Even though perceptual asymmetries in a population may depend on a functionally asymmetric nervous system, individual differences in perceptual asymmetry are not valid measures of individual differences in cerebral lateralization.

SOME GENERAL CONSIDERATIONS

The Diversity of Learning Disabilities

Perhaps because the problem of measuring lateralization is so challenging and intriguing, investigators almost unanimously overlook the possibility that learning-disabled children are a heterogeneous group with respect to cerebral organization. If some children with learning disabilities in fact do have anomalous cerebral representation of cognitive functions, these children may constitute only a small minority of cases. Alternatively, some children may have incomplete language (left-hemispheric) lateralization and others may have incomplete visuospatial (right-hemispheric) lateralization. Since reading has linguistic and visuospatial components (Sparrow and Satz 1970), both groups might display reading difficulties but they might show opposite patterns of perceptual asymmetry. Another possibility is that the results of laterality studies will vary depending on whether children with neurological damage are included or excluded. If selection criteria do not exclude such children, their influence will depend on factors such as their number, lateralization of lesions, and age at which damage occurred.

These possibilities lead us, of course, to the question of how learning disabilities are to be defined. Its crucial importance to laterality research prompts us to state a few general principles.

Definitions serve a purpose; and they can be evaluated only in terms of their usefulness. Consequently, the researcher with his or her own objectives in mind must define a problem in such a way that those objectives can be served. In the case of learning disability, the investigator should not automatically adopt a definition that was established for a different purpose. Presumably, governmental agencies and educational systems arrive at definitions that best serve their purposes and that can be justified in terms of their criteria. However, such definitions may fail to include distinctions that are important to the researcher. For instance, if the established definition of learning disability includes children across a wide spectrum of IQ scores, the investigator should not assume that either behavioral or neurological characteristics will be identical for children with low IQs and those with average IQs. The fact that a definition causes dissimilar children to be combined into a category should not prevent the researcher from using a more restrictive definition.

For the researcher with an interest in the cerebral organization of learning disabled children, there are two basic aspects to the matter of defining the target population. First, criteria must be established to distinguish between children with learning disabilities and all other children; then it may be necessary to divide the population of learning-disabled children into more homogeneous subgroups.

It is a common practice to define learning disabilities by exclusion (Gaddes 1976; McCarthy and McCarthy 1969; Rourke 1975): A child has a learning disability if he or she is an academic underachiever according to some set of criteria and if that underachievement cannot be explained in terms of certain specified variables. This generic definition can generate

a large number of specific definitions, depending on the criteria for underachievement and the explanatory factors to be included or excluded.
At the most inclusive extreme, one might identify children whose achievement in one or more specified academic subjects is significantly lower
than would be expected on the basis of IQ criteria. Such a definition
clearly would be too broad to be useful in neuropsychological research, as
it fails to exclude confounding factors such as emotional disturbance, cultural deprivation, instructional inadequacy, and known neurological damage. If anything is to be learned about cerebral organization in learning-
disabled children, the selection criteria must be more restrictive.

Even after the population has been defined satisfactorily, it may be
necessary to determine whether it can be further decomposed into more
homogeneous sub-groups (Boder 1970; Kinsbourne and Warrington
1963; Myklebust 1965; Spreen 1976). It would be advantageous to separate children whose underachievement is selective from those (e. g., hyperactive children) whose difficulties are not restricted to any one academic
skill or set of related skills. The criteria for creating sub-groups will vary
according to the nature of the investigation. For example, it is unlikely
that a classification based on arousal level (Ferguson, Simpson, and
Trites 1976) or responsiveness to stimulant medication (Wender 1976)
would be useful in answering questions about cerebral lateralization. On
the other hand, it may be quite appropriate to identify "language-type"
and "developmental Gerstmann" cases on the basis of achievement profiles, IQ profiles, error patterns, and developmental characteristics (Kinsbourne 1976) and to distinguish these children from those showing other
patterns. Since both language-type and Gerstmann characteristics presumably are related to left hemispheric dysfunction, it is these children
who should display anomalous laterality if the lateralization hypothesis
has merit.

Children with learning disabilities are a diverse group with great
variation in the quantity and quality of their deficits. Even if their deficits
are brain-based in all cases, it is unlikely that the same brain dysfunction
invariably is involved. The tendency of investigators to treat all learning
disabled children as if they were alike has impeded the attempt to establish a relationship between learning disability and cerebral lateralization.

The Consequences of Deviant Lateralization

Attempts to implicate anomalous lateralization as a causal factor in
learning disabilities are based on the assumption—whether explicit or

implicit—that anomalous lateralization *per se* is maladaptive. Orton (1937) specified output competition as the maladaptive feature of incomplete dominance, but other models could be constructed. The critical question is whether deviant lateralization actually implies cognitive deficit; the answer would seem to be that it does not.

The investigator confronts a dilemma in attempting to ascertain whether deviant lateralization is associated with intellectual deficiency. One needs to study people with no evidence of brain pathology but, as we have pointed out, there are no noninvasive measures of cerebral lateralization that can be relied upon to determine a person's pattern of lateralization. The only measures with the necessary precision involve medical procedures to which normal subjects cannot ethically be subjected. Fortunately, nature has provided us an experiment. If virtually all right-handers but fewer than two-thirds of left-handers have left hemispheric speech, then there is a much greater proportion of left-handers than right-handers with anomalous language lateralization (*i.e.*, bilateral and right lateralized speech). If cognitive deficiency is associated with anomalous lateralization, *normal* left-handers should display cognitive performance that is characterized by (a) lower mean scores than those of right-handers and (b) more variability than that of right-handers.

In general, research has failed to reveal any significant differences between left- and right-handers in cognitive ability. However, two studies (Levy 1969; Miller 1971) have generated considerable interest, as they reported significantly lower nonverbal ability in left-handers or mixed-handers than in right-handers. Similarly, Nebes (1971) found a visuospatial deficiency (in part-whole matching) among left-handers. Levy (1969) interpreted her findings as evidence that left-handers' bilateral representation of language disrupts the holistic processing thought to be characteristic of the nondominant hemisphere. Although this is an intriguing hypothesis, the findings themselves are suspect. The Miller and Levy findings are based on small samples of university undergraduate and graduate students, respectively; the intellectual level of Levy's subjects, in particular, is entirely unrepresentative of the general population. Other studies, many of which have used much larger and more representative samples, have failed to find any notable deficiency among left-handers in either general intelligence or nonverbal ability (Fagin-Dubin 1974; Hardyck, Petrinovich, and Goldman 1976; Keller, Croake, and Riesenman 1973; Newcombe and Ratcliff 1973; Orme 1970; Roberts and Engle 1974; Wilson and Dolan 1931). For example, Newcombe and Ratcliff failed to find significant differences in either verbal or performance IQ among twenty-six left-handers, 139 mixed-handers, and 658 right-handers. Scores of pure left-handers were notable only for their *low* degree of variability. An exhaustive study was described by Roberts and Engel (1974) in a United States Government National Health Survey report. Wechsler Block Design and Vocabulary tests were given to more than 7,000 children who were carefully selected as a representative sample of the national population between the ages of 6 and 11 years. The 762 children identified as left-handers could not be differentiated from the right-handers on the basis of either Block Design or Vocabulary scores.

In view of the preponderance of negative findings, especially from studies in which large and representative samples were used, it seems prudent to conclude that left-handers in the general population are as intelligent as their right-handed counterparts. Consequently, nature's experiment seems to have yielded negative results. When anomalous lateralization is found in the absence of brain pathology, there appear to be no unfavorable consequences insofar as intellectual ability is concerned.

The Paradox of Left-Handedness

Despite the findings from normal samples, it is impossible to dismiss completely the claim that there is a disproportionately high number of left-handers in certain abnormal groups. In our discussion of handedness and learning disability, we were unable to rule out the possibility that the incidence of deviant handedness is elevated among children with learning disabilities. We noted Yule and Rutter's (1976) observation that associations between deviant handedness and learning disability are reported in clinical studies but not in studies of entire populations. There is even stronger evidence that left-handedness is frequent among the mentally retarded (Bakwin 1950; Burt 1950; Doll 1933; Gordon 1920; Hicks and Barton 1975; Wilson and Dolan 1931; Zangwill 1960). Deviant handedness also has been associated with epilepsy (Bolin 1953) and with various motor and language difficulties (Morley 1965).

Is it possible that both generalizations are correct, *i.e.,* that left-handers in the general population are as intelligent as right-handers, but that left-handedness nonetheless is associated with various kinds of pathology? These seemingly contradictory conclusions can both be accommodated by a model that specifies two different etiologies for left-handedness.

Most left-handers owe their left-handedness to normal variation. Whether the source of that variation is genetic, environmental, or an interaction between genotype and environment is not entirely clear. Family studies show significant parent-offspring correlations for handedness (Annett 1973, 1974; Bakan, Dibb, and Reed 1973; Chamberlain 1928;

Falek 1959), but these results do not allow us to discriminate between genetic and environmental explanations. There is some evidence for genetic inheritance of handedness (Annett 1973; Hicks and Kinsbourne 1976a, 1976b), but a fully satisfactory genetic model has not been developed (cf. Annett 1964, 1972; Hudson 1975; Levy and Nagylaki 1972). Moreover, cultural factors (Teng, Lee, Yang, and Chang 1976) and other environmental variables may influence the expression of hand preference (Collins 1975; Morgan and Corballis 1978). Thus, our present level of knowledge does not allow us to specify the mechanism or mechanisms responsible for left-handedness in the general population. We can conclude only that this benign and common deviation from the norm probably is a result of natural variation.

Left-handedness also can result from brain damage. Whereas "pathological left-handedness" (Satz 1972, 1973) probably is rare in the general population, it may be a major factor in explaining left-handedness in abnormal groups. Prenatal or perinatal insult to the brain, even if subtle, may be sufficient to effect a shift in handedness. Left lateralized injury would impair right-hand performance and lead to pathological left-handedness; right lateralized injury similarly would lead to pathological right-handedness. Even if left-sided damage and right-sided damage are equally common, this pathological mechanism would produce far more left-handers than right-handers simply because the baseline incidence of right-handedness in the population greatly exceeds the baseline incidence of left-handedness. If 90 or 95 percent of all infants are predisposed to become right-handers and only 5 or 10 percent are predisposed to become left-handers, then most of the infants who acquire shifted handedness as the result of lateralized brain damage will be natural right-handers who have become left-handed. Actually, the disparity in number between pathological left-handers and pathological right-handers is exacerbated by physiological factors that make the left hemisphere more vulnerable to injury than the right (Kinsbourne and Hiscock 1977).

The distinction between natural left-handedness and pathological left-handedness allows us to explain why left-handedness may be associated with cognitive deficit in certain abnormal groups but not in unselected samples from the general population (e.g., Annett 1970; Annett and Turner 1974). It should be emphasized, however, that the concept of pathological left-handedness pertains to groups that are deviant on grounds other than handedness. The hypothesis that all left-handers are neurologically damaged (Bakan 1971; Bakan et al. 1973) has not been substantiated by subsequent research (Hicks, Evan, and Pellegrini 1978; Hubbard 1971; Schwartz 1977; Teng et al. 1976). Also, the concept of pathological left-handedness should not be misconstrued so that left-handedness is considered to be a cause of cognitive insufficiency in any individual or group. Left-handedness is an effect rather than a cause. The immature nervous system is vulnerable to various kinds of subtle insult, which may or may not lead to left-handedness and which may or may not lead to significant intellectual impairment. If there is a statistical association between intellectual deficiency and left-handedness, that association might be attributed to a common cause (*i.e.,* early cerebral insult) but the intellectual deficiency should not be attributed to the left-handedness.

The Question of Ontogeny

Orton (1937, pp. 48–51) assumed that cerebral dominance is absent in infants but develops with increasing age. In fact, that assumption rarely has been questioned until recent years. The assumption of "progressive lateralization" is essential to Orton's model and to more recent models (Bakker 1973; Bakker, Smink, and Reitsma 1973; Sparrow and Satz 1970) that specify a differential relationship between reading and cerebral lateralization, depending on the child's age or stage of reading acquisition. Consider the implications if the assumption is incorrect. If the infant brain is lateralized from the time of birth, it would make no sense to speak of delayed lateralization or of an optimal degree of lateralization for each stage of language development. There would be no reason to attempt to accelerate the course of lateralization through special training or other environmental manipulation. Indeed, there would be only two possible conclusions that one could reach regarding the cerebral lateralization of children with learning disabilities: That the brains of these children are lateralized in the usual manner and to the usual degree, or that at least some of these children are born without the usual form of cerebral lateralization and will reach maturity without acquiring the usual form of cerebral lateralization. Clearly, our hypotheses about the relationship between cerebral lateralization and learning disabilities depend on the assumptions we make about how and when the brain becomes lateralized in normal children.

Equipotentiality, the principle of functional equivalency of the two cerebral hemispheres in infancy, has been an established neurological doctrine since the nineteenth century. This assertion that the left and right halves of the infant brain are equally good substrates for language development seems to have been based partly on early observations that the cerebral hemispheres of the neonate are anatomically identical and partly on clinical evidence (see Dennis and Whitaker 1977). The clinical evidence consists mainly of case reports of acquired aphasia in children (*e.g.,* Basser 1962; Hecaen 1976; Lenneberg 1967), from which it was concluded that language is represented bilaterally in the young child.

Lenneberg (1967) put forth a well-articulated and influential argument for the concepts of hemispheric equipotentiality and progressive lateralization. Drawing upon his own cases and those of others (*e.g.,* Basser 1962), Lenneberg described the course of recovery from aphasia thought to be typical of children at different ages. He pointed out that, relative to aphasia in adults, aphasia in children (a) tends to be less severe and more transitory and (b) is much more likely to result from right-hemispheric damage. These observations led to the conclusion that language is represented bilaterally in the brain of the young child but gradually becomes lateralized to the left hemisphere as the child matures. In other words, during the time between the beginning of language acquisition and pubescence, the linguistic role of the right hemisphere decreases until language ultimately is represented only in the left hemisphere.

Lenneberg's hypothesis has many weaknesses. The clinical evidence itself is questionable in many respects (see Kinsbourne 1975*c*; Kinsbourne and Hiscock 1977). Woods and Teuber (1978) suggest that the older aphasia literature contains many cases in which, even though a focal lesion in the right hemisphere may have been evident, the aphasia can be attributed instead to an associated pathology of the left hemisphere. In the more recent literature, the incidence of aphasia in children, following right-sided damage, has dropped to about the level reported for adults (Woods and Teuber 1978). Even if we were to accept Lenneberg's data base at face value, we would take issue with his major conclusions. The developmental trend reported in the recovery from aphasia can be explained more satisfactorily in terms of the well-established principle of decreasing neurological plasticity than in terms of a shrinking brain base for language (Kinsbourne and Hiscock 1977).

The argument against equipotentiality and progressive lateralization is not limited to criticism of observations about aphasia in children. On the contrary, the argument rests primarily on recent experimental demonstrations of hemispheric specialization very early in life (see Segalowitz and Gruber 1977). Firstly, the early claims of anatomical symmetry have been disproven. At least some of the cerebral regions associated with speech are larger on the left side than on the right in the brains of most adults and infants (Galaburda, Le May, Kemper, and Geschwind 1978; Geschwind and Levitsky 1968; Teszner, Tzavaras, Gruner, and Hecaen 1972; Wada *et al.* 1975; Witelson and Pallie 1973; Yeni-Komshian and Benson 1976). Using electrophysiological techniques, investigators have discovered that the left and right sides of the infant brain respond differentially to speech and nonspeech stimuli (Gardiner and Walter 1976; Molfese 1973, 1977; Molfese, Freeman, and Palermo 1975). Molfese and his colleagues, for example, report that speech stimuli yield higher amplitude evoked potentials from the left side than from the right, but that music and noise yield higher amplitude potentials from the right side than from the left. These asymmetries were reported to be *greater* in magnitude than similar asymmetries found in adults. Asymmetries in posture and head-turning (Gesell and Ames 1947; Liederman and Kinsbourne in press; Siqueland and Lipsitt 1966; Turkewitz, Gordon, and Birch 1965) suggest that the left side of the brain is prepotent at the time of birth if not before birth. Even predominant right-handedness can be demonstrated in young infants if an appropriate measure of handedness is used (Caplan and Kinsbourne 1976). There have been two recent demonstrations of listening asymmetries in infants. In these experiments, techniques for recording recovery from either sucking habituation (Entus 1977) or cardiac habituation (Glanville, Best, and Levenson 1977) were used to measure the infant's detection of a transition from one sound to another. When speech sounds were presented in dichotic competition, transitions were most likely to be detected if they entered the right ear. Conversely, musical transitions were better detected if they entered the left ear.

In our own work with preschool children, we repeatedly have found clearcut listening asymmetries (Hiscock and Kinsbourne 1977; Kinsbourne and Hiscock 1977). Results of three experiments are summarized in Table 10.1. Each of these three experiments was designed specifically for young children. Instead of having to recall long lists of stimuli, the children were presented only two digit names at a time. In the first experiment, only a "yes" or "no" response was required to indicate whether a specified digit name had been heard at either ear. In the two subsequent experiments, children were instructed to listen to one ear at a time and to report only the digit name heard at that ear. All three experiments yielded statistically significant right-ear advantages. In fact, the magnitude of right-ear advantage was substantially greater than that usually obtained using standard dichotic listening procedures with older children and adults.

Other investigators also have reported significant auditory asymmetries in young children (Bever 1971; Gilbert and Climan 1974; Ingram 1975; Nagafuchi 1970). The various demonstrations of functional asymmetry in infants and young children constitute compelling evidence that language is lateralized in the human brain long before the child is ready to learn to read. Nevertheless, it may be argued that the degree of lateralization increases as the child grows older. This modified form of the progressive lateralization hypothesis—*i.e.,* early lateralization that becomes increasingly complete with increasing age—is difficult to evaluate. At the

TABLE 10.1

Listening Asymmetries in Preschool Children

Experiment	Task	Subjects	Results
Kinsbourne, Hotch & Sessions, Experiment I (see Kinsbourne & Hiscock 1977)	Detection of target digits	20 children 3-5 years	37% misses from right ear; 53% misses from left ear
Kinsbourne, Hotch & Sessions, Experiment II (see Kinsbourne & Hiscock 1977)	Selective listening for digits	16 3-year olds	67% correct responses from right ear; 26% correct responses from left ear
Hiscock & Kinsbourne 1977	Selective listening for digits	12 3-year olds	43% correct responses from right ear; 27% correct responses from left ear
		14 4-year olds	56% correct responses from right ear; 36% correct responses from left ear
		16 5-year olds	55% correct responses from right ear; 51% correct responses from left ear

theoretical level, the concept is ambiguous. Does representation of language within the dominant hemisphere become more concentrated or does the nondominant hemisphere simply lose its linguistic capacity? If the concept of increasing lateralization refers only to the nondominant hemisphere's capacity for assuming linguistic functions after injury to the dominant hemisphere, then the concept of decreasing plasticity is a more parsimonious alternative. Is functional lateralization a unitary characteristic that undergoes a quantitative change over time, or do different capacities become lateralized at different stages of development (see Porter and Berlin 1975)? If different functions become lateralized at different times, then one must be careful to distinguish between the development of lateralization for a function and the development of that function. Lateralization of a function (*e.g.,* writing) may precede the full expression of that function, but behavioral asymmetries may be demonstrable only after the function has developed to the point that it can be measured reliably. These theoretical ambiguities make it difficult to put the progressive lateralization hypothesis to an empirical test. In addition, the researcher faces problems, discussed previously, such as having to compare groups that are disparate in overall performance. The same task may measure different processes at different age levels. Even if asymmetries are greater among older children then among younger children, it may be impossible to isolate lateralization effects from other variables such as strategy and differential experience.

The merits of the progressive lateralization hypothesis have been debated on the basis of dichotic listening data. Longitudinal data are not available, but most cross-sectional studies of dichotic listening performance in children do not show an age-related increase in asymmetry (Berlin, Hughes, Lowe-Bell, and Berlin 1973; Goodglass 1973; Kimura 1963, 1967; Knox and Kimura 1970; Nagafuchi 1970). A minority of studies, however, do suggest that the magnitude of the right-ear advantage increases with increasing age (Bryden 1970; Bryden and Allard 1978; Satz, Bakker, Teunissen, Goebel, and Van der Vlugt 1975). Thus, the question of ontogenetic changes in listening asymmetry remains an open question (Porter and Berlin 1975; Satz et al. 1975). Our own research, in which we used both free recall and selective listening tasks with digit names as stimuli, has shown no increase in the magnitude of the right-ear advantage between the ages of 3 and 12 years (Hiscock and Kinsbourne 1978b; Kinsbourne and Hiscock 1977). In addition, we have demonstrated a developmental invariance for verbal-manual time-sharing asymmetries. The rationale underlying the time-sharing task is that speech, if left-lateralized, should interfere with skilled activity programmed by the left hemisphere (e.g., right-handed activity) more than it interferes with activity programmed by the right hemisphere (e.g., left-handed activity). Asymmetries of this nature have been found in right-handed adults (Hicks 1975; Kinsbourne and Cook 1971; Lomas and Kimura 1976) and kindergarten children (Kinsbourne and McMurray 1975), and the magnitude of this asymmetry remains constant between the ages of 3 and 12 years (Hiscock and Kinsbourne 1978a, in press; White and Kinsbourne 1978).

The ontogeny of cerebral lateralization is not fully understood. Not only is more research needed, but also more sophisticated and explicit models of cerebral organization and cognitive development are needed so that research findings may be interpreted correctly. However, rapid progress is being made. The picture today is much different from that of Orton's time or even from that of ten years ago. It is clear that the infant brain is anatomically and functionally asymmetrical. The influential reports concerning asphasia in children seem to reflect the plasticity of the young brain but not a lack of hemispheric specialization. Even if one accepts measures of auditory asymmetry or time-sharing asymmetry as indices of the degree to which speech is lateralized, the developmental trends provide little basis on which to argue that the degree of lateralization increases wtih increasing age. Those investigators who seek to understand the cerebral organization of children with learning disabilities must consider the likelihood that hemispheric specialization is an invariant characteristic of the normal child from the time of birth.

The Concept of Lateralization

Cerebral lateralization is a hypothetical construct. It refers to a pattern of brain organization that cannot be observed directly but must be inferred from indirect evidence. Lateralization of function may be defined in terms of lateralization of deficit: A particular function is lateralized if it is "asymmetrically represented in the two halves of the brain so that equivalent unilateral lesions do not produce equivalent effects" (Zangwill 1962, p. 105). If lateralization is defined in terms of deficits, clinical observations, in theory, may constitute relatively direct evidence of lateralization. However, in practice, the vagaries of clinical evidence (*e.g.,* ill-defined or nonequivalent lesions; pre-existing brain pathology; individual differences in localization of function) place severe constraints on the validity of this evidence. Moreover, the clinical evidence indicates lateralization of deficit; functional lateralization in the normal, intact brain remains a hypothetical construct that is unavailable to direct observation. In other words, statements about normal lateralization are inferences even when they are based on strong clinical evidence. Statements based on behavioral asymmetries also are inferences, and the justification for these inferences often is questionable.

Let us consider, for example, the data summarized in Table 10.2. These data reflect the performance of 20 hyperactive children who were administered dichotic digit tasks with both free-report and selective-listening instructions (Hiscock, Kinsbourne, Caplan, and Swanson 1979). For this small clinical sample of children, the right-ear advantage for the free-report task did not reach an acceptable level of statistical significance. Consequently, if we were to confuse observable date (the right-ear advantage) with a hypothetical construct (lateralization of speech perception), we might claim that hyperactive children are not completely lateralized for speech perception. That claim would not be justified in light of selective listening data from the same children, which do show a significant right-ear superiority. Perhaps the selective listening task is a more sensitive measure of asymmetry or perhaps differences between the free-

TABLE 10.2

Dichotic Listening Asymmetries in Hyperactive Children

Free Recall Correct Responses		Selective Listening Correct Responses		Selective Listening Intrusion Errors	
Left Ear	Right Ear	Left Ear	Right Ear	Left Ear	Right Ear
69%	74%	75%	84%	13%	22%
$F (1, 19) = 1.34$		$F (1, 18) = 7.38$		$F (1, 18) = 7.78$	
$p > .25$		$p < .025$		$p < .025$	

Source: Hiscock, Kinsbourne, Caplan, and Swanson (1978).

report and selective-listening findings can be attributed to some characteristic of hyperactive children, such as an inability to focus attention in a consistent manner. The important point is that no single behavioral measure is sufficient to define individual or group differences in cerebral lateralization. The finding that young children or dyslexic children fail to show the expected asymmetry on a particular task does not mean that those children are anomalously lateralized. Claimed differences in lateralization must be substantiated by convergent evidence from different tasks.

An author's choice of terminology should make clear the distinction between observable and unobservable events. In addition, different terms imply different concepts of cerebral organization. As described by Zangwill (1962), the term "lateralization" implies only that functions are represented unequally in the two hemispheres. The term "dominance," however, also implies that one hemisphere is the executive hemisphere which exerts its mastery over the other. The notion that the dominant hemisphere exercises control over its counterpart appears to be incorporated into Orton's (1937) concept of dominance, but there is little empirical support for this notion. Also, it is not clear how the nondominant hemisphere would gain the opportunity to perform the tasks for which it is specialized.

As Semmes (1968) has pointed out, the concept of cerebral specialization is little more than a label until the mechanism or mechanisms of lateralization can be specified. There have been at least two preliminary attempts to explain hemispheric specialization in terms of general properties that differentiate the two hemispheres. Kimura (1977) suggests that parts of the left hemisphere are specialized for the control of motor sequencing, and that specialization for linguistic functions is a secondary consequence of that more fundamental specialization. Semmes (1968) argues that sensorimotor functions are represented focally in the left hemisphere but diffusely in the right, and that this fundamental difference in neural organization leads to differential capabilities. Although hypotheses such as these ultimately may lead to a better understanding of what it is that is lateralized, they are unlikely to provide insight into the manner in which the two specialized brain halves communicate, co-operate, and interfere with each other in the neurologically intact child or adult. In other words, lateralization cannot be understood solely on the basis of what each hemisphere does well or the manner in which each hemisphere processes information. It is necessary to understand how both hemispheres together contribute to the overall, moment-to-moment functioning of the person.

Interaction between the cerebral hemispheres forms the basis for a model that can account for behavioral asymmetries and for many of the apparent inconsistencies in the perceptual literature reviewed earlier (see also Studdert-Kennedy 1975). This model (Kinsbourne 1970, 1973, 1974, 1975b) begins with the proposition that a fundamental function of each hemisphere is the direction of orientation toward the contralateral side of space. Differential activation of the hemispheres results in an overt or covert shift of attention away from the side of the more highly activated hemisphere. For instance, the solving of a verbal problem, which presumably involves heightened activation of the left hemisphere, has been shown to bias eye and head turning toward the right (Kinsbourne 1972; Kocel, Galin, Ornstein, and Merrin 1972).

According to this model, behavioral asymmetry is not an invariant function of some fixed characteristic of the nervous system. Individual differences in magnitude of asymmetry are not determined by "degree of lateralization" or by any structural property of the brain. Instead, the magnitude of behavioral asymmetry is influenced largely by the balance of activation between the hemispheres at the time the asymmetries are measured; and the balance of activation, in turn, depends on the manner in which the stimulus or task is being processed. Thus, factors such as strategy, expectancy, and past experience with the material or task contribute directly to the manner in which the task is accomplished and indirectly to the likelihood that behavioral asymmetries will be observed.

Our study of listening asymmetries in hyperactive children (Hiscock et al. 1979) illustrates the importance of nonstructural variables as determinants of perceptual asymmetry. For the selective listening portion of the experiment, the children were instructed to attend primarily to one ear for 12 trials and then to attend to the opposite ear for 12 trials. Nine children attended first to the right ear and eleven attended first to the left ear. The same order of selective listening was maintained during each of four

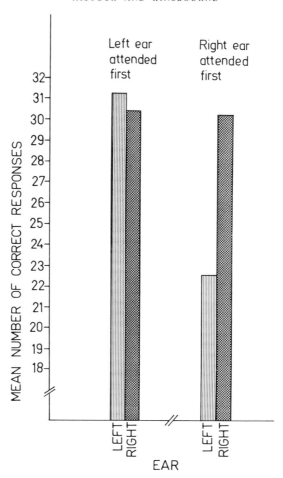

FIGURE 10.1 Mean number of left-ear and right-ear correct responses for hyperactive children who attended first to the left ear and for those who attended first to the right ear (Hiscock *et al.* 1979).

experimental sessions. As shown in Figure 10.1, the order in which the ears were attended had a great influence on the results. A significant right-ear advantage was shown by those children who listened first to the right ear, but the other group showed no appreciable asymmetry. The two groups differed significantly in left-ear but not right-ear performance. These findings do not reflect some peculiarity of hyperactive children, since a large sample of normal children showed a very similar effect (Hiscock and Kinsbourne 1978*b*) and the effect cannot be attributed to fatigue, since right-ear performance was invariant irrespective of whether the right ear was the first or second ear to be monitored. Also, intrusion errors from the unattended right ear accounted for the poor performance from the left ear when the left ear was attended after the right. We seem to have discovered a "priming effect" that makes it difficult to attend to a verbal stimulus at the left ear after gaining experience in attending to the right. Currently, we are attempting to elucidate further the nature of this effect, but it seems clear that this strong influence on perceptual asymmetry cannot be explained readily on the basis of structural variables. It seems quite likely that the child's set, or expectancy, plays a major role.

Regardless of how lateralization is conceptualized, solid evidence of a relationship between lateralization and learning disability is lacking. However, we should not dismiss the possibility that learning disabilities are the result of delayed maturation of the nervous system. The maturational lag concept assumes that increasing levels of cerebral organization are necessary for normal cognitive development, and that delayed maturation of the nervous system will result in cognitive deficits (Kinsbourne 1975a). If the language substrate in the left hemisphere is retarded in development, selective deficits in speech, reading, or spelling may result. Consequently, some forms of learning disability may be associated with a delay in left-hemispheric maturation. Although this possibility, i.e., delayed left-hemispheric maturation, is easily confused with the delayed lateralization hypothesis, the two concepts are entirely independent. The lateralization model concerns only the cerebral space in which language is represented; the maturation model concerns only the adequacy of the neuronal equipment subserving language.

Both models are depicted schematically in Figure 10.2. Dark shaded areas, in the left half of Figure 10.2, depict cerebral regions in which the language substrate is mature and normal. The incompletely lateralized brain, illustrated in the right half of Figure 10.2a, has its language-processing capacity spread across both hemispheres. Presumably, if both left-and-right-hemispheric language areas were consolidated in the left hemisphere, the brain would become normal. In other words, the neuronal equipment is adequate but it is spread too diffusely throughout the cerebrum and consequently cannot be used efficiently. The delayed maturation model is depicted in Figure 10.2b. The immature brain, shown at the right, is fully lateralized for language but the neuronal equipment is inadequate. All linguistic processes are represented in the usual location, but the immaturity of the substrate prevents normal development of linguistic processes. In order to function normally, the language-processing capacity must be increased; simply compressing the existing processor into a smaller space would not improve performance.

Orton's hypothesis regarding cerebral dominance and learning dis-

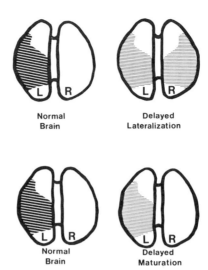

FIGURE 10.2 Schematic diagrams illustrating delayed lateralization and delayed maturation models of language representation in the brains of learning-disabled children. In the case of delayed lateralization (top right), the light shading indicates that language processing capacity is spread across both hemispheres, even though the total capacity is not necessarily deficient. The lightly shaded region of the delayed maturation model (bottom right) indicates a normally lateralized but deficient language processor.

abilities seems simplistic and essentially incorrect in the light of current evidence and concepts. However, we may reject his specific model without rejecting his more general position that learning disabilities have a brain basis and that emotional factors usually are consequences rather than causes of these disabilities (J. L. Orton 1966). In particular, we should not reject the possibility that at least some forms of learning disability, and perhaps most forms, are the result of a delay in the maturation of the nervous system.

REFERENCES

Annett, M. Handedness in families. *Annals of Human Genetics,* 1973, *37,* 93–105.

Annett, M. Handedness in the children of two left-handed parents. *British Journal of Psychology,* 1973, *65,* 129–131.

Annett, M. A model of the inheritance of handedness and cerebral dominance. *Nature,* 1964, *204*, 59-60.

Annett, M. The growth of manual preference and speed. *British Journal of Psychology,* 1970, *61,* 545-558.

Annett, M. The distribution of manual asymmetry. *British Journal of Psychology,* 1972, *63,* 343-358.

Annett, M. Hand preference and the laterality of cerebral speech. *Cortex,* 1975, *11,* 305-328.

Annett, M. A coordination of hand preference and skill replicated. *British Journal of Psychology,* 1976, *67,* 587-592.

Annett, M., Hudson, P. T. W., & Turner, A. The reliability of differences between the hands in motor skill. *Neuropsychologia,* 1974, *12,* 527-531.

Annett, M., & Turner, A. Laterality and the growth of intellectual abilities. *British Journal of Educational Psychology,* 1974, *44,* 37-46.

Bakan, P. Birth order and handedness. *Nature,* 1971, *229,* 195.

Bakan, P., Dibb, G., & Reed, P. Handedness and birth stress. *Neuropsychologia,* 1973, *11,* 363-366.

Bakker, D. J. Hemispheric specialization and stages in the learning-to-read process. *Bulletin of the Orton Society,* 1973, *23,* 15-27.

Bakker, D. J. Perceptual asymmetries and reading proficiency. In M. Bortner (Ed.), *Toward theories of cognitive development.* Herbert G. Birch Memorial Volume (in press).

Bakker, D. J., Smink, T., & Reitsma, P. Ear dominance and reading ability. *Cortex,* 1973, *9,* 301-312.

Bakker, D. J., Van der Vlugt, H., & Claushuis, M. The reliability of dichotic ear asymmetry in normal children. *Neuropsychologia,* 1978, *16,* 753-757.

Bakwin, H. Psychiatric aspects of pediatrics: Lateral dominance, right- and left-handedness. *Journal of Pediatrics,* 1950, *36,* 385-391.

Balow, I. H. Lateral dominance characteristics and reading achievement in the first grade. *Journal of Psychology,* 1963, *55,* 323-328.

Bartholomeus, B. Effects of task requirements on ear superiority for sung speech. *Cortex,* 1974, *10,* 215-223.

Basser, L. S. Hemiplegia of early onset and the faculty of speech with special reference to the effects of hemispherectomy. *Brain,* 1962, *85,* 427-460.

Belmont, L., & Birch, H. G. Lateral dominance, lateral awareness, and reading disability. *Child Development,* 1965, *36,* 57-72.

Benton, A. R. Developmental Dyslexia: Neurological Aspects. In W. J. Friedlander (Ed.), *Advances in neurology* (Vol. 7). New York: Raven Press, 1975.

Berlin, C. I., & Cullen, J. K., Jr. Acoustic problems in dichotic listening tasks. In S. J. Segalowitz & F. A. Gruber (Eds.), *Language development and neurological theory.* New York: Academic Press, 1977.

Berlin, C. I., Hughes, F., Lowe-Bell, S., Berlin, L. Dichotic right ear advantage in children 5 to 13. *Cortex,* 1973, *9,* 393–401.

Berlin, C. I., Lowe-Bell, S. S., Cullen, J. K., Jr., Thompson, C. L., & Loovis, C. F. Dichotic speech perception: An interpretation of right-ear advantage and temporal offset effects. *Journal of the Acoustical Society of America,* 1973, *53,* 699–709.

Berlin, C. I., & McNeil, M. R. Dichotic listening. In N. J. Lass (Ed.), *Contemporary issues in experimental phonetics.* New York: Academic Press, 1976.

Bever, T. G. The nature of cerebral dominance in speech behaviour of the child and adult. In R. Huxley & E. Ingram (Eds.), *Language acquisition: models and methods.* London: Academic Press, 1971.

Bever, T. G., & Chiarello, R. J. Cerebral dominance in musicians and non-musicians. *Science,* 1974, *185,* 537–539.

Blumstein, S., Goodglass, H., & Tartter, V. The reliability of ear advantage in dichotic listening. *Brain & Language,* 1975, *2,* 226–236.

Boder, E. Developmental dyslexia: A new diagnostic approach based on the identification of three subtypes. *Journal of School Health,* 1970, *40,* 289–290.

Bolin, B. J. Left handedness and stuttering as signs diagnostic of epileptics. *Journal of Mental Science,* 1953, *99,* 483–488.

Bryden, M. P. Order of report in dichotic listening. *Canadian Journal of Psychology,* 1962, *16,* 291–299.

Bryden, M. P. Tachistoscopic recognition, handedness, and cerebral dominance. *Neuropsychologia,* 1965, *3,* 1–8.

Bryden, M. P. An evaluation of some models of laterality effects in dichotic listening. *Acta Oto-Laryngologica,* 1967, *63,* 595–604.

Bryden, M. P. Laterality effects in dichotic listening: Relations with handedness and reading ability in children. *Neuropsychologia,* 1970, *8,* 443–450.

Bryden, M. P. Measuring handedness with questionnaires. *Neuropsychologia,* 1977, *15,* 617–624.

Bryden, M. P., & Allard, F. Dichotic listening and the development of linguistic processes. In M. Kinsbourne (Ed.), *The asymmetrical function of the brain.* New York: Cambridge University Press, 1978.

Buffery, W. H. H. Sex differences in the neuropsychological development of verbal and spatial skills. In R. M. Knights & D. J. Bakker (Eds.), *The neuropsychology of learning disorders.* Baltimore: University Park Press, 1976.

Burt, C. The backward child, (3rd Ed.). London: University of London Press, 1950.

Caplan, B., & Kinsbourne, M. Hemispheric specialization and cognitive style in children with reading disability (submitted).

Caplan, P. J., & Kinsbourne, M. Baby drops the rattle: asymmetry of duration of grasp by infants. *Child Development,* 1976, *47,* 532–534.

Chamberlain, H. D. Inheritance of left-handedness. *Journal of Heredity,* 1928, *19,* 557–559.

Clark, M. M. *Reading difficulties in schools.* Harmondsworth: Penguin Books, 1970.

Coleman, R. I., & Deutch, C. P. Lateral dominance and left-right discrimination: A comparison of normal and retarded readers. *Perceptual and Motor Skills,* 1964, *19,* 43–50.

Collins, R. L. When left-handed mice live in right-handed worlds. *Science,* 1975, *187,* 181–184.

Coren, S., & Kaplan, C. P. Patterns of ocular dominance. *American Journal of Optometry and Archives of the American Academy of Optometry,* 1973, *50,* 283–292.

Critchley, M. *The dyslexic child* (2nd Ed.). London: Heinemann, 1970.

Cullen, J. K., Jr., Thompson, C. L., Hughes, L. F., Berlin, C. I., & Sampson, D. The effects of varied acoustic parameters on performance on dichotic speech perception tasks. *Brain and Language,* 1974, *1,* 307–322.

Curry, F. W. K. A comparison of left handed and right handed subjects on verbal and non-verbal dichotic listening tasks. *Cortex,* 1967, *3,* 343–352.

de Hirsch, K., Jansky, J. J., & Langford, W. S. *Predicting reading failure.* New York: Harper & Row, 1966.

Dennis, M., & Whitaker, H. A. Hemispheric equipotentiality and language acquisition. In S. J. Segalowitz & F. A. Gruber (Eds.), *Language development and neurological theory.* New York: Academic Press, 1977.

Doll, E. A. Psychological significance of cerebral birth lesions. *American Journal of Psychology,* 1933, *45,* 444–452.

Entus, A. K. Hemispheric asymmetry in processing of dichotically presented speech and nonspeech stimuli by infants. In S. J. Segalowitz & F. A. Gruber (Eds.), *Language development and neurological theory.* New York: Academic Press, 1977.

Fagan-Dubin, L. Lateral dominance and development of cerebral specialization. *Cortex,* 1974, *10,* 69–74.

Falek, A. Handedness: A family study. *American Journal of Human Genetics,* 1959, *11,* 52–62.

Ferguson, H. B., Simpson, S., & Trites, R. L. Psychophysiological study of methylphenidate responders and nonresponders. In R. M. Knights & D. J. Bakker (Eds.), *The neuropsychology of learning disorders.* Baltimore: University Park Press, 1976.

Fleishman, E. A. On the relation between abilities, learning and human performance. *American Psychologist,* 1972, *27,* 1017–1032.

Freides, D. Do dichotic listening procedures measure lateralization of information processing or retrieval strategy? *Perception and Psychophysics,* 1977, *21,* 259–263.

Gaddes, W. H. Prevalence estimates and the need for definition of learning disabilities. In R. M. Knights & D. J. Bakker (Eds.), *The neuropsychology of learning disorders.* Baltimore: University Park Press, 1976.

Galaburda, A. M., LeMay, M., Kemper, T. L., & Geschwind, N. Right-left asymmetries in the brain. *Science,* 1978, *199,* 852–856.

Gardiner, M. F., & Walter, D. O. Evidence of hemispheric specialization from infant EEG. In S. Harnad, R. W. Doty, L. Goldstein, J. Jaynes & G. Krauthmer (Eds.), *Lateralization in the nervous system.* New York: Academic Press, 1977.

Geschwind, N., & Levitsky, W. Human brain: Left-right asymmetries in temporal speech region. *Science,* 1968, *161,* 186–187.

Gesell, A., & Ames, L. B. The development of handedness. *Journal of Genetic Psychology,* 1947, *70,* 155–175.

Gilbert, J. H. V., & Climan, I. Dichotic studies in 2-3 year olds: A preliminary report. Speech communication seminar, Stockholm, August 1-3, 1974.

Glanville, B. B., Best, C. T., & Levenson, R. A cardiac measure of cerebral asymmetries in infant auditory perception. *Developmental Psychology,* 1977, *13,* 54–59.

Gloning, I., Gloning, K., Haub, G., & Quatember, R. Comparison of verbal behavior in right handed and non-right handed patients with anatomically verified lesion of one hemisphere. *Cortex,* 1969, *5,* 41–52.

Goldstein, L., & Lackner, J. R. Sideways look at dichotic listening. *Journal of the Acoustical Society of America,* 1974, *55,* Supplement S10(A).

Goodglass, H. Developmental comparison of vowels and consonants in dichotic listening. *Journal of Speech and Hearing Research,* 1973, *16,* 744–752.

Gordon, H. Left-handedness and mirror writing especially among defective children. *Brain,* 1920, *43,* 313–368.

Guyer, B. L., & Friedman, M. P. Hemispheric processing and cognitive styles in learning-disabled and normal children. *Child Development,* 1975, *46,* 658–668.

Haggard, M. P., & Parkinson, A. M. Stimulus and task factors as determinants of ear advantage. *Quarterly Journal of Experimental Psychology,* 1971, *23,* 168–177.

Hardyck, C., & Petrinovich, L. F. Left-handedness. *Psychological Bulletin,* 1977, *84,* 385–404.

Hardyck, C., Petrinovich, L., & Goldman, R. Left-handedness and cognitive deficit. *Cortex,* 1976, *12,* 255–279.

Harris, A. J. Lateral dominance, directional confusion and reading disability. *Journal of Psychology,* 1957, *44,* 283–294.

Harshman, R., & Krashen, S. An "unbiased" procedure for comparing degree of lateralization of dichotically presented stimuli. Paper presented at the 83rd meeting, Acoustical Society of America, April, 1972.

Hecaen, H. Acquired aphasia in children and the ontogenesis of hemispheric functional specialization. *Brain and Language,* 1976, *3,* 114-134.

Hecaen, H., & Sauget, J. Cerebral dominance in left-handed subjects. *Cortex,* 1971, *7,* 19-48.

Hellige, J. B., & Cox, P. J. Effects of concurrent verbal memory on recognition of stimuli from the left and right visual fields. *Journal of Experimental Psychology: Human Perception and Performance,* 1976, *2,* 210-221.

Heron, W. Perception as a function of retinal locus and attention. *American Journal of Psychology,* 1975, *70,* 38-48.

Hicks, R. A., Evans, E. A., & Pellegrini, R. J. Correlation between handedness and birth order: Compilation of five studies. *Perceptual and Motor Skills,* 1978, *46,* 53-54.

Hicks, R. E., Intrahemispheric response competition between vocal and unimanual performance in normal adult human males. *Journal of Comparative and Physiological Psychology,* 1975, *89,* 50-60.

Hicks, R. E., & Barton, A. K. A note on left-handedness and severity of mental retardation. *Journal of Genetic Psychology,* 1975, *127,* 323-324.

Hicks, R. E., & Kinsbourne, M. Human handedness: A partial cross-fostering study. *Science,* 1976, *192,* 908-910(a).

Hicks, R. E., & Kinsbourne, M. On the genesis of human handedness: A review. *Journal of Motor Behavior,* 1976, *8,* 257-266(b).

Hicks, R. E., & Kinsbourne, M. Human handedness in M. Kinsbourne (Ed.) *The asymmetrical function of the brain.* New York: Cambridge University Press, 1978.

Hines, D. A brief reply to McKeever, Suberi, and Van Deventer's comment on "Bilateral Tachistoscopic Recognition of Verbal and Nonverbal Stimuli." *Cortex,* 1972, *8,* 480-482.

Hines, D. & Satz, P. Cross-modal asymmetries in perception related to asymmetry in cerebral function. *Neuropsychologia,* 1974, *12,* 239-247.

Hiscock, M., & Kinsbourne, M. Selective listening asymmetry in preschool children. *Developmental Psychology,* 1977, *13,* 217-224.

Hiscock, M., & Kinsbourne, M. Ontogeny of cerebral dominance: Evidence from time-sharing asymmetry in children. *Developmental Psychology,* 1978, *14,* 321-329(a).

Hiscock, M., & Kinsbourne, M. The right ear advantage in children: Studies of selective listening. Paper presented at the annual meeting of the International Neuropsychology Society, Minneapolis, February, 1978(b).

Hiscock, M., & Kinsbourne, M. Asymmetry of verbal-manual time sharing in children: A follow-up study. *Neuropsychologia,* in press.

Hiscock, M., Kinsbourne, M., Caplan, B., & Swanson, J. M. Auditory attention in hyperactive children: Effects of stimulant medication on dichotic listening performance. *Journal of Abnormal Psychology,* 1979, *88,* 27-32.

Hubbard, G. I. Handedness not a function of birth order. *Nature,* 1971, *232,* 276–277.

Hudson, P. T. W. The genetics of handedness: A reply to Levy and Nagylaki. *Neuropsychologia,* 1975, *13,* 331–339.

Inglis, J., & Sykes, D. H. Some sources of variation in dichotic listening performance in children. *Journal of Experimental Child Psychology,* 1967, *5,* 480–488.

Ingram, D. Cerebral speech lateralization in young children. *Neuropsychologia,* 1975, *13,* 103–105.

Johnson, P. R. Dichotically-stimulated ear differences in musicians and non-musicians. Paper presented at the annual meeting of the Canadian Psychological Association, Vancouver, June, 1977.

Johnson, W., & Duke, D. Revised Iowa hand usage dextrality quotients of six-year-olds. *Journal of Educational Psychology,* 1940, *31,* 45–52.

Johnson, W., & King, A. An angle board and hand usage study of stutterers and non-stutterers. *Journal of Experimental Psychology,* 142, *31,* 293–311.

Keller, J. F., Croake, J. W., & Riesenman, E. Relationships among handedness, intelligence, sex, and reading achievement of school age children. *Perceptual and Motor Skills,* 1973, *37, 159–162.*

Kimura, D. Cerebral dominance and the perception of verbal stimuli. *Canadian Journal of Psychology,* 1961, *15,* 166–177(a).

Kimura, D. Some effects of temporal-lobe damage on auditory perception. *Canadian Journal of Psychology,* 1961, *15, 156–165.*

Kimura, D. Speech lateralization in young children as determined by an auditory test. *Journal of Comparative and Physiological Psychology,* 163, *56,* 899–902.

Kimura, D. Left-right differences in the perception of melodies. *Quarterly Journal of Experimental Psychology,* 1964, *14,* 355–358.

Kimura, D. Dual functional asymmetry of the brain in visual perception. *Neuropsychologia,* 1966, *4,* 275–285.

Kimura, D. Functional asymmetry of the brain in dichotic listening. *Cortex,* 1967, *3,* 163–178.

Kimura, D. The neural basis of language qua gesture. In H. Avakian-Whitaker & H. A. Whitaker (Eds.), *Studies in neurolinguistics.* New York: Academic Press, 1977.

Kimura, D., & Durnford, M. Normal studies on the function of the right hemisphere in vision. In S. J. Diamond & J. G. Beaumont (Eds.), *Hemisphere function in the human brain.* New York: Halsted Press, 1974.

Kinsbourne, M. The cerebral basis of lateral asymmetries in attention. *Acta Psychologica,* 1970, *33,* 193–201.

Kinsbourne, M. Eye and head turning indicates cerebral lateralization. *Science,* 1972, *176,* 539–541.

Kinsbourne, M. The control of attention by interaction between the cerebral hemispheres. In S. Kornblum (Ed.), *Attention and performance IV*. New York: Academic Press, 1973.

Kinsbourne, M. Mechanisms of hemispheric interaction in man. In M. Kinsbourne & W. L. Smith (Eds.), *Hemispheric disconnection and cerebral function*. Springfield, Illinois: Charles C. Thomas, 1974.

Kinsbourne, M. Cerebral dominance, learning and cognition. In R. Myklebust (Ed.), *Progress in learning disabilities,* Vol. III, New York: Grune & Stratton, 1975(a).

Kinsbourne, M. The mechanism of hemispheric control of the lateral gradient of attention. In P. M. A. Rabbitt & S. Dornic (Eds.), *Attention and performance V*. London: Academic Press, 1975(b).

Kinsbourne, M. The ontogeny of cerebral dominance. *Annals of the New York Academy of Sciences,* 1975, *263*, 244–250(c).

Kinsbourne, M. Selective difficulties in learning to read, write, and calculate. In *Learning disabilities and related disorders,* edited by J. G. Millichap. Chicago: Yearbook Medical Publishers, 1976.

Kinsbourne, M., & Cook, J. Generalized and lateralized effects of concurrent verbalization on a unimanual skill. *Quarterly Journal of Experimental Psychology,* 1971, *23*, 341–345.

Kinsbourne, M., & Hiscock, M. Does cerebral dominance develop? In S. J. Segalowitz & F. A. Gruber (Eds.), *Language development and neurological theory*. New York: Academic Press, 1977.

Kinsbourne, M., & McMurray, J. The effect of cerebral dominance on time sharing between speaking and tapping by preschool children. *Child Development,* 1975, *46*, 240–242.

Kinsbourne, M., & Warrington, E. Developmental factors in reading and writing backwardness. *British Journal of Psychology,* 1963, *54*, 145–156.

Kinsbourne, M., & Warrington, E. K. The developmental Gerstmann syndrome. In J. Money (Ed.), *The disabled reader*. Baltimore: Johns Hopkins Press, 1966.

Kirstein, E., & Shankweiler, D. Selective listening for dichotically presented stop consonants and vowels. Haskins Laboratories Status report on speech research, 1969, *SR-17/18,* 133–141.

Knights, R. M., & Bakker, D. J. (Eds.), *The neuropsychology of learning disorders*. Baltimore: University Park Press, 1976.

Knox, C., & Kimura, D. Cerebral processing of nonverbal sounds in boys and girls. *Neuropsychologia,* 1970, *8*, 227–237.

Kocel, K., Galin, D., Ornstein, R., & Merrin, E. L. Lateral eye movement and cognitive mode. *Psychonomic Science,* 1972, *27*, 223–224.

Krueger, L. E. Evidence for directional scanning with the order-of-report factor excluded. *Canadian Journal of Psychology,* 1976, *30*, 9–14.

Kuhn, G. M. The PHI coefficient as an index of ear differences in dichotic listening. *Cortex,* 1973, *9,* 450–456.

Lake, D. A., & Bryden, M. P. Handedness and sex differences in hemispheric asymmetry. *Brain and Language,* 1976, *3,* 266–282.

Lenneberg, E. H. *Biological foundations of language.* New York: Wiley, 1967.

Levy, J. Possible basis for the evolution of lateral specialization of the human brain. *Nature,* 1969, *224,* 614–615.

Levy, J. Psychobiological implications of bilateral asymmetry. In S. J. Dimond & J. G. Beaumont (Eds.), Hemisphere function in the human brain. London: Paul Elek, 1974.

Levy, J., & Nagylaki, T. A model for the genetics of handedness. *Genetics,* 1972, *72,* 117–128.

Liederman, J., & Kinsbourne, M. The mechanism of the rightward neonatal turning bias: a sensory or motor effect? *Infant Behavior and Development,* in press.

Lomas, J., & Kimura, D. Intrahemispheric interaction between speaking and sequential manual activity. *Neuropsychologia,* 1976, *14,* 23–33.

Lowe, S. S., Cullen, J. K., Jr., Berlin, C. I., Thompson, C. L., & Willett, M. E. Perception of simultaneous dichotic and monotic monosyllables. *Journal of Speech and Hearing Research,* 1970, *13,* 812–822.

Luria, A. R. *Traumatic aphasia: its syndromes, psychology and treatment,* Trans., Douglas Bowden. Paris: Mouton, 1970.

Lyle, J. G. Reading retardation and reversal tendency: A factorial study. *Child Development,* 1969, *40,* 833–843.

Malmquist, E. *Factors related to reading disabilities in the first grade of elementary school.* Stockholm: Almquist & Wiksell, 1958.

Marshall, J. C., Caplan, D., & Holmes, J. M. The measure of laterality. *Neuropsychologia,* 1975, *13,* 315–321.

McCarthy, J. J., & McCarthy, J. F. *Learning Disabilities.* Boston: Allyn & Bacon, 1969.

Miller, E. Handedness and the pattern of human ability. *British Journal of Psychology,* 1971, *62,* 111–112.

Molfese, D. L. Central asymmetry in infants, children and adults: auditory evoked responses to speech and music. *Journal of the Acoustical Society of America,* 1973, *53,* 363–373.

Molfese, D. L. Infant cerebral asymmetry in S. J. Segalowitz & F. A. Gruber, (Eds.), *Language development and neurological theory.* New York: Academic Press, 1977.

Molfese, D. L., Freeman, R. B., Jr., & Palermo, D. S. The ontogeny of brain lateralization for speech and nonspeech stimuli. *Brain and Language,* 1975, *2,* 356–368.

Morais, J. The effects of ventriloquism on the right-side advantage of verbal material. *Cognition,* 1975, *3,* 127–139.

Morais, J., & Bertelson, P. Spatial position versus ear of entry as determinant of the auditory laterality effects: A stereophonic test. *Journal of Experimental Psychology: human perception and performance,* 1975, *1,* 253–262.

Morgan, M. J., & Corballis, M. C. On the biological basis of human laterality: II. The mechanisms of inheritance. *The Behavioral and Brain Sciences,* 1978, *2,* 270–277.

Morley, M. E. *The development and disorders of speech in childhood,* 2nd Ed. Baltimore: Williams & Wilkins, 1965.

Myklebust, H. *Development and disorders of written language, Volume 1, picture story language test.* New York: Gruen & Stratton, 1965.

Nagafuchi, M. Development of dichotic and monaural hearing abilities in young children. *Acta Oto-Laryngologica,* 1970, *69,* 409–414.

Nebes, R. D. Handedness and the perception of part-whole relationships. *Cortex,* 1971, *7,* 350–356.

Newcombe, F., & Ratcliff, G. Handedness, speech lateralization and ability. *Neuropsychologia,* 1973, *11,* 399–407.

Oldfield, R. C. The assessment and analysis of handedness: The Edinburgh inventory. *Neuropsychologia,* 1971, *9,* 97–113.

Orme, J. E. Left-handedness, ability and emotional instability. *British Journal of Social and Clinical Psychology,* 1970, *9,* 87–88.

Orton, J. L. The Orton-Gillingham approach. In J. Money (Ed.), *The disabled reader.* Baltimore: Johns Hopkins Press, 1966.

Orton, S. T. "Word-blindness" in school children. *Archives of Neurology and Psychiatry,* 1925, *14,* 581–615.

Orton, S. T. Reading, writing and speech problems in children. New York: Norton, 1937.

Papcun, G., Krashen, S., Terbeek, D., Remington, R., & Harshman, R. Is the left hemisphere specialized for speech, language and/or something else? *Journal of the Acoustical Society of America,* 1974, *55,* 319–327.

Pizzamiglio, L., De Pascalis, Corradino, & Vignati, A. Stability of dichotic listening test, *Cortex,* 1974, *10,* 203–205.

Porac, C., & Coren, S. Is sighting dominance a part of generalized laterality? *Perceptual and Motor Skills,* 1975, *40,* 763–769.

Porac, C., & Coren, S. The dominant eye. *Psychological Bulletin,* 1976, *83,* 880–897.

Porter, R. J., Jr., & Berlin, C. I. On interpreting developmental changes in the dichotic right-ear advantage. *Brain and Language,* 1975, *2,* 186–200.

Provins, K. A., & Cunliffe, P. The reliability of some motor performance tests of handedness. *Neuropsychologia,* 1972, *10,* 199–206.

Raczkowski, D., Kalat, J. W., & Nebes, R. Reliability and validity of some handedness questionnaire items. *Neuorpsychologia,* 1974, *12,* 43–47.

Rasmussen, T., & Milner, B. Clinical and surgical studies of the cerebral speech areas in man. In K. J. Zuelch, O. Creutzfeldt, & G. Galbraith (Eds.), *Cerebral localization: an Otfried Foerster Symposium.* Heidelberg: Springer-Verlag, 1975.

Richardson, J. T. E. How to measure laterality. *Neuropsychologia,* 1976, *14,* 135–136.

Roberts, J., & Engel. A. *Family Background, Early Development, and Intelligence of children 6-11 years: United States.* National Center for Health Statistics, vital and health statistics: data from the National Health Survey, series 11, No. 142, Dhew Publication No. (HRA) 75-1624. Washington, D.C.: U.S. Government Printing Office, 1974.

Roberts, L. Aphasia, apraxia and agnosia in abnormal states of cerebral dominance. In P. J. Vinken & G. W. Bruyn, (Eds.), *Handbook of Clinical Neurology,* Vol. 4. Amsterdam: North Holland, 1969.

Rossi, G. F., & Rosadini, G. Experimental analysis of cerebral dominance in man. In C. H. Millikan & F. L. Darley (Eds.), *Brain mechanisms underlying speech and language.* New York: Grune & Stratton, 1967.

Rourke, B. P. Brain-behavior relationships in children with learning disabilities. *American Psychologist,* 1975, *30,* 911–920.

Rutter, M., Tizard, J., & Whitmore, K. (Eds.), *Education, health, and behavior.* London: Longmans, 1970.

Satz, P. Pathological left-handedness: an explanatory model. *Cortex,* 1972, *8,* 121–135.

Satz, P. Left-handedness and early brain insult: an explanation. *Neuropsychologia,* 1973, *11,* 115–117.

Satz, P. Cerebral dominance and reading disability: an old problem revisited. In R. M. Knights & D. J. Bakker (Eds.), *The Neuropsychology of learning disorders.* Baltimore: University Park Press, 1976.

Satz, P. Laterality: an inferential problem. *Cortex,* 1977, *13,* 208–212.

Satz, P., Achenbach, K., & Fennel, E. Correlations between assessed manual laterality and predicted speech laterality in a normal population. *Neuropsychologia,* 1967, *5,* 295–310.

Satz, P., Bakker, D. J., Teunissen, J., Goebel, R., & Van Der Vlugt, H. Developmental parameters of the ear asymmetry: a multivariate of approach. *Brain and Language,* 1975, *2,* 171–185.

Schwartz, M. Left-handedness and high-risk pregnancy. *Neuropsychologia,* 1977, *15,* 341–344.

Searleman, A. A review of right hemisphere linguistic capabilities. *Psychological Bulletin,* 1977, *84,* 503–528.

Segalowitz, S. J., & Gruber, F. A. (Eds.), *Language development and neurological theory.* New York: Academic Press, 1977.

Semnes, J. Hemispheric specialization: a possible clue to mechanism. *Neuropsychologia,* 1968, *6,* 11–26.

Shankweiler, D., & Studdert-Kennedy, M. A continuum of lateralization for speech perception? *Brain and Language,* 1975, *2,* 212–225.

Siqueland, E. R., & Lipsitt, L. P. Conditioned head turning in human newborns. *Journal of Experimental Child Psychology,* 1966, *4,* 356–357.

Sparrow, S., & Satz, P. Dyslexia, laterality, and neuropsychological development. In D. J. Bakker & P. Satz (Eds.), *Specific reading disability: advances in theory and method.* Rotterdam: Rotterdam University Press, 1970.

Spellacy, Frank, & Blumstein, S. The influence of language set on ear preference in phoneme recognition. *Cortex,* 1970, *6,* 430–439.

Spreen, O. Neuropsychology of learning disorders: post-conference review. In R. M. Knights & D. J. Bakker (Eds.), *The neuropsychology of learning disorders.* Baltimore: University Park Press, 1976.

Studdert-Kennedy, M. Dichotic studies II: two questions. *Brain and Language,* 1975, *2,* 123–130.

Studdert-Kennedy, M., & Shankweiler, D. Hemispheric specialization for speech perception. *Journal of the Acoustical Society of America,* 1970, *48,* No. 2, Part 2, 579–594.

Teng, E. L., Lee. P.-H., Yang, K.-S., & Chang, P. C. Handedness in a Chinese population: biological, social, and pathological factors. *Science,* 1976, *193,* 1148–1150.

Teng, E. L., Lee, P.-H., Yang, K.-S., & Chang. P. C. Lateral preferences for hand, foot and eye, and their lack of association with scholastic achievement in 4143 Chinese. *Neuropsychologia,* 1979, *17,* 41–48.

Teszner, D., Tzavaras, A., Gruner, J., & Hecaen, H. L'asymetrie droite-gauche du planum temporale. A propos de l'etude anatomique de 100 cerveaux. *Revue Neurologique,* 1972, *126,* 444–449.

Turkewitz, G., Gordon, E. W., & Birch, H. G. Head turning in the human neonate: effect of prandial condition and lateral preference. *Journal of Comparative and Physiological Psychology,* 1965, *59,* 189–192.

Van Lancker, D., & Fromkin, V. A. Hemispheric specialization for pitch and "tone": Evidence from Thai. *Journal of Phonetics,* 1977, *1,* 101–109.

Vernon, M. D. *Backwardness in reading.* Cambridge: Cambridge University Press, 1957.

Vernon, M. D. *Reading and its difficulties.* London: Cambridge University Press, 1971.

Wada, J., Clarke, R., & Hamm, A. Cerebral hemispheric asymmetry in humans. *Archives of Neurology,* 1975, *32,* 239–246.

Wada, J., & Rasmussen, T. Intracarotid injection of sodium amytal for the lateralization of cerebral speech dominance. *Journal of Neurosurgery,* 1960, *17,* 266–282.

Webster, W. G., & Thurber, A. D. Problem-solving strategies and manifest brain asymmetry. *Cortex,* 1978, *14,* 474–484.

Wender, P. H. Hypothesis for a possible biochemical basis of minimal brain dysfunction. In R. M. Knights & D. J. Bakker (Eds.), *The neuropsychology of learning disorders.* Baltimore: University Park Press, 1976.

White, M. J. Laterality differences in perception: a review. *Psychological Bulletin,* 1969, *72,* 387–405.

White, N., & Kinsbourne, M. Does speech output control lateralize over time? Evidence from verbal-manual time-sharing tasks. *Brain and Language,* in press.

Wilson, M. O., & Dolan, L. B. Handedness and ability. *American Journal of Psychology,* 1931, *43,* 261–268.

Witelson, S. F. Hemispheric specialization for linguistic and nonlinguistic tactual perception using a dichotomous stimulation technique. *Cortex,* 1974, *10,* 3–17.

Witelson, S. F. Abnormal right hemisphere specialization in developmental dyslexia. In R. M. Knights & D. J. Bakker (Eds.), *The neuropsychology of learning disorders.* Baltimore: University Park Press, 1976 (a).

Witelson, S. F. Sex and the single hemisphere: right hemisphere specialization for spatial processing. *Science,* 1976, *193,* 425–427 (b).

Witelson, S. F. Developmental dyslexia: two right hemispheres and none left. *Science,* 1977, *195,* 309–311.

Witelson, S. F., & Pallie, W. Left hemisphere specialization for language in the newborn: neuroanatomical evidence of asymmetry. *Brain,* 1973, *96,* 641–646.

Witelson, S. F., & Rabinovitch, M. S. Children's recall strategies in dichotic listening. *Journal of Experimental Child Psychology,* 1971, *12,* 106–113.

Woo, T. L., & Pearson, K. Dextrality and sinistrality of hand and eye. *Biometrika,* 1927, *19,* 165–199.

Woods, B. T., & Teuber, H. L. Changing patterns of childhood aphasia. *Annals of Neurology,* 1978, *3,* 273–280.

Yeni-Komshian, G. H., & Benson, D. A. Anatomical study of cerebral asymmetry in the temporal lobe of humans, chimpanzees, and rhesus monkeys. *Science,* 1976, *192,* 387–389.

Yule, W., & Rutter, M. Epidemiology and social implications of specific reading retardation. In R. M. Knights & D. J. Bakker (Eds.), *The Neuropsychology of learning disorders.* Baltimore: University Park Press, 1976.

Zangwill, O. L. *Cerebral dominance and its relation to psychological function.* London, Oliver & Boyd, 1960.

Zangwill, O. L. Dyslexia in relation to cerebral dominance. In J. Money (Ed.), *Reading disability*. Baltimore: Johns Hopkins Press, 1962.

Zangwill, O. L. Speech and the minor hemisphere. *Acta Neurologica et Psychiatrica Belgica,* 1967, *67,* 1013–1020.

11

Development of Cerebral Dominance in Learning Disabled Children

Evidence from Dichotic Listening and Time-Sharing Asymmetries

John E. Obrzut, George W. Hynd, and Ann Obrzut

HEMISPHERE SPECIALIZATION has been a perennial issue in neuropsychology. There have been numerous comprehensive summaries of research and theoretical statements concerning cerebral lateralization in adults (Dimond and Beaumont 1974; Kinsbourne and Smith 1974; White 1969). In adults, at least, each hemisphere appears dominant or specialized for specific cognitive functions. However, the development of hemisphere specialization during childhood still has not been firmly established. Two theoretical positions exist at present. Kinsbourne (1975) has hypothesized that left hemispheric specialization exists at birth and does not undergo subsequent developmental change. Lennenberg (1967) theorized that at birth and during early childhood there is a bilateral representation of language; however, as the child grows, the linguistic processes gradually become lateralized to the left hemisphere. To date, most research has addressed the question of the development of hemisphere specialization in normal children (Hiscock and Kinsbourne 1978; Hynd and Obrzut 1977; Kinsbourne and Hiscock 1977), although beginning attempts to apply this knowledge to special populations such as the learning disabled were initiated almost four decades ago.

Orton (1937) was the first to suggest a relationship between cerebral dominance and numerous functions such as speech, writing, reading, and spelling. He conceptualized the reading process as one of the complex linguistic-cognitive functions subserved by the left hemisphere. He noted a similarity in reading errors made by adults with known unilateral left hemisphere injury and children with specific reading disorders (dyslexics). He hypothesized that the reversals and mirror images of letters made by children were a result of competing images in both hemispheres because of a lack of lateralization of linguistic processes. He attributed the reading impairment in adults to a pathological defect (lesion) and by contrast in children, he postulated a physiological defect that prevented the normal establishment of unilateral cerebral dominance. His distinction between a pathological and physiological etiology was particularly optimistic to educators in that with training and possibly maturation the situation might improve. However, many of his original hypotheses regarding the neuropsychological correlates of learning disabilities still have not been empirically established.

In an attempt to explain some of the cognitive and performance deficits which learning disabled children show, much research of late has focused on abnormalities in the development of lateralized cerebral functions (Dimond and Beaumont 1974). Initial studies have attempted to relate handedness and/or mixed dominance to anomalies of lateralization (Belmont and Birch 1965; Coleman and Deutsch 1964; Orton 1937). Specifically researchers have attempted to relate left handedness to learning disability. For example, many authors have reported an elevated incidence of left handers among their dyslexic samples. Others have reported a high incidence of weak laterality or ambidexterity in this clinical group. However, research has failed to produce substantial agreement that mixed dominance is directly related to learning disability. Basically there is no evidence that handedness is related to degree of lateralization. Results from case reports and invasive techniques (Wada and Rasmussen 1960) indicate that right handers have their language represented in the left cerebral hemisphere in children and adults. But if preference is for the left hand no statement about language can be made. Presumably mixed dominance and inconsistent sidedness suggests incomplete lateralization, but many normal students have crossed eye-hand dominance and many learning disabled do not.

In recent years, perceptual asymmetry tasks (dichotic listening, visual half-field presentation, verbal-manual time-sharing) have been used in the study of cerebral lateralization. The assumption is that these are more direct measures and yield better information about brain organization than traditional measures of handedness.

One of the most frequently used techniques is the dichotic listening procedure which involves a simultaneous presentation of two different acoustic signals (stop-consonants, words, digits), one to each ear. Most normal adults and children report right ear stimuli more accurately than left. This right ear advantage (REA) is thought to reflect left hemisphere representation for language. Satz (1976) has extensively reviewed dichotic studies relating cerebral dominance and reading disability. Briefly, several of these studies (Bryden 1970; Leong 1975; Satz, Rardin, and Ross 1971; Sparrow and Satz 1970) revealed an REA in reading disabled children. However, other studies revealing no perceptual asymmetry (REA) in disabled readers were marred by procedural artifacts which may be responsible for the inconsistent findings (Witelson and Rabinovitch 1972; Zurif and Carson 1970).

While the dichotic listening technique has been useful in contributing information about the development of cerebral dominance, it presents certain shortcomings. For example, reliability of ear asymmetry is not very high (.60–.75 with adults) (Blumstein, Goodglass, and Tartter 1975). Hiscock and Kinsbourne (1978) recently found that only 60 percent of their children reported a right ear advantage (REA) for verbal stimuli which was similar to the findings of Bryden and Allard (1978). It is likely that developmental studies utilizing dichotic listening have encountered floor and ceiling effects (Satz 1976) and this together with irrelevant factors such as attentional deficits (Kinsbourne 1970), acoustical characteristics of stimulus materials (Berlin and Cullen, Jr. 1977), and statistical treatment of the data (Bryden and Allard 1978) may prevent underlying patterns of language lateralization from being revealed.

Time-sharing is one of the most recent perceptual asymmetry techniques utilized with children and may be less susceptible to situational bias. Unlike the strictly auditory perceptual phenomena used in dichotic studies, this technique makes use of motor concomitants of lateralized cerebral processes which may allow for a more sensitive measure of developmental trends in lateralized function. It is a type of experiment that contrasts subjects' ability to perform concurrent activities when they are programmed in the same hemisphere (e.g., speaking and right manual activities) and when they are programmed in separate hemispheres (speaking and left manual activities). The mechanism of this effect of "hemisphere sharing" appears to be competition and "cross-talk" between incompatible timing mechanisms hierarchically organized in the brain (Kinsbourne and Cook 1971; Kreuter, Kinsbourne, and Trevarthen 1972).

Results from studies using this technique have indicated greater decrement of right than left hand performance in adults (Briggs 1973; Hicks 1975; Kantowitz and Knight 1974; Kinsbourne and Cook 1971; Kreuter, Kinsbourne and Trevarthen 1972) and in children (Hiscock and Kinsbourne 1978; Kinsbourne and McMurray 1975).

The following study was an attempt to investigate the performance of both normal and learning disabled children on a time-sharing and dichotic listening task. Specifically, it was of interest to examine (1) speech lateralization (REA and asymmetry of interference), (2) the consistency of measurement using both perceptual techniques, and (3) developmental trends evidenced in either population.

METHOD

Subjects

A sample of 96 white middle class students ranging in age from 7-0 to 11-10 participated voluntarily in the study. Forty-eight subjects were selected on the basis of their placement in learning disabled programs in Greeley, Colorado. All of these students demonstrated at least average intelligence on the Wechsler Intelligence Scale for Children-Revised (WISC-R) the mean intelligence quotients were: verbal $\overline{X} = 101.2$ (S.D. = 11.9); performance $\overline{X} = 103.3$ (S.D. = 14.4); and full scale $\overline{X} = 102.4$ (S.D. 12.3). In addition, each of these subjects had a minimum two year achievement deficit on the Woodcock Reading Mastery Test and the Key Math Diagnostic Test. Forty-eight normal students were subsequently matched with the learning disabled group according to age, sex and handedness. All normals were reading at or above their grade placement according to the Wide Range Achievement Test.

Handedness was established by observing the hand each child used in eight activities selected from the Edinburgh Handedness Inventory (Oldfield 1971). All 96 subjects preferred their right hand, using a cutoff of five out of eight activities being performed with the dominant hand. Left-handed children were automatically replaced in view of equivocal findings relating to interpretation of their hemispheric specialization. The mean laterality quotients (LQ) were as follows: normal LQ $\overline{X} = 94.27$ (S.D. 16.37); learning disabled LQ $\overline{X} = 92.71$ (S.D. 14.03).

Prior to testing, subjects passed an audiometric screening test for the octave audiometric frequencies from 500 Hz through 8,000 Hz at a hearing threshold level of 5db (ANSI-1969). Criteria for passing was failure at no more than one frequency, each ear, and at no greater level than 20db HTL. Students failing the screening were eliminated. This screening was conducted in a Tracoustics Sound Suite (meeting ANSI specifications for ambient noise levels) on a Grason-Stadler 1701 audiometer.

To facilitate an analysis for a developmental trend in the establishment of cerebral speech lateralization, the 48 learning disabled subjects were divided into three age levels of sixteen children. All normal subjects were matched for age and divided into the same three age levels. The means were as follows: Level 1: $\overline{X} = 8.0$ years (range 7-0 to 8-5); Level 2: $\overline{X} = 9$-5 years (range 8-6 to 10-4); Level 3: $\overline{X} = 11$-0 years (range 10-5 to 11-11).

Materials and Apparatus

The instruments utilized in the time-sharing technique consisted of a telegraph key and a stereo tape recorder. The telegraph key controlled an audio oscillator which was fed into one channel of the tape recorder as the child performed the tapping task. The child spoke into a microphone which was recorded onto the second channel in the concurrent verbal-manual task condition. A stopwatch was used for timing.

The source of dichotic stimuli was a synthesized tape which was prepared at Kresge Hearing Research Laboratory, New Orleans, Louisiana. Thirty pairs of voiced CV syllables (/ba/ka/da/pa/ga/ta) were presented through a MAICO-24 audiometer using a SONY TC560 tape recorder. The presentation of dichotic stimuli represented all possible non-identical pairings of the CV syllables. The test stimuli were received through TDH-39 earphones at a hearing threshold level of 55db. Each channel of the recording was monitored at the "O" VU on the audiometer with the calibration tone on the tape recording as the reference tone.

Procedure

All testing was conducted in a Tracoustics Sound Suite. The subjects were tested in a counter-balanced order during one experimental session on the dichotic and time-sharing tasks.

The time-sharing procedure was very similar to that employed by Hiscock and Kinsbourne (1978). Each child received a practice trial in which they were asked to tap with one hand, then to tap while reciting the names of vegetables. When it was clear that the child understood the task, the experimental task was introduced. There were two control conditions (RC, LC) in which the child tapped each index separately as rapidly as possible without verbalizing. These control trials were used to establish a base tapping rate per hand. There were two experimental conditions (RV, LV) where the child tapped while concurrently verbalizing animal names, one trial with the right index (RV) and one with the left index (LV). Alternate subjects performed one of the following sequences: RC, LV, RV, LC: LC, RV, LV, RC. Each of the four trials lasted 15 seconds. The tapes were played at half-speed and blindly scored by two independent observers. The inter-scorer reliability coefficient was r = .99 for each of the trials.

The procedures for the dichotic listening task included presenting each child with a strip of tagboard on which the six CV syllables were printed. The examiner then pronounced each syllable with the subject repeating after him. Each child then received three practice trails followed with the 30 pairs of voiced CV syllables in the tradition of dichotic studies.

RESULTS

Time-Sharing–Control Condition

The mean number of taps per subject per condition for each hand and developmental level by diagnostic group is presented in Table 11.1.

A 3 x 2 x 2 (developmental level x diagnostic group x control condition) analysis of variance revealed three significant main effects and no significant interactions. A main effect for developmental level, F (2,

TABLE 11.1

**Mean Number of Taps Per Second for Each Hand by
Diagnostic Group and Developmental Level**

Developmental Level (Age Range)	N	Control Condition		Verbal Interference	
Normal		*Left Hand* (LC)	*Right Hand* (RC)	*Left Hand* (LV)	*Right Hand* (RV)
Level I (7.0–8.5)	16	3.86	4.40	2.95	2.92
Level II (8.6–10.4)	16	4.99	5.33	3.30	3.03
Level III (10.5–11.11)	16	4.73	6.08	3.10	2.96
Learning Disabled					
Level I (7.0–8.5)	16	2.79	3.06	0.84	0.86
Level II (8.6–10.4)	16	3.26	3.98	1.04	1.01
Level III (10.5–11.11)	16	3.38	4.17	1.58	1.77

90) = 14.62, p < .01, reflects an increase in tapping rate with increasing age, and a main effect for hand, $F(1, 90) = 30.49$, p < .01, reflects a right hand superiority for tapping speed in both normal and learning disabled children. The main effect for diagnostic groups, $F(1, 90) = 72.78$, p. < .001, indicates that normal children outperform learning disabled in tapping rate. Although there was a significant difference between these two groups in tapping speed, a non-significant Age x Hand interaction, $F(2, 90) = 2.79$, p > .05, Age x Group interaction, $F(2, 90) = .58$, p > .05, and Group x Hand interaction, $F(1, 90) = .37$, p > .05 was found. These results suggest that while there may be differences between the performance of normal and learning disabled in tapping rates in the control condition, that is, without interference, both groups show strong right hand laterality and that the tapping rate for both hands increases with age.

Time-Sharing–Verbal-Interference Condition

The analysis of asymmetry of interference is accomplished by determining the degree to which the concurrent task (RV, LV) depresses tapping rate for either hand as compared to the control tapping condition (RC, LC). Scores were converted to an "interference index" representing the proportionate decrease (expressed as percent reduction) in tapping rate in the concurrent vocalization condition relative to the tapping rate with that hand in the control condition (see Kinsbourne and Hiscock 1977). Subsequently these percent decrease scores were transformed using arcsine transformations for purposes of statistical analysis.

Figure 11.1 shows the findings for the concurrent verbal interference task. Values in the figure represent the percentage decrease in tapping rate for the right and left hands. It can be seen that the right-hand decrement exceeds the left-hand decrement at all age levels in normal and learning disabled children. The 3 x 2 x 2 (developmental level x diagnostic group x interference condition) analysis of variance revealed two significant main effects and no significant interactions. There was a significant main effect for hand, $F(1, 90) = 16.37$, p < .01. Thus concurrent speech decreased right-hand control tapping speed (a mean decrease of 40% for normals and 67% for learning disabled) significantly more than left-hand control tapping speed (a mean decrease of 31% for normals and 63% for learning disabled). A significant main effect for diagnostic groups, $F(1, 90) = 19.84$, p < .01, confirms the observed tendency for normals to outperform learning disabled. It was of particular interest that no develop-

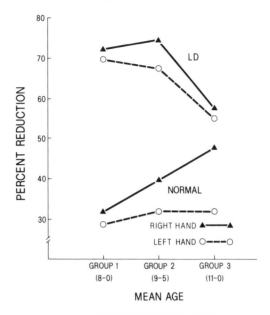

FIGURE 11.1 Mean reduction in right-hand and left-hand tapping rate, relative to the control condition, when the concurrent task was recitation of animal names

mental trend, $F(2, 90) = .29$, p > .05, was found. In addition, and similar to the results for the control condition, there was an absence of an Age x Hand interaction, $F(2, 90) = 1.24$, p > .05, Age x Group Interaction, $F(2, 90) = 1.98$, p > .05, and Group x Hand interaction, $F(1, 90) = 1.49$, p > .05. The presence of a verbal secondary task appears to differentiate the performance of normal from learning disabled children and interferes with right-hand tapping to a greater extent than left-hand tapping for both groups regardless of developmental level. Thus, the time-sharing technique did reflect asymmetry of interference for both diagnostic populations.

Dichotic Ear Laterality

All subjects were free to recall either one or both of the CV syllables on each trial. These scores are reported in Table 11.2 according to devel-

TABLE 11.2

**Mean Number of Correctly Reported CV Syllables for Each Ear
by Diagnostic Group and Developmental Level**

Developmental Level		Left Ear		Right Ear	
(Age Range)	N	X̄	S.D.	X̄	S.D.
Normal					
Level I (7.0–8.5)	16	8.69	2.33	15.50	3.06
Level II (8.6–10.4)	16	9.88	2.55	13.88	3.14
Level III (10.5–11.11)	16	9.31	2.68	14.19	2.29
Learning Disabled					
Level I (7.0–8.5)	16	10.61	2.31	11.19	3.06
Level II (8.6–10.4)	16	9.13	2.94	12.50	2.83
Level III (10.5–11.11)	16	8.56	4.15	12.25	6.04

A total score of 30 was possible for each ear.

opmental levels for both the normal and learning disabled children.

A 3 x 2 x 2 (developmental level x diagnostic group x ear) analysis of variance with repeated measures using the correct only scores revealed two significant main effects and one significant interaction. While both the normal and learning disabled children demonstrated a significant right ear effect, $F(1, 90) = 45.75$, p < .001, there was a significant difference between these two groups in their performance on the dichotic task, $F(1, 90) = 12.35$, p < .01. The only other significant effect was a Group x Ear interaction, $F(1, 90) = 5.47$, p < .05. It appears that some learning disabled children reported more left ear stimuli than their normal counterparts (see Table 11.2). However, no developmental trend, $F(2, 90) = .12$, p > .05, or other significant interactions were evidenced. These results indicate that while there may be differences between the performance of normal and learning disabled on a dichotic task, both are lateralized for speech representation and do not show an increase in dichotic recall with age.

In an effort to resolve some of the methodological shortcomings that have been suggested recently by Bryden and Allard (1978) as being partly responsible for the inconsistent findings on dichotic data, this study also measured ear laterality with the percentage of error (POE) index (Harshman and Krashen 1972; Millay, Roeser, and Godfrey 1977).

Mean POE is shown for the recall of CV syllables according to developmental level in Figure 11.2. The ordinate (POE) indicates mean percentage of error contributed by the left ear; scores above 50 percent reflect a right ear advantage (REA), scores below 50 percent, a left ear advantage (LEA). The fact that both the normal and learning disabled children are lateralized across developmental levels is demonstrated by the REAs in Figure 11.2. Normal children show a POE index range of 59 percent (for the youngest) to 56 percent (for the oldest) which decreases as age increases while learning disabled children's POE index ranges from 51 percent (for the youngest) to 55 percent (for the oldest) and appears to increase slightly with age.

As with the dichotic correct scores, an identical three-way analysis of variance with repeated measures was computed on POE scores which had been transformed using arcsine transformations. This analysis yielded one significant main effect and one significant interaction. While the sig-

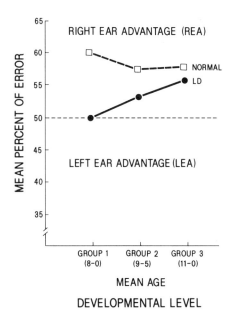

FIGURE 11.2 Mean dichotic percent of error (POE) contributed by the left ear across age groups

nificant ear effect, F (1, 90) = 43.36, p < .001, was still evident, the apparent difference between the performance of the normal and learning disabled children was no longer significant, F (1, 90) = 1.06, p > .05. However, the significant Group x Ear interaction, F (1, 90) = 5.22, p < .05, remained. Again, no developmental trend, F (2, 90) = .92, p > .05, or other significant interactions were noted. These results, although similar to the findings when using dichotic correct scores, suggest that the significant differences originally reported between the normal and matched learning disabled children may be attributed to the effects of guessing rather than to actual differences in the relative degree of cerebral speech lateralization.

DISCUSSION

The time-sharing and dichotic listening techniques used to assess perceptual asymmetries in normal and learning disabled children yielded the following findings: (1) both groups demonstrated lateralization of language function, (2) no developmental trends were evident, and (3) the normal children had different performance characteristics on the tasks.

The first finding that learning disabled children demonstrate speech lateralization disputes the theoretical position that these children suffer from a failure of the two hemispheres to differentiate function as suggested by Orton (1937) and many others. To date, the time-sharing technique has not been reported in studies with learning disabled children although the dichotic technique has been utilized. The asymmetry found with the dichotic technique corroborates other studies involving learning disabled (e.g., Hynd, Obrzut, Weed, and Hynd in press; Obrzut in press). However, utilization of the time-sharing technique offers a unique contribution because it involves a speech production component whereas the dichotic measure requires speech reception. Therefore it is suggested that learning disabled children are lateralized in some aspects of the receptive and expressive areas of language.

Although lateralization existed, the finding that some learning disabled children reported more left ear stimuli on the dichotic task might be a result of the free recall procedure. In free recall there is no way to assure that a subject is not shifting attention from the left to the right ear either out of boredom, motivation, or inability to concentrate. Learning disabled children have well documented attentional deficits and as a result may shift attention from ear to ear. This may help explain the weak but significant group by ear interaction effect found on the dichotic results.

The second finding that no developmental trend existed on either task disputes Lenneberg's (1967) hypothesis describing cerebral specialization as a developmental process. The data supports the "developmental invariance" hypothesis which states that left hemispheric specialization exists at birth and does not undergo subsequent developmental change (Kinsbourne 1975). This study concurs with other research in which no developmental trends have been found using dichotic stimuli with normal (Hynd and Obrzut 1977; Kinsbourne and Hiscock 1977) and learning disabled children (Hynd *et al.* in press). In addition, the results from the time-sharing task also lend support to the notion that lateralization of language is not a developmental process. Although a developmental trend was evidenced in the tapping rate for both hands (RC, LC), no trend was found when a language production component was introduced in the tapping asymmetry task. This finding is significant in view of the fact that it has been suggested that different components of language abilities lateralize at different times (Geffner and Hockberg 1971). However, one of the most significant results of this study suggests that no developmental trends were evident on either speech reception or speech expression in normal or learning disabled children seven years of age and older.

The third finding that normal and learning disabled children differ quantitatively may contribute to further understanding of how they differ neuropsychologically. First, the learning disabled had a dramatically reduced tapping rate when the concurrent verbal task was introduced in time-sharing (see Figure 11.1). The time-sharing task is based on the functional distance model predicting that a concurrent verbal task will interfere with right-hand performance more than left, because the right-hand control center is functionally closer than the left-hand control center to the speech area in the cerebral cortex. When two tasks are performed concurrently "cross-talk" is averted centrally by an inhibitory barrier (Powell and Mountcastle 1959). The maintenance of this barrier consumes neural capacity, thus leaving less available for expenditure on two performances. Perhaps the neural structures in learning disabled children are less able to meet the demands of maintaining this inhibitory barrier and as a result they cannot mediate a simultaneous task involving speech and motor behavior. Second, the overall results of the POE index on the dichotic data suggest that there are no differences between the performances of normal and learning disabled children. However, inspection of the correct scores (Table 11.2) reported from both groups suggest that normals differ slightly in correct right-ear report. Perhaps, as Kinsbourne (1970) has suggested, a verbal set induces greater left-hemisphere activity and hence a greater sensitivity to right-ear stimuli. In other words, the normal children may employ a verbal strategy which activates the left hemisphere and positively influences their processing ability. The time-sharing results would support this notion by the fact that the normals were much better able to process the concurrent task in the left hemisphere than were learning disabled.

Further inspection of Table 11.2 indicates that actual between ear difference scores decrease with age in normal children while an increase is noted in learning disabled children. This increase with age in learning disabled children may be due to the suppression of left ear stimuli whereas with normal children the between ear differences may be due to an increase in left ear recognition of stimuli.

The results reported here strongly question the explanation which attributes learning disabilities to incomplete or delayed language lateralization and lend support to the notion that cerebral lateralization is not a developmental phenomena. They offer some explanation as to how learning disabled and normal children differ neuropsychologically in their ability to utilize a "verbal strategy" and process simultaneous information in the left hemisphere. Further research examining the verbal performance of learning disabled children on neuropsychological measures is needed to explain their qualitative differences.

REFERENCES

Belmont, L., and Birch, H. G. (1965). Lateral Dominance, Lateral Awareness, and Reading Disability. *Child Development* 36: 57–72.

Berlin, C. I., Cullen, J. K., Jr. (1977). Acoustical Problems in Dichotic Listening Tasks. In S. J. Segalowitz and F. A. Gruber, eds. *Language Development and Neurological Theory.* New York: Academic Press.

Blumstein, S., Goodglass, H., and Tartter, V. (1975). The Reliability of Ear Advantage in Dichotic Listening. *Brain and Language* 2: 226–36.

Briggs, G. G. (1973). The Effects of Cerebral Organization on the Control of Fine Movements. Durham, N.C.: Doctoral Dissertation, Duke University.

Bryden, M. P. (1970). Laterality Effects in Dichotic Listening: Relations with Handedness and Reading Ability in Children. *Neuropsychologia* 8: 443–50.

Bryden, M. P., and Allard, F. (1978). Dichotic Listening and the Development of Linguistic Processes. In M. Kinsbourne, ed., *Asymmetrical Function of the Brain.* Cambridge: Cambridge University Press.

Coleman, R. L., and Deutch, C. P. (1964). Lateral Dominance and Left-right Discrimination: A Comparison of Normal and Retarded Readers. *Perceptual and Motor Skills* 19: 43–50.

Dimond, S. J., and Beaumont, J. G., eds. (1974). *Hemisphere Function in the Human Brain.* London: Paul Elek.

Geffner, D. S., and Hockberg, I. (1971). Ear Laterality Performance of Children from Low and Middle Socioeconomic Levels on a Verbal Dichotic Listening Task. *Cortex* 7: 193-203.

Harshman, R., and Krashen, S. (1972). An "Unbiased" Procedure for Comparing Degree of Lateralization of Dichotically Presented Stimuli. Paper presented at the 33rd Meeting of the Acoustical Society of America.

Hicks, R. E. (1975). Intrahemispheric Response Competition Between Vocal and Unimanual Performance in Normal Adult Human Males. *Journal of Comparative and Physiological Psychology* 89: 50-60.

Hiscock, M., and Kinsbourne, M. (1978). Ontogeny of Cerebral Dominance: Evidence from Time-sharing Asymmetry in Children. *Developmental Psychology* 14: 321-29.

Hynd, G. W., and Obrzut, J. E. (1977). Effects of Grade Level and Sex on the Magnitude of the Dichotic Ear Advantage. *Neuropsychologia* 15: 689-92.

Hynd, G. W., Obrzut, J. E., Weed, W., and Hynd, C. R. (in press). Development of Cerebral Dominance: Dichotic Listening Asymmetry in Normal and Learning Disabled Children. *Journal of Experimental Child Psychology.*

Kantowitz, B. H., and Knight, J. L., Jr. (1974). Testing Tapping Timesharing. *Journal of Experimental Psychology* 103: 331-36.

Kinsbourne, M. (1970). Cerebral Basis of Asymmetries in Attention. *Acta Psychologia* 33: 193-201.

_____ (1975). The Ontogeny of Cerebral Dominance. In D. Aaronson and R. W. Rieber, eds., Developmental psycholinguistics and communication disorders. *Annals of the New York Academy of Sciences* 263: 244-50.

Kinsbourne, M., and Cook, J. (1971). Generalized and Lateralized Effect of Concurrent Verbalization on a Unimanual Skill. *Quarterly Journal of Experimental Psychology* 23: 341-43.

Kinsbourne, M., and Hiscock, M. (1977). Does Cerebral Dominance Develop? In A. J. Segalowitz and F. A. Gruber, eds., *Language Development and Neurological Theory.* New York: Academic Press.

Kinsbourne, M., and McMurray, J. (1975). The Effects of Cerebral Dominance on Time-Sharing between Speaking and Tapping by Preschool Children. *Child Development* 46: 240-42.

Kinsbourne, M., and Smith, W. L., eds. (1974). *Hemispheric Disconnection and Cerebral Function.* Springfield, Ill.: Thomas.

Kreuter, C., Kinsbourne, M., and Trevarthen, C. (1972). Are Disconnected Cerebral Hemispheres Independent Channels? A Preliminary Study of the Effect of Unilateral Loading on Bilateral Finger Tapping. *Neuropsychologia* 10: 453-61.

Lenneberg, E. (1967). *Biological Foundations of Language*. New York: Wiley.

Leong, C. K. (1976). Lateralization in Severely Disabled Readers in Relation to Functional Cerebral Development and Synthesis of Information. In R. M. Knights and D. J. Bakker, eds. *The Neuropsychology of Learning Disorders*. Baltimore: University Park Press.

Millay, K., Roeser, R. J., and Godfrey, J. J. (1977). Reliability of Performance for Dichotic Listening Using Two Response Modes. *Journal of Speech and Hearing Research* 20: 510–18.

Obrzut, J. E. (in press). Dichotic Listening and Bisensory Memory Skills in Qualitatively Diverse Dyslexic Readers. *Journal of Learning Disabilities*.

Oldfield, R. C. (1971). The Assessment and Analysis of Handedness: The Edinburgh Inventory. *Neuropsychologia* 9: 97–113.

Orton, S. T. (1937). *Reading, Writing, and Speech Problems in Children*. New York: Norton.

Powell, T. P. S., and Mountcastle, V. P. (1959). Some Aspects of the Functional Organization of the Cortex of the Postcentral Gyrus of the Monkey, a Correlation of Findings Obtained in a Single Unit Analysis with Cytoarchitecture. *John Hopkins Bulletin* 105: 133.

Satz, P. (1976). Cerebral Dominance and Reading Disability: An Old Problem Revisited. In R. M. Knights and D. J. Bakker, eds., *The Neuropsychology of Learning Disorders*. Baltimore: University Park Press.

Satz, P., Rardin, D., Ross, J. (1971). An Evaluation of a Theory of Specific Developmental Dyslexia. *Child Development* 42: 2009–21.

Sparrow, S., and Satz, P. (1970). Dyslexia, Laterality and Neuropsychological Development. In D. J. Bakker and P. Satz, eds., *Specific Reading Disability: Advances in Theory and Method*. Rotterdam: Rotterdam University Press.

Wada, J., and Rasmussen, T. (1960). Intracarotid Injection of Sodium Amytal for the Lateralization of Cerebral Speech Dominance: Experimental and Clinical Observations. *Journal of Neurosurgery* 17: 266–72.

White, M. G. (1969). Laterality Differences in Perception: A Review. *Psychological Bulletin* 72: 387–405.

Witelson, S. F., and Rabinovitch, M. S. (1972). Hemispheric Speech Lateralization in Children with Auditory Linguistic Deficits. *Cortex* 8: 412–26.

Zurif, E. B., and Carson, G. (1970). Dyslexia in Relation to Cerebral Dominance and Temporal Analysis. *Neuropsychologia* 8: 351–61.

Children learn spontaneously through active interaction with the

12

The Application of Research to the Design of Therapeutic Play Environments for Exceptional Children

Gary T. Moore

SCOPE AND IMPORTANCE OF THE TOPIC

THE PLIGHT OF HANDICAPPED CHILDREN—both physically and mentally handicapped—has led to a major national and international commitment to programs for early diagnosis and education. During the last decade there has been a remarkable growth of interest in the preschool education of exceptional children. This problem is not minor: at the time of the last national census, 1970, there were approximately one million preschool children and another 6 million school age children suffering from a handicapping condition (Martin 1971; Melcher 1977). Estimates are that at any point in time, 7.5–8.5 percent of the school-age population require some form of special program for a developmental disability (Melcher 1977).

There is a growing awareness among people who work directly with exceptional children—teachers, parents, therapists, and other professionals —that the physical environment may play a role in helping children to overcome developmental disabilities (Cruickshank and Quay 1970; Rho and Drury n.d.). Many educators and child psychologists have believed that only the social environment is important in learning, while others like architects have had the feeling that the physical environment plays an important role. Nevertheless, there has been little in the way of research findings and research-based design criteria on which to base judgments

Presentations on which this chapter is based were done in collaboration with Leland G. Shaw, to whom I owe thanks. Much of the work underlying the chapter was developed in concert with my colleagues Uriel Cohen, Lani van Ryzin, Jeffrey Oertel, and other members of Team 699 at the University of Wisconsin–Milwaukee. Though I take full responsibility for the ideas expressed herein, I gratefully acknowledge their collaboration on the initial work. Sincere thanks to Eli Tash, Sr. Joanne-Marie Kleibhan, and the staff of the St. Francis Center for their cooperation, interest, and encouragement throughout this project. Without their support and enthusiasm, the project never would have been realized.

about which aspects of space matter and which are superfluous.

There is, however, considerable evidence from the emerging inter-disciplinary field of environment-behavior studies, and from the study of child-environment relations in particular, that space does play a role in education (*e.g.,* David and Wright 1974; Coates 1974), and this leads nat-urally to the assumption that space might also play a critical role in the de-velopment of children with learning and other developmental disabilities.

The questions thus arise: What is the role of space in the learning of the exceptional child? What particular environmental variables are criti-cal? And how can we conceptualize their impacts?

Since the exceptional child is constantly engaged with the physical environment as part of any interaction with a parent or professional, and as he or she often has some difficulty adapting to that environment, ex-ceptional education research and theory—and architectural practice—are obliged to give consideration to the role of the environment in develop-ment. Not only may the environment operate directly to affect develop-ment and exceptional education, but the total environmental setting—both physical and social—also provides or withholds the resources staff, par-ents, and child find it useful to call upon. Said differently, the environ-ment may exert a direct therapeutic effect on exceptional children, or it may provide settings conducive to the functioning of different educa-tional programs. Some authors have advocated the first, or therapeutic view (*e.g.,* Bayes 1967), while others have taken the second, more moder-ate, environment-as-mediator view (*e.g.,* Sanoff 1977).

Based on one or the other of these positions—most often held im-plicitly, without analysis—designers have recently begun to recommend a range of criteria for the design of environments for handicapped children (*e.g.,* Texas A&M University 1969; Bednar and Haviland 1969; Bayes and Francklin 1971; Nellist 1970; Shaw forthcoming) and to show examples of their work which they think meets the needs of handicapped children (Rho and Drury n.d.).

But very little of this work has been based on research; even less is evaluated after construction. Design wisdom and a casual look 'round of-ten substitute for what should be careful, empirical evaluation. There are notable exceptions to this rule, of which Shaw and Robertson's (nd) de-velopment of a quasi-rigorous environmental analysis test is a prime ex-ample. But direct empirical evidence on the role of the physical environ-ment in exceptional education is sparse. Most statements about the role of space in the learning of developmentally-disabled children and most crite-ria for the design of environments for exceptional children are anecdotal, based on experience, unsubstantiated by systematic research.

The position is taken here that the experience of good designers and design theoreticians can become the basis for research hypotheses. The results of applied empirical research can provide the basis for the development of new design criteria and design applications. Research and design operate in a feedback loop—every design decision is based on an implicit hypothesis about how children will react to their environment, and every design decision, therefore, is testable. A body of empirical research and theory are necessary in order to more rationally base design interventions on empirical evidence. As designers and as researchers, we are fundamentally concerned with a research basis for design and with research that aids the design professional in solving problems. We have been advocating —and our research, professional work, and teaching are directed toward —a collaborative effort between applied researchers and behaviorally-oriented designers to develop a body of empirical knowledge about child-environment relations and their application to exceptional education, to derive new design criteria based on that knowledge, and to evaluate completed designs either in the field or in controlled experimental situations. The cycle of research-design-evaluation which we have therefore proposed is shown in Figure 12.1.

A COGNITIVE-DEVELOPMENTAL MODEL OF
THERAPEUTIC PLAY ENVIRONMENTS

To underlie both applied research and research applications in exceptional education and the environment, it will be useful to articulate a general theoretical position about development and the environment. In past research applications, the most neglected area has been the absence of systematic concern for an overall conception of how the physical environment and child development interact. Space does not permit the full development of a theory here, so only the most important assumptions about child-environment relations will be outlined.

Environment is a very broad term, encompassing many meanings, ranging from distant events (e.g., landscapes) to those that are quite immediate (the shape of a room). There is no logical or theoretical reason to separate the physical from the social environment. Events occur in a total context—a milieu. Though designers can only directly manipulate the physical environment, any comprehensive theory of child-environment relations must include the total ensemble of the social and physical environment.

A strict causal, explanatory model is not appropriate—at least at

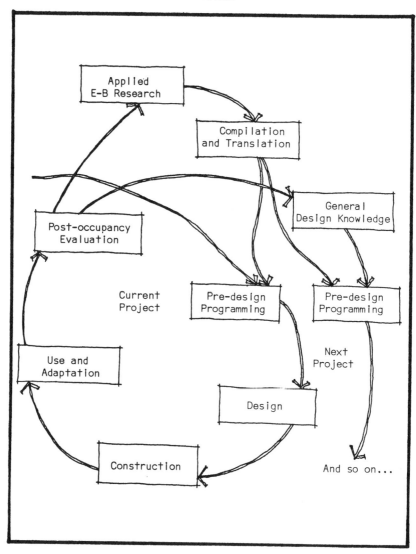

FIGURE 12.1 Model of the cycle of research, design, and evaluation

this stage—to the understanding of child-environment relations. Careful observations and systematic description must precede explanation. An ecological model where the total ensemble of social and physical variables are related holistically seems more appropriate than a strict cause-effect model. Such an approach would also focus on the processes mediating between variables (such processes as the child's cognitive structuring of the situation and the role this plays in his or her total behavior and development; cf. Moore 1976). How the total collection of variables interacts in an ongoing transaction between the child and the environment must be our first concern.

With regard to *development,* a cognitive-developmental approach is favored for a variety of reasons (see Moore 1976; Moore and Shaw Note 2). Looked at developmentally, the physically handicapped, learning disabled, or mildly retarded child is not basically different from other children. Certain developmental differences do stand in the way of average rates of development, but as Kirk (1972) has shown, there are more similarities between the exceptional and the average child than there are differences. The pattern of intra-individual differences is what must interest us if we are to aid development of the full child. But the stages of development are the same for all children; certain developments are only more difficult for the developmentally-disabled child. For exceptional environmental design, then, every design decision must be thought out more carefully so that the environment can pace developmental progressions from sub-stage to sub-stage.

Children learn through a series of interactions with the social and physical environment—the staff, the curriculum, and space. The child is not a passive being to be bombarded with stimuli. The child is an active agent in his or her own development—exploring, discovering, testing, trying things out, imitating, fantasizing, and developing—and in all of this, he or she is not only interacting with the social environment of people, staff, and other children, but also with the physical environment. It is through this dynamic interaction with the total social and physical environment, and from feedback on his or her actions, that development occurs (Piaget 1963; cf. also Gordon 1972; Hart and Moore 1973).

Major developmental theories—from Berlyne's stimulus-seeking theory applied to play (Ellis 1973) to Garvey's (1977) social learning theory and Piaget's (1962) cognitive developmental theory of play—all hold that play is integral to development; it is through unstructured, child-initiated play that the child is often freest to explore, to test, and to learn from feedback on his or her own actions.

Quite often children with developmental disabilities are over-sheltered by well-meaning parents and staff, and this may hinder development. As Lady Allen (1968) said: "It is important to insure that the handicapped child can have rich, varied, and spontaneous experiences wherever they are." Gordon (1972) advocates that disabled children should be able to experience the natural diversity and change which only the natural out-of-doors can provide.

Looked at in this context, it is absolutely amazing how little most playgrounds offer to children. Less cognitive and social play are observed on traditional, fixed-in-place play apparatus, and children spend considerably less time on them than they do at other types of playgrounds, like adventure playgrounds (Hayward, Rothenberg, and Beasley 1974). Recent field observations at 26 playgrounds around the United States and Canada have shown that very few existing play environments support the full range of developmental needs of growing children (Cohen, Moore, and McGinty 1978). Fewer still meet the needs of exceptional children (Moore, Cohen, Oertel, and Van Ryzin 1979) (see Figures 12.2–12.5).

RESEARCH-BASED DESIGN CRITERIA

There is considerable evidence that the physical environment has a rich impact on learning (David and Wright 1974; Prescott and David Note 3;

FIGURE 12.2 An example of a traditional playground and of primarily motor activity observed on such playgrounds. Fort Lewis Child Care Center, Fort Lewis, Washington. *All photographs are by the author, unless otherwise noted.*

FIGURE 12.3 An example of a contemporary playgound, primarily motor (or no) activity. Jacob Riis Houses, New York City; *M. Paul Friedberg and Associates, Architects.*

Altman and Wohlwill 1979). Unfortunately there is less evidence about particular environment-behavior relations with respect to exceptional children. This is a much-needed area of basic and applied environment-behavior research. Based on the above general theoretical position, and on an exhaustive review of the research literature, we have been able to derive a set of research-based criteria for the design of indoor and outdoor environments for exceptional children.

A number of other behaviorally-oriented designers have also articulated design concepts for play environments for mentally and physically handicapped children (*e.g.,* Bayes 1967; Allen 1968; Bednar and Haviland 1969; Gordon 1972; Shaw Note 4).

Method

Our approach at the University of Wisconsin–Milwaukee has been to develop a set of design criteria arising from a research application and

FIGURE 12.4 An example of an adventure playground, and of the results of children's self-initiated activity with loose parts. Irvine Adventure Playground, Irvine, California.

design project for exceptional children. No first-hand empirical research was conducted. The project involved the collection of design-relevant research information from a variety of sources and the translation of that information into design guidelines.

User information on the spatial behavior and developmental difficulties encountered in different environments by exceptional children was collected and analyzed. Sources included the existing research literatures in exceptional education, architecture and landscape architecture, and environment-behavior studies (child-environment relations). As very little substantive research has been conducted on the role of the physical environment in exceptional education, most of this information was gathered from neighboring fields, making the translation to design somewhat speculative. As the exceptional education literature tended to treat the child without considering his or her environmental context, and as the architecture literature tended to treat buildings without any systematic reference to users, the most valuable literature was found to be that in child-environment relations.

Other sources of information included interviews and participatory

FIGURE 12.5 An example of a playground supposedly planned for handicapped children from "Big Toys" manufactured parts. Children's Mid-Peninsula Health Center, Palo Alto, California; *Jay Beckwith, Designer.*

games with the staff and administration of the St. Francis Children's Activity and Achievement Center in Milwaukee and from informal observation of children at the Center.

A set of design criteria was derived from this analysis together with specific user requirements for designing new environments. These criteria have been brought together as a general design guide for play/learning environments—indoor and outdoor—for all handicapped children (Moore *et al.* 1979).

Finally, an actual design of an outdoor play/learning environment was created for the St. Francis Center *to implement the theoretical concepts and to provide an opportunity to evaluate their effectiveness in a real field situation.*

It must be pointed out, in reference to Figure 12.1 above, that, though derived from empirical research, these criteria have not been directly tested. They thus have the status of hypotheses, and await evaluation in a quasi-experiment field situation. The cycle of research and design is not complete until evaluation has been completed and hypotheses either corroborated or falsified, the results being then fed back into additional basic and applied research. In this way, research and design can contribute to each other, design decisions can be research-based, applied research can be influenced by problems facing practitioners, and the whole area of exceptional education and the physical environment can move forward on a firm footing.

DESIGN PRINCIPLES AND USER REQUIREMENTS

To illustrate the above theoretical and methodological position, let us examine two empirically-derived design principles and their application in a specific design context.

A major characteristic of our approach to design for handicapped children is the development of what we have come to call *design principles*. The notion owes a considerable amount to the work of Christopher Alexander and his colleagues in developing what he calls "patterns" (Alexander, Ishikawa, and Silverstein 1977). Our design principles have certain similarities to patterns, but they also have some intentional differences from them, as I'll show.

Design principles respond to and are derived from an analysis of developmental goals for exceptional children and research information articulating these goals and suggesting interactions with the physical environment. A summary description of developmental goals, derived design ideas, and the arguments linking the two comprise what we refer to as a *generic, behaviorally-based design guide* (an example of which is Moore *et al.* 1979).

We may define design principles in the following more precise way:

1. Design principles must respond to critical environment-behavior problems in humanistic terms.

2. They must either provide settings which will enclose but not encumber children's activities and behaviors conducive to the attainment of specified developmental goals (environment-as-mediator) or they must facilitate development goals by direct environmental stimulation (therapeutic environment).

3. They must generate specific design solutions and must be able to be used in explaining these solutions.

4. They must be based on the latest and best research information.

5. They must be testable.

6. They must be stated in environmental terms, not behavioral terms, i.e., they must specify in what ways the environment is to be designed.

7. They must be intentionally open-ended; they are intended to sug-

gest form, and to stimulate the designer's imagination and intuition, while avoiding overly doctrinaire and absolute solutions that might inhibit design innovation.

Two examples will illustrate the notion and its use.

Paced Alternatives

Problem and Developmental Goals

Environments with which the average child can cope are often frustrating or impossible for a child with reduced competence. The exceptional child should not be frustrated by the environment. On the other hand, the environment should have prosthetic qualities to suit user groups but still provide enough challenges to stimulate and maintain activity.

Design Principle

All play environments should have a variety of graded challenges and paced alternatives for children of varying abilities. Some challenges should be easy, while other challenges of the same play type should be more difficult (e.g., a gentle crawling ramp and a steeper set of stairs for the perceptual-motor handicapped child). The entire play environment should be designed to stimulate and advance children's skills but not put unreasonable demands on their ability if they can't keep up with the pace.

Justification

Children have a great need to gain self-confidence and a positive self-image, and this is often more difficult for the exceptional child than for the average child. Feelings and self-concept can be seriously damaged if children never reach goals they set for themselves (McCandless and Evans 1973). Maximum development results from an optimal discrepancy between the child's current abilities and demands by the environment (Hunt 1965)—challenges are made to existing motor, cognitive, and social schemes, motivating the child from one level of development to the next. Low self-concept reduces incentive to perform mental and motor tasks; to step up performance, children should be given tasks at which they can succeed—the success will lead them to attempt more difficult tasks (Cratty 1974; Ayers 1972). This required intensity of challenge can be called "the pacer." Success at such paced alternatives can also help to break the frustration cycle so common to exceptional children (St. Francis Center Note 5). Therefore, graded challenge and paced alternatives assure the involvement of all children, motivate children to further development, and support a positive self-concept (See Figures 12.6–12.8).

Supporting User Requirements

1. Small parts of the environment should provide challenge to develop long-range skills.

2. Challenge should be experienced in a variety of ways.

3. For each type of activity, there should be several levels of accomplishment, *e.g.,* climbing steps, climbing a ladder, climbing a cargo net, climbing a fireman's pole, etc.

4. Play experiences should provide an awareness of challenges ahead without being intimidating—children should be able to see new challenges and accomplishment points ahead when completing a cycle of activities.

5. Interest and success must be maintained by activities and space.

6. There should be some portions of the environment designed to the scale and skill level of infants as well as for children of all developmental levels up to 13 years of age.

7. Older children require less emphasis on balance, general coordination, and general physical activities; more emphasis should be placed on complex cognitive challenges.

8. Play environments should provide for similar activities to occur at different rates without interfering with each other.

Example Application

A design project was developed to implement this and other principles. The project was for the St. Francis Children's Activity and Achievement Center in Milwaukee, a center for exceptional children between the ages of infancy and about 10 years of age. A model outdoor play/learning environment was designed (see accompanying plan in Figure 12.9) and was summarized as a case study in design application (Moore *et al.* 1979).

The principle of paced alternatives had a large influence on the design of an interconnected series of built structures on the west side of the

FIGURE 12.6 Paced alternatives

site (left side of the plan in Figure 12.9). A central set of climbing towers adjacent to a sand pit unifies this area, with other built structures feeding out from them. This section includes a toddler area, a dual-functioning observation and play deck, a water play area with handicapped access, a maze, a loose parts building area, a major integrated series of towers, large-muscle area, an emotional release area, a viewing tower, a social play area, and various levels of sand and rocks.

Applying the principle of paced alternatives to just one portion of this environment, that of the central climbing tower and slides (see Figures 12.10–12.11), it became evident that several factors needed to be considered within this overall experience:

1. Climbing and entry points would have to accommodate different

FIGURE 12.7 An example of the principle of paced alternatives in a play environment designed for exceptional children. Miami Cerebral Palsy Association Exterior Sensory Learning Environment, Miami, Florida; Leland Shaw and Nan Plessas, Architects; *photograph courtesy of Leland Shaw.*

levels of motor skills. Height, pitch, and width of the slides would have to provide graded challenge.

2. Several modes of entry are possible in the structure illustrated, offering the child a choice of difficulty. Simple stairs, pitched ladders, a climbing arch, and a rope rail up the slide require varying degrees of skill and confidence, but all provide access to the slides.

paced alternatives

FIGURE 12.8 Paced alternatives; *freehand sketches courtesy of Tim McGinty.*

3. Three sliding surfaces vary in height, all allowing the whoosh feeling of sliding, but in varying degrees of "thrillingness."

4. Secure protective edges, wide platforms, and ample handrails and grips are provided at the junction points—those places where a child must reposition him or herself from the climb up to get into a sliding posture; confidence at these points is necessary for the child to continue with the challenge.

5. Air mattresses, mats, and sand are offered as alternative landing surfaces; the child can choose between the complete security of the softest air mattress landing, or the more challenging sand pit which requires some balance.

Loose Parts

Problem and Developmental Goals

Children learn spontaneously through active interaction with the

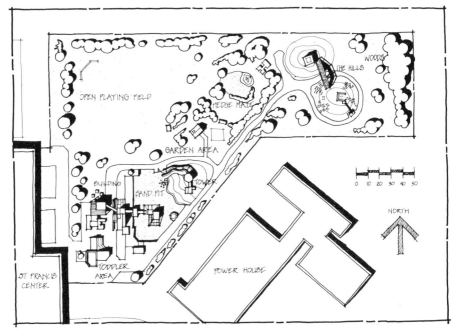

FIGURE 12.9 Site plan for the proposed St. Francis Center Outdoor Play/Learning Environment. *Architectural graphics courtesy of Jeffrey Oertel.*

environment around them, yet so many environments designed for children are static and rigid. One of the most important things about growing up is having the opportunity to experiment on the world, to change it, to see the results of these changes, and to learn from the total experience.

Design Principle

In any play area for exceptional children, an area should be put aside for creative play with a variety of loose parts. The parts should be dynamic, interchangeable, and manipulable. There are three different types of loose parts: (a) manufactured objects in which the child realizes an invariable finished form (e.g., a three-dimensional spatial puzzle); (b) a manufactured kit of parts in which the finished form is variable (*e.g.,* a large, outdoor set of unit blocks); and (c) discarded, natural, and found objects that can be used in any number of creative ways (*e.g.,* tires,

FIGURE 12.10 The central tower, slides, and sand pit area

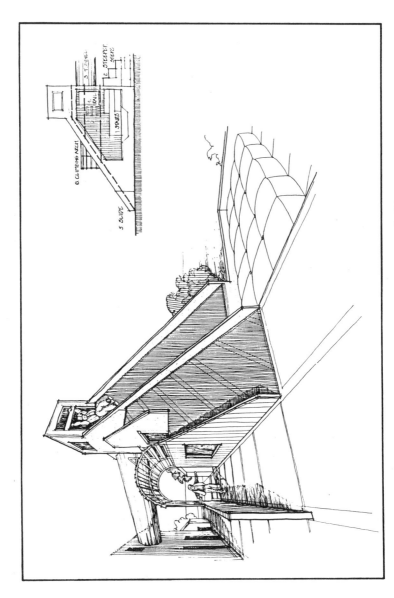

FIGURE 12.11 Paced alternatives applied to the climbing tower and slides

boards, spools, sand, gravel, material, old clothes, and props of various kinds).

Justification

Children need to satisfy their curiosity and to experience the pleasure derived from discovery and invention. Through unstructured play, children learn new skills, gain self-confidence, take pride in their achievements, build up a picture of reality, sort out fact from fantasy, and extend their knowledge of the real world.

Children learn spontaneously through active interaction with the environment around them (Piaget 1963), and need therefore to be able to manipulate the environment around them.

Although handicapped children require special care and attention, they too can cope with and gain from a "rough and ready" atmosphere that is different from the usual supervised, structured playground (Handicapped Adventure Playground Association n.d.), and should be provided with a full range of challenging experiences which they can structure for themselves (Allen 1968).

The most articulate statement of the need for manipulable or loose parts comes from the British designer, Simon Nicholson (1971): "There is evidence that all children love to interact with variables, such as materials and shapes; physical phenomena such as electricity, magnetism, and gravity; media such as gasses and fluids; sounds, music, and motion; chemical interactions, cooking, and fire; and other people, animals, plants, words, concepts, and ideas. With all these things all children love to play, experiment, discover and invent, and have fun" (p. 30).

From this beginning, Nicholson has developed a hypothesis about loose parts, which suggests, quite simply, the following: "In any environment, both the degree of inventiveness and creativity, and the possibility of discovery, are directly proportional to the number and kind of variables in it" (p. 30).

A number of other writers have advocated the value of loose, manipulable parts, including for exceptional children. Lady Allen of Hurtwood, a lifelong advocate for children and the founder of several adventure playgrounds for exceptional children, suggests that manipulative objects should be provided in all play spaces for exceptional children (Allen 1968). Moran and Kalakian (1974) recommend the provision of at least two manipulative or loose parts areas in school buildings and playgrounds for handicapped children—one for advanced building systems and another for other manipulative and tactile experiences of a simpler nature. Ellis (1972) summarizes the argument: "The essential characteristic for a playground is that it should elicit new responses from the child as he plays, and that these responses increase in complexity as play proceeds" (p. 4). The principles of loose parts is an ideal design response to this goal (see Figures 12.12–12.14).

Supporting User Requirements

1. Offer opportunities for manipulation.
2. Provide manipulative objects which demand self-initiated activity (e.g., sand, dirt, informal loose parts, props, etc.).

FIGURE 12.12 Loose parts

FIGURE 12.13 An example of loose parts in a play environment called a Creative Playground based on a Swedish model. The author's daughter at Harbourfront Creative Playground, Toronto, Ontario; *William Rock, Landscape Architect.*

3. Provide the opportunity for the child's awareness of a finished form before constructing it from a kit of parts (may even mean involving children in design and construction of the kit of parts).

4. Provide space and materials to build undetermined structures.

5. Provide manipulative and tactile experiences separate from the more advanced building area.

6. Include provisions for storage, activity space, and tools for children's use with found objects such as tires, boards, bricks, etc.

7. Provide exceptional children with manufactured sets of loose parts such as giant Tinker Toys, large outdoor modular blocks, etc.

8. Zone the play area so that high activity loose parts areas (e.g., an adventure playground for handicapped children) are away from less intense loose parts areas (e.g., a creative play area) and from quieter retreat and observational areas.

Example Application

In providing loose parts in the St. Francis Center play environment,

(after lady Allen, 1968.)

FIGURE 12.14 Different types of loose parts possible in a play/learning environment for exceptional children

several factors needed to be considered. Children need to be able to handle a wide range of materials, to experience a wide range of textures, smells, forms, shapes, and plasticity, and to discover what different items can do. Ground surface materials, sand, gravel, bark chips, as well as water, all respond to this principle and encourage creative play. Preformed construction sets and free-form building materials and tools can be provided and contained within a designated loose parts area (see Figures). The interconnected play area of the St. Francis scheme—as well as each of the other areas of the total play environment—provided several opportunities to include these features:

    1. An extensive sand pit is centrally positioned allowing easy access and ample space for a large number of children to experience the special plasticity of sand play. An additional elevated sand area allows barrier-free access for physically handicapped children.

    2. A wide variety of water-play experiences is possible in the system of interconnected pools and water tables provided. Nearby storage is provided for cups, funnels, shovels, and other items for sand and water play.

    3. A specially designated loose parts building area is set aside for more active construction with modular or free-form loose parts. Storage is again provided for tools and materials. The area is zoned away from quieter play areas and observation areas by being on the northwest side of the maze structure.

    4. Landscaping throughout and surrounding the interconnected series of built structures provides numerous incidental loose parts in the

way of leaves, twigs, and grass, and this is even more prevalent as the child moves east on the site away from the indoor center toward the nature woods area (see Figures 12.15 and 12.16).

FIGURE 12.15 Climbing rocks, changes in grade, and an "emotional release" area constructed of light-weight, air-filled bags at the proposed St. Francis Center Outdoor Play/Learning Environment

Design Principles and Developmental Goals

As shown in the above examples, design principles are made in response to developmental goals, and are derived by design intuition based on research information on child-environment relations. A complete set of principles for the design of environments for mentally and physically handicapped children is shown in Figure 12.17.

SUMMARY

It is possible to derive criteria for the better design of play/learning en-

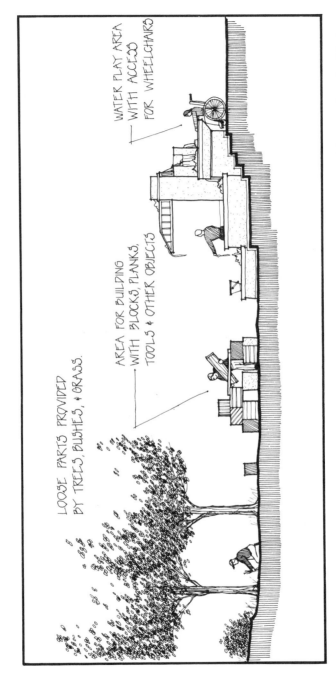

LOOSE PARTS PROVIDED
BY TREES, BUSHES, & GRASS.

AREA FOR BUILDING
WITH BLOCKS, PLANKS,
TOOLS & OTHER OBJECTS

WATER PLAY AREA
WITH ACCESS
FOR WHEELCHAIRS

FIGURE 12.16 Examples of the use of loose parts in a designated area, plus a water play area with access for wheelchairs, for the eastern side of the St. Francis site (see site plan, Figure 12.9)

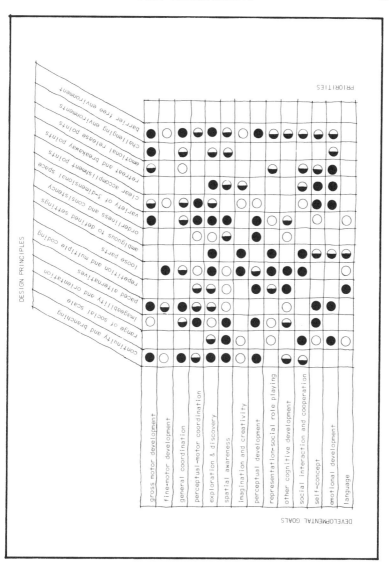

FIGURE 12.17 Matrix showing the entire set of 14 design principles for the design of therapeutic environments for exceptional children and the developmental goals from which they were derived. This matrix is also the basis for post-occupancy evaluation, as it shows the collection of hypotheses being made about the role of the physical environment in exceptional education. From G. T. Moore, U. Cohen, J. Oertel, and L. van Ryzin, *Designing Environments for Handicapped Children,* Educational Facilities Laboratories, 1979.

vironments for exceptional children on the basis of existing research literature, especially in the child-environment area, supplemented with information from other sources like observations of children and interviews with professionals involved in exceptional education. Furthermore, a powerful and scientific way of presenting these design criteria is in the form of testable design principles. They are powerful in that they provide the designer with wide latitude for creative design, and yet provide him or her with a conceptualized statement and image about certain characteristics of the exceptional child's environment thought to be important to development. They are scientific in that they are testable, and thus are open to both corroboration or falsification in the light of an empirical study either in a laboratory setting or a natural field setting. As illustrations of this notion, two design principles were presented together with their supporting data and arguments. The design principles are based on a theoretical conception of the exceptional child and his or her interaction with the physical environment. This conception holds that active commerce with the environment is critical to development, that all children—exceptional or not—pass through the same developmental stages, and that an adequate play/learning environment must provide a full range of opportunities for cognitive, social, and physical play.

It is absolutely amazing to this writer that the role of space in the learning and development of exceptional children has not yet been studied systematically. Sensitive teachers all "know" how important the environment of childhood is, how it can facilitate or hinder the curriculum and activities planned for handicapped children, how the children themselves are often frustrated by the environment around them, and how space can have a direct stimulus or therapeutic value. Empirical research on this topic is sadly lacking. The above is only one way of thinking about space/behavior relations and clearly is influenced by our desire to develop somewhat better play/learning environments even before the last work is in from the research community. Other conceptual approaches to the child-environment relation in the context of exceptional children are needed, as are carefully designed empirical studies. One approach which fascinates us in this latter regard is to develop a program of research or a demonstration program testing some of the many hypotheses between environment and development represented in Figure 12.17. Such a program could then lead also to new theory tailored to the special conditions of the exceptional child and the environment, and to design criteria which could be updated continuously and systematically.

REFERENCES

Alexander, C.; Ishikawa, S.; and Silverstein, M. (1977). *A Pattern Language: Towns, Buildings, Construction.* New York: Oxford University Press.

Allen, Lady, of Hurtwood (1968). *Planning for Play.* Cambridge, Mass.: MIT Press.

Altman, I. and Wohlwill, J. F., eds. (1979). *Human Behavior and Environment,* Vol. 3. *Children and the Environment.* New York: Plenum.

Ayers, A. J. (1972). *Sensory Integration and Learning Disorders.* Los Angeles: Western Psychological Services.

Bayes, K. (1967). *The Therapeutic Effect of Environment on Emotionally Disturbed and Mentally Subnormal Children.* Old Woking, England: Unwin.

Bayes, K., and Francklin, S., eds. (1971). *Designing for the Handicapped.* London: George Godwin.

Bednar, M. J., and Haviland, D. S. (1969). *Role of the Physical Environment in the Education of Children with Learning Disabilities.* Troy, N.Y.: Rensselaer Polytechnic Institute, Center for Architectural Research.

Bureau of Education for the Handicapped (1969, 1970). *Better Education for the Handicapped.* Washington, D.C.: USGPO.

Coates, G., ed. (1974). *Alternative Learning Environments.* Stroudsburg, Pa.: Dowden, Hutchinson & Ross.

Cohen, U.; Moore, G. T.; and McGinty, T. (1978). *Case Studies of Child Play Areas and Child Support Facilities.* Milwaukee: University of Wisconsin-Milwaukee, Center for Architecture and Urban Planning Research.

Cratty, B. J. (1970). *Perceptual and Motor Development in Infants and Children.* New York: Macmillan.

Cruickshank, W. M. (1977). *Learning Disabilities in Home, School, and Community.* Syracuse: Syracuse University Press.

_____, and Quay, H. C. (1970). Learning and Physical Environment: The Necessity for Research and Research Design. *Exceptional Children* 37: 261–68.

David T. G., and Wright, B. D., eds. (1974). *Learning Environments.* Chicago: University of Chicago Press.

Ellis, M. J. (1972). Play: Theory and Research. In W. J. Mitchell, ed., *Environmental Design: Research and Practice,* Vol. 1. Los Angeles: University of California, School of Architecture and Urban Planning.

Garvey, C. (1977). *Play.* Cambridge, Mass.: Harvard University Press.

Gordon, R. (1972). *The Design of a Preschool Therapeutic Playground: An Outdoor "Learning Laboratory."* New York: New York University Medical Center, Institute of Rehabilitation Medicine, Rehabilitation Monograph 47.

Handicapped Adventure Playground Association (nd). *Adventure Playgrounds for Handicapped Children.* London: Author.

Hart, R. A., and Moore, G. T. (1973). The Development of Spatial Cognition: A Review. In R. M. Downs and D. Stea, eds., *Image and Environment.* Chicago: Aldine.

Hayward, D. G.; Rothenberg, M.; and Beasly, R. R. (1974). Children's Play and Urban Play Environments: A Comparison of Traditional, Contemporary, and Adventure Playground Types. *Environment and Behavior* 6: 131–68.

Hunt, J. McV. (1965). Intrinsic Motivation and its Role in Psychological Development. *Nebraska Symposium on Motivation* 13: 189–282.

Kirk, S. A. (1972). *Educating Exceptional Children,* 2nd ed. Boston: Houghton Mifflin.

Martin, E. W. (1971). Bureau of Education for the Handicapped Commitment and Program in Early Childhood Education. *Exceptional Children* 38: 661–64.

Moore, G. T. (1976). Theory and Research on the Development of Environmental Knowing. In G. T. Moore and R. G. Golledge, eds., *Environmental Knowing: Theories, Research, and Methods.* Stroudsburg, Pa.: Dowden, Hutchinson & Ross.

————, and Cohen, U. (1978). Exceptional Education and the Physical Environment: Toward Behaviorally-based Design Principles. In W. E. Rogers and W. H. Ittelson, eds., *New Directions in Environmental Design Research.* Washington, D.C.: Environmental Design Research Association Publications.

Moore, G. T.; Cohen, U.; Oertel, J.; and van Ryzin, L. 1979). *Designing Environments for Handicapped Children.* New York: Educational Facilities Laboratories.

Moore, G. T., and Smith, D. (1975). Evaluating the Built Environment. *Architecture in Australia* 64(6): 65–68.

Moran, J. M., and Kalakian, L. H. (1974). *Movement Experiences for the Mentally Retarded or Emotionally Disturbed Child.* Minneapolis: Burgess.

Nellist, I. (1970). *Planning Buildings for Handicapped Children.* Springfield, Ill.: Thomas.

Nicholson, S. (1971). How Not to Cheat Children: The Theory of Loose Parts. *Landscape Architecture* 62(5): 30–34.

Piaget, J. (1962). *Play, Dreams, and Imitation in Children.* New York: Norton.

———— (1963). *The Origins of Intelligence in Children.* New York: Norton.

Rho, L., and Drury, F. (nd). *Space and Time in Early Learning.* Hartford, Conn.: Connecticut State Department of Education.

Sanoff, H. (1977). *Methods of Architectural Programming.* Stroudsburg, Pa.: Dowden, Hutchinson & Ross.

Shaw, L. G., and Robertson, M. F. (nd). *The Playground: The Child's Creative Learning Space.* Gainsville, Fla.: University of Florida, College of Architecture, Bureau of Research.

Texas A&M University (1969). *Environmental Criteria: MR Preschool Day Care Facilities.* College Station, Tex.: Texas A&M University, College of Architecture and Environmental Design.

U.S. Department of Housing and Urban Development (1978). *A Playground for All Children,* 3 Vols. Washington D.C.: USGPO.

13

One Tiger to a Hill

James C. Chalfant

Today, we are standing on the threshold of one of the most challenging and exciting eras of special education. I have been asked to highlight what I perceive to be some of the key issues in implementing the federal mandate for learning disabled children. I have, therefore, identified seven problem areas which lay before us in the field of special education and commented on what I think needs to be done to overcome these obstacles so we can achieve the intent of Public Law 94-142 for handicapped children.

RELUCTANCE TO CHANGE

In 1908 a man named Vilhjalmur Stefansson trekked to the Arctic Circle where he lived four years with the Eskimos. Stefansson was one of the greatest scientist-explorers of the twentieth century, and his book, *My Life with the Eskimos,* is considered a classic by both sociologists and scientists.

The reason I mention Stefansson is that he relates a number of experiences about Eskimo life on the Arctic ice which seem similar to the experiences many of us are currently having on the educational tundra of Public Law 94-142. For example:

One day Stefansson and his guide entered a valley which contained a glacial lake. A small community of Eskimos was living by the lake. There was a serious shortage of food in the village and the Eskimos were nearing starvation. Stefansson asked if they could catch fish in the lake. They said, "No, there were no fish in the lake." Stefansson asked whether they had been able to kill caribou in the adjacent valley. Again, they said, "No, there are no caribou in the valley."

That evening Stefansson was walking by the lake and saw a fish jump. He unpacked his fishing tackle and within a short time caught a large number of fish. The Eskimos were overjoyed and everyone began

231

fishing. Stefansson said, "I thought you told me there were no fish in the lake." "Ahhh," said the head of the village, "no one has ever caught a fish in that lake." The next day Stefansson hunted caribou in the adjacent valley and was successful in killing several, and for the first time in many weeks, there was meat in the village.

After reading several such episodes, I concluded that there are at least three similarities between Eskimo life at the turn of the century and the life of the special educator today.

Both the Eskimo and the special educator are living a marginal existence. Conditions on the Arctic ice in 1908 were so harsh and severe that much of the Eskimos' energy was spent on basic survival. Today, teachers spend much of their energy coping with federal and state rules and regulations and with day to day survival in the classroom.

Both Eskimos and teachers are creatures of habit, even when another alternative might be better. In 1908 Eskimos used those practices in obtaining shelter, hunting, fishing, and travel, which previous experience over many years insured some degree of success and survival. Similarly, teachers continue to use practices which have provided some degree of success and survival in the classroom.

Neither Eskimos nor teachers receive very much reinforcement for showing initiative, creativity, or doing things in a different way. The Eskimo might perish on the ice and the teacher might lose her job for diverging from the usual practices.

In order to meet the challenge and intent of Public Law 94-142 during the 1980s, we cannot respond like Stefansson's Eskimos and fail to use our initiative and creativity to seek more efficient and more effective ways of meeting the needs of handicapped children. We cannot afford to cling to comfortable and familiar practices which we know in our hearts are less than efficient, less than effective, and less than successful. Perhaps like Stefansson's Eskimos, many of us may be a little fearful of changing the world we have made for ourselves.

There are several difficult facts all of us must learn to accept: First, both federal and state laws mandate certain changes. There is no choice. We will comply. Second, financial support for education is being cut back every year. We cannot expect more money in the future. In fact, we can expect less. Third, I see schools closing and special education staffs being cut back across the country. It seems we are being asked to do more with fewer resources.

So, like Stefansson's Eskimos, we administrators and teachers can sit by our respective lakes and bemoan our misfortune. Or, we can accept the situation and begin using our initiative and creativity to make these rules and regulations work. This will require flexibility for change.

TERRITORIALITY

Perhaps the greatest obstacle to quality special education services today are the territorial wars. Many special educators seem to be working alone and within their separate disciplines, and sometimes there seems to be more competition than cooperation. In Kipling's East there is an old saying: "One Tiger to a Hill." This refers to the geographic hunting territory needed to provide the food supply for one animal.

The territorial phenomenon also extends to human behavior. We seem to have an all-powerful instinct for territorial possession and to protect what is ours. In fact, recognition of territorial rights seems to be one of the most significant attributes of civilization and religion (e.g., Thou shalt not steal.) In addition, territorial rights yield economic benefits, survival of the species, jobs for all, and professional status.

Exclusive testing-teaching territory is valuable property on the educational tundra. In the State of Arizona, for example, how many children are consumed in the case load of an average specialist? How many children does it take to support: A flock of guidance counselors? A herd of resource teachers? A gaggle of speech pathologists? A covey of learning disabilities teachers? or A tribe of school psychologists?

Many of us in special education seem to be engaged in a great, but undeclared, civil war testing whether this professional group or that professional group shall have the right to test or teach certain children. The competition for the right to test and teach children is not only going on in our schools, it is occurring in our universities, and in Washington, D.C., where professional organizations are lobbying to secure jobs for their respective memberships.

Is this child advocacy? I think not. We cannot be child advocates if we continue to compete for the reserved right to test or teach children. We cannot continue to have five or six specialists competing for children, and we cannot competitively resolve the problem of who should serve handicapped children, because there is no competitive solution.

When I see the divisiveness in special education, I sometimes wonder if our professional organizations and the Divisions of the Council for Exceptional Children haven't done their work too well. Our problem is not decategorizing the children. Our problem is decategorizing ourselves.

OVER-IDENTIFICATION

During the past seven years I have studied the prevalence of handicapped children who have been identified as needing special education services. The rate of identification ranged from 17 percent to 22 percent of the school population base. Obviously this excessively high rate of identification includes many slow learners and conduct problems. Many children currently being identified are not special education's responsibility. Over-referral wastes staff time and increases costs. There are a number of factors contributing to this situation.

Inability to Cope

There are many reasons why teachers refer children for special help. Perhaps the most basic reason is the inability to cope with a child's problem within the framework of the regular classroom. Each teacher must decide for himself whether or not he can successfully deal with a given child's problem within the classroom setting.

Teachers may not feel qualified to deal with a child's problem, because they lack training and/or experience to cope with certain kinds of learning or behavior problems. There are situations when a teacher simply has difficulty relating to a child and personality conflicts enter into the decision to refer. Each teacher has his own tolerance level for noise, movement, and classroom disruptions. Some teachers have a lower tolerance level than others. Sheer frustration because of continued failure to cope with a learning or behavior problem is often the cause of a referral.

Lack of Time

The reason mentioned most frequently is "lack of time" to plan for and teach a child differently from the rest of the class. How many teachers have said, "Yes, but I have 29 other children to teach. There just isn't time." It is true that many teachers do have large classes. It is also true that many teachers are required to cover a specified amount of curricular material during the school year. In addition, teachers have many extra-curricular assignments to perform such as playground duty, lunchroom duty, collecting the milk money, etc. All of these activities reduce the amount of time available for planning and meeting the individual differences of children in the classroom.

Low Expectations for Children

Some children seem so different in comparison to the rest of the children in the class that teachers sincerely believe these children cannot learn in the classroom and should be placed in a special class. Children whose interests and value systems are much different from the teachers may be referred more quickly than others.

Occasionally a teacher may develop a stereotyped picture of a child based on one personal experience or from the child's cumulative folder. When this occurs, the teacher often has difficulty thinking about the child in an objective way. As children become older, they may become a threat to the teacher's authority and control in the classroom and the tendency is to want to get the child out of the regular classroom.

Parental Pressure

Parental pressure is another factor in referral. Children who have a few minor problems are sometimes referred because of parental anxiety and pressure.

Teachers Have Been Conditioned to Refer

Another factor contributing to over-referral is that many special educators inadvertently have conditioned teachers to refer every child experiencing a problem, which deviates from the usual problems in the classroom. It should not be surprising, therefore, that many teachers have taken the position, "These children are not my responsibility," and promptly refer all children who are having difficulty to speech correctionists, remedial reading personnel, learning disability teachers, guidance counselors, psychologists, social workers, etc., without first trying to help the child within the classroom.

Multiple Identification Systems

Many school districts have made the mistake of permitting each specialist to devise his or her own screening and referral system for categorical handicaps. The end result is a multiple screening and referral system which duplicates time and effort. For purposes of improving the efficiency of the identification process, it is recommended that a school district establish a single system for identifying high risk children. This means that the various disciplines working with handicapped children in a particular school district must agree on the system to be used and the specialists in each system will have to have their activities defined and coordinated as needed. A single coordinated screening system avoids duplication of effort, simplifies scheduling, and saves time for both regular education and special education staff.

Loose Referral Systems

Referral procedures generally need to be tightened. In one large midwestern city, referral forms are kept in the teachers' lounge. To refer a child, the teacher simply checks the appropriate behaviors and completes the identifying information. There were 11,500 children on the waiting list. The work required to assess these children will be very costly. There are several ways a referral system might be tightened. First, have one form, not five or six forms. Second, conduct in-service on what is or is not an appropriate referral. Third, each building should screen all referrals before forwarding them to special education. Fourth, teachers must be trained to individualize instruction for problem children in their classrooms. All of these procedures will help reduce referrals.

ASSESSMENT

The assessment of learning disabled children is a highly controversial subject as evidenced in our professional journals. I have selected five issues for discussion which I believe have grave implications for assessing learning disabled children.

Exclusion of the Learning Disabilities Specialist

A major issue confronting our field is whether or not learning disabilities specialists will be included on the multidisciplinary team. The Rules and Regulations for PL 94-142 published August 23, 1977, stated: "The evaluation is made by a multidisciplinary team or group of persons, including at least one teacher or other specialist with knowledge in the area of suspected disability" (121a.532).

My interpretation of this regulation led me to believe that a certified professional in learning disabilities would be on the multidisciplinary team for those children suspected of having a specific learning disability.

These Rules and Regulations were amended on December 29, 1977, to read:

> In evaluating a child suspected of having a specific learning disability, in addition to the requirements of 121a.532, each public agency shall include on the multidisciplinary evaluation team:
> (a) (1) The child's regular teacher; or
> (2) If the child does not have a regular teacher, a regular classroom teacher qualified to teach a child of his or her age; and
> (3) For a child of less than school age, an individual qualified by the state educational agency to teach a child of his or her age; and
> (b) At least one person qualified to conduct individual diagnostic examinations of children, such as a school psychologist, speech-language pathologist, or remedial reading teacher. (121a.540)

Although regular teachers, school psychologists, speech-language pathologists, and remedial reading teachers are mentioned in the amendment, there is no mention of the learning disabilities specialist.

I cannot imagine Rules and Regulations written for the speech impaired, deaf, blind, or emotionally disturbed children not including the specialist in those areas as members of the multidisciplinary team.

If the various disciplines were not engaged in territorial wars, I could accept the "intent" of the Rules and Regulations to include specialists in learning disabilities. But we are engaged in territorial wars and state departments and local educational agencies can interpret the Rules and Regulations as they see fit. The fact is that learning disabilities specialists can be omitted from the team as long as there is someone with "knowledge in the area of disability" on the team. The definition of the term "knowledge" remains undefined.

The Board of Directors of ACLD, the Professional Advisory Board of ACLD, and the Division of Learning Disabilities of CEC are aware of this situation and are preparing position papers which will clarify the field's position on this issue and to help correct this oversight.

Piecemeal Assessment

Observation of current assessment practices in schools leaves me with the impression that specialists who are diagnosing children are dividing them into parts and assessing on a piecemeal basis. Each discipline has developed useful diagnostic procedures and trained its members to assess limited or selected territories of performance.

Despite the individual diagnostic contributions of each specialist on the team, our fragmented assessment practices do not lead to integrated diagnostic conclusions and program plans for children.

Federal and state regulations require specialists to work on teams in our public schools, yet many of our university training programs continue to train specialists in isolation rather than in multidisciplinary training centers. If professionals are expected to work together in our schools, they should be trained together in our universities and colleges.

The Rigid Use of Test Batteries

Most people like to do that which is comfortable and that which they do best. This principle probably extends to test giving as well. Using a standard battery of tests on every child may provide a sense of comfort and security to administrators and examiners, and if enough tests are given the shotgun effect will occur—chances are you will hit something. Despite the false sense of security a "standard battery" might create, the automatic, indiscriminate use of a single battery of tests contributes to unnecessary testing and a needless waste of staff time and money by giving tests which may not be appropriate for a given child. The alternative to the test battery is to individualize testing procedures for each child which requires some thought, planning, and administrative flexibility.

Overreliance on Test Scores

Too many placement decisions and individualized education programs are made solely on the basis of test scores. Children are not digits and effective IEPs cannot solely be based on numbers derived from the tests currently available to us. Continual pressures for accountability and quantification for categorizing children for state reimbursement has reduced many of our assessment programs to number games. The observations of parents and teachers for planning must be given more credence, whether or not their information is "quantifiable." If the observations of a parent or teacher are markedly different from the behavior elicited in a testing situation, then the test score should be considered "suspect" until the disparities in the child's behaviors in both situations can be explained.

Failure to Assess How a Particular Child Learns

Educators typically plan educational programs for teachers by:
1. Determining the child's current level of achievement,
2. Identifying the kinds and frequency of inappropriate behaviors which occur,
3. Administering psychological tests to generate a profile of abilities and disabilities.
4. Establishing instructional or behavioral objectives, and
5. Studying the learning environment.

While these procedures are important for planning, these kinds of information and/or data do not necessarily tell us how a child learns or how he or she should be taught.

Teachers seem to worry about the products of learning far more than the worry about the learning process itself. Most of life is made up of the process of getting there, not the actual achievement. Sir Edmund Hillary, for example, spent less than an hour on the summit of Mt. Everest, yet he invested years in training, months in planning, days in the ascent, and remained on the summit a short time. Olympic medalists train for years, yet a world record performance takes only a few seconds or minutes.

Perhaps we, as teachers, would be more effective if we followed the athlete's example and spent a little less time worrying about the mountain tops and gold medals (the products of learning) and invested more time in thinking about the best way to get there (the process of learning). If we can discover how an individual child learns best, then we can make better decisions as to how he can be taught.

THE MULTIDISCIPLINARY STAFFING

The fourth major obstacle which we must overcome is to streamline the multidisciplinary staffing. Chief among my concerns are:

Membership on Multidisciplinary Teams

When I see professionals from different disciplines attending staff-ings, who: (a) have not tested the child; (b) are unable to offer relevant in-put for the program recommendations; and (c) are unfamiliar with the child's case—one cannot help but wonder why all of these people are there. Are they protecting their territories? Do administrators lack ration-ale for convening multidisciplinary team members who are relevant for a specific child?

The number of members on a multidisciplinary team should be lim-ited to those who have relevant data or information with respect to assess-ment, eligibility, placement, or individual programming. This point of view requires that the number and kinds of personnel making up the mul-tidisciplinary team to vary from case to case.

Inefficient Staffings

All of us have attended staffings where little or no advance prepara-tion was done by either the group leader or the participants. Unfortunately many staffings are conducted in an information sharing format and amount to little more than adult "Show and Tell" sessions, where each member of the team orally reviews his or her findings and conclusions about the child. This "sharing" can be a great time waster and can take up to 15 or 20 minutes per report. After listening to unintegrated data and in-formation for an hour or an hour and a half, many listeners wonder "So what! What does it all mean?"

We must become more efficient and reduce the duration of our meetings by:

1. Reducing the number of specialists in attendance to those whose input is relevant to the child in question.

2. Sharing our written findings and conclusions with our colleagues prior to the multidisciplinary staffing. This means we will have to become more efficient in writing reports.

3. Reading our colleague's reports prior to the meeting and prepare for discussion of key points and recommendations.

4. Using the staffing for the final integration of data and decision making.

To accomplish these tasks training should be given in the principles of Group Dynamics. How can a number of individuals be shaped into a team? How can we run efficient meetings? How can we work with and relate more effectively to our colleagues? How can we diagnose why a group is ineffective? What interventions can we use to change an ineffective group into an effective and efficient group? There is much to be learned from the field of group dynamics which has positive implications for application in our field.

The Great Professional Game

I am also concerned about the great professional games which occur in so many of our meetings. Many of us sometimes feel as if we have to generate an image of infallible expertise. Some of us take definitive stands about what to do with a child. Some of us fail to ask important questions because we want to appear knowledgeable and confident. Sometimes we act as if we really know—when we don't.

Let me tell you a secret. My bachelor's degree taught me certain facts. My master's degree taught me the questions. My doctorate taught me that no one really knows the answers to many, many questions. I don't know. You don't know. And the person next to you doesn't know either. You can't imagine the confidence the doctorate has given me, because I don't have to be an expert anymore. Now I have the confidence to ask all those "dumb" questions I used to keep to myself.

There is a simple solution to the great professional game. We can begin by being honest with ourselves and our colleagues. Honesty in our staffings is imperative if we are to make the best decisions for children.

The Writing of Annual Goals and Short-Term Objectives

Looking to the future, I see teachers writing goals and objectives which are: (1) observable and easily defined, (2) easy to measure, and (3) which probably can be achieved. In contrast, there may be many annual goals and short term objectives which may never be written or taught because they are: (1) poorly defined at a verbal level; (2) not readily observable; (3) elusive in terms of measurement; and (4) difficult to achieve.

Legally, the Individualized Education Program is a good faith agreement, and teachers are expected to try to achieve goals and objectives. Parents, principals, supervisors, and state and federal officials will be monitoring the IEP to insure the IEP is appropriate and being implemented. It is only natural that many teachers and administrators will be threatened by any kind of monitoring and will protect themselves by not risking the writing of any goal or objective that might be difficult to achieve.

If pressure for accountability is exerted at any level, many teachers will work with single-minded purpose on goals and objectives which are written and spend very little time or effort teaching children content that is not on the IEP, regardless of how relevant that content might be for a particular child.

The individuals who are responsible for monitoring and supervising teachers must be aware of how teachers view the "good faith agreement" concept. If teachers believe they are to be held accountable, the way they will write IEPs will be influenced greatly. More important, still, is the need for those in authority to stand behind our teachers and support them and insure that the "good faith agreement" remains exactly that. Only when teachers have confidence that they won't be held strictly accountable for a child learning each objective will the IEP be used appropriately and accomplish the intent of the law.

DELIVERY OF INSTRUCTIONAL SERVICES

Of all the issues surrounding the actual delivery of instruction, I have selected only five for comment. My rationale for selecting these five issues, rather than others, is that these five issues are often the source of many of our instructional problems.

Categorical vs. Functional Grouping

Special education services have been provided by: a) placing children in special classes or schools according to a defined handicapping condition; b) randomly placing handicapped children in classes taught by a "regular special educator," who knows a little bit about everything, but lacks in-depth expertise; c) taking handicapped children out of regular classes part-time and providing various kinds of tutoring by different specialists; and d) placing handicapped children in the regular classroom and consulting with the teacher.

I believe it is high time we begin grouping children for instructional purposes on the basis of how they function and learn. There are at least four criteria for the functional grouping of children: (1) level of academic achievement; (2) socioemotional compatibility with peers and adults; (3) communication ability for receiving and sending information; and (4) cognitive learning style. If we are going to group and serve children on a functional rather than on a diagnostic condition level, then we are going to have to specify the criteria for grouping, stop traditional categorical training and begin preparing teachers according to the new or altered services.

The Desire to Change Children

Practically all of the instructional objectives and methods we use are directed toward changing children into something they are not and, in some cases, into something they may never become. Typical examples are changing a non-reader into a reader, an acting out child into a well behaved child, and a non-fluent child into a fluent child.

Too often, we teachers care, not about the child as he is, but an idealized concept of what that child will become under our care and teaching. This is a tragic mistake. The desire and intent to change a child into something he is not is acceptable and desirable, provided we show the child we love him and accept him the way he is.

The Continuum of Special Education Services

The continuum of special education services model, which is presented in Figure 13.1, is based upon the kinds of service delivery alternatives necessary to meet the needs of special education students. Each level of the model, beginning with the Preventative Intervention Level and progressing through Level V (Residential, Hospital or State Operated Programs), represents an increasing amount of special education service. The concept of placing students in the least restrictive alternative refers to the practice of placing a student in a program appropriate for his/her needs and removed as little as possible from the regular school program. Once a student is placed at a particular program level, the goal of special education services is to help the student successfully move to the next lowest level of service until the student is fully returned to the regular classroom and no longer requires any kind of special education service. It should be noted that the five kinds of alternatives necessary to meet the needs of special education students can be implemented for preschool,

FIGURE 13.1

A Continuum of Educational Program Alternatives

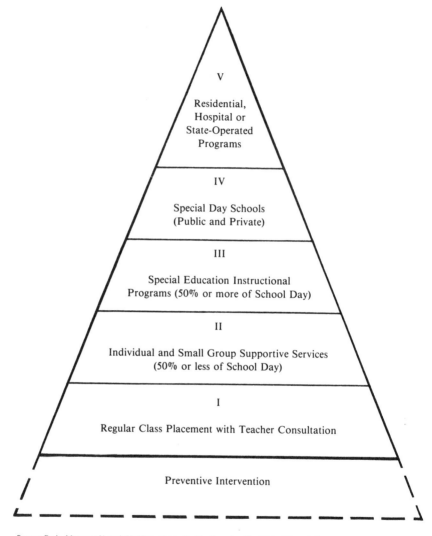

Source: Pysh, Margaret V. and Chalfant, James C. *The Learning Disabilities Manual: Recommended Procedures and Practices.* State Board of Education, Illinois Office of Education, Springfield,.Illinois, May, 1978, p. 72

elementary, and junior or senior high school students who need special help. We must avoid placing children at one level and leaving them there.

The Routine Automatic Use of Materials, Kits, etc.

Too many of us have become overly dependent upon tests, materials, kits, cookbooks, and educational materials. Too often these items are used routinely and mechanically with little thought or preparation. This situation can be overcome by writing specific assessment objectives or instructional objectives and having a logical rationale for every material chosen for use.

Failure to Focus on Individual Needs

A teacher who teaches each child in the same way is like a doctor who treats each patient in the same way. If physicians try to recognize different symptoms of physical illness in their patients and use different treatments, teachers should be able to apply the knowledge from psychology, education, child development, etc., to recognize that children have different problems, learn differently, and require different instructional methods in order to learn at their maximum rate.

I will never forget the classroom teacher in a very small rural school who was asked to do something special for a handicapped child in her class. "Yes, I understand the need, but you must remember I have four other children in my second grade classroom." Most teachers do not individualize in their classes because they don't know how. They were never taught. This means that massive in-service must occur in our schools and that college and university pre-service training must be revised to include individualization.

The Need for More Teacher Initiative

Too many of us are waiting: waiting for guidelines from the state or federal government; waiting for administrators to make decisions; waiting for a psychologist to give a test; or waiting for publishing houses to produce those materials and kits which will solve these children's problems. We keep trying to find answers to our daily problems in books. It is a fantasy to believe someone else is going to solve our problems for us.

When we are confronted with a problem or a dilemma, we can certainly seek help, but if it isn't forthcoming, we can't just stand there. We have to show initiative and do something. As the tactical officers at Fort Benning say to Officer Candidates who have to make decisions on field problems "Don't just stand there, candidate; do something, even if it's wrong."

If there is a problem with one of our cases, and we are in this field of learning disabilities, then it is our responsibility, yours and mine, to do something. That something is to use our initiative, our logic, and our energies to try and make the difference for that child and his parents.

MAINSTREAMING

The concept of mainstreaming refers to placing children who qualify for special education services in the regular classroom for part of their educational program. Many parents advocate mainstreaming because the children remain closer to the regular school curriculum. The parents feel more secure because their child's education is not that different from other children, and the transition back to the regular classroom from special services is easier.

Many administrators advocate mainstreaming because they think it will cost less, reduce the special education staff, and make less demands on the physical plant in terms of space. Actually, the costs are about the same, and the special education staff will be necessary except their roles will require more consultation with teachers and less direct teaching with children.

Many special education teachers support mainstreaming because they do not have to carry the sole responsibility for the child. Transitioning back to the regular classroom is easier, and special and regular education are brought closer together.

But what do regular classroom teachers say about mainstreaming? A list of their most frequent questions follows: (1) How will the presence of these handicapped children in my classroom affect the progress of my normal and gifted students? (2) How many handicapped children will be placed in my classroom? (3) How severe will they be? (4) Will the number of students in my class be readjusted for each handicapped child I accept? (5) Will I be given released time to plan daily work, attend staffings, and do the required paper work? (6) What kind of follow-up will I receive in terms of aides, para-professional, demonstration teaching, consultation, crisis intervention? (7) How can I group these children for instruction in my room? (8) How can I learn about their problems and characteristics? (9) How can I learn the techniques for individualizing instruction? (10) To what extent will the parents be involved? (11) Handicapped children are absent a lot. What do I do about make-up work? (12) How do I grade them? (13) What impact will the rest of my children have on the handicapped child who is mainstreamed? (14) Who has the final responsibility for these children?

Regular teachers have been assigned the mainstream responsibility by federal, state, and local educational officials. Many teachers are resentful, angry, and often hostile. Despite all the problems, most teachers are reasonable and will try almost anything to help a child, provided they are: (1) told what to do; (2) shown how to do it; (3) given support when they need it; and (4) reinforced and appreciated for their efforts.

Special educators often have unrealistic expectations as to what a classroom teacher can do to help a learning disabled child in the classroom. Many of us who talk or write about mainstreaming have never really done it. Yet, many of us have taken moral positions about what regular teachers should do. We cite principles of behavior modification and make platitudinous statements. We offer regular teachers advice, counsel, and encouragement—but very little else. We must ask ourselves what we are doing to actually make the mainstreaming concept work for the child and his teacher.

RECOMMENDATIONS

The past has demonstrated time and time again that our problems cannot be solved by working alone. The federal government cannot solve our problems through dictatorial and regulatory action. The universities are busy training and certifying teachers. The state departments are busy coping with the federal mandates and the local educational agencies. The public schools are busy serving thousands of children. There is not enough time and most public school personnel are bending to a breaking point under a cross of paper.

It is my impression that the reason the federal and state governments keep generating rules and regulations for all of us to implement is because our field has not gotten our act together in any integrated fashion and gone to the federal and state governments and told them exactly what we want to do and what we will need to achieve our goals.

It is time for those of us who do the day to day work in our field to take the initiative. Let us give the state and federal government an opportunity to listen and react to us for a change—and they will listen, provided we speak in one voice and support our concepts and requests for help with data.

The obstacles I have described this evening will eventually be overcome through gradual, evolutionary change, and it will take at least twenty years to do it. I am, therefore, taking this opportunity to make two overall recommendations which might accelerate a more rapid change. The first recommendation is at a systems level and the second recommendation is at a personal level.

A Systems Recommendation

In order to overcome the major problem of territoriality in identification, assessment, multidisciplinary staffings, delivering instructional services and mainstreaming, I am recommending that each state create a problem solving consortium, which incorporates the resources and capabilities of the State Office of Education, the institutions of higher education, and the local education agencies. Such a consortium could consist of three state office personnel, three university representatives, six to twelve persons from public and private schools. Regular teachers, special education teachers, administrators, supervisors, parents, members of boards of education might belong.

The mission of this consortium would be twofold: First, to provide a mechanism for identifying the critical problems in the state and setting priorities through state-wide need surveys, and contacts from school districts, intermediate units, and regions. Second, the consortium would generate constructive approaches and to obtain sanction to conduct experimental field tests to evaluate new approaches to old problems. Such a group could meet every two months and appoint subgroups to work on specific tasks.

A problem solving group offers a number of benefits. Rather than each interest group trying to solve common problems alone, collective problem solving, if done properly, can be more efficient and effective. Different disciplines can gain empathy and understanding for one another through cooperation. The projects of the consortium could be included in the annual state plan.

Such a group could give a state a quantum leap into the future. In order for a consortium to work properly requires the leadership and personal commitment of each member to the common cause.

A Personal Recommendation

If we are to meet the challenge of the 1980s and resolve these problems, all of us will have to change our behavior.

We must begin questioning some of the practices we have been advocating for so long.

We must begin listening to the ideas of others and try to relate our science to theirs.

We must sit down together and decide what is best for the learning disabled children and youth all of us are trying to serve.

At this point in time our field is standing on the shoulders of people like Cruickshank, Kirk, Myklebust, Frostig, Birch, Getman, Kephart, Strothers, Rabinovitch and others, as well as all of the parents and teachers who have worked so hard for these children. It is up to each of us to try and go beyond their contributions and advance the present status of knowledge in our field.

If we are to succeed we must have the courage to take a long look at ourselves and what we are doing; the personal honesty to admit what is or is not good for children; and the strength of character to discard familiar and comfortable practices and seek more effective alternatives. But if we continue to behave as we have in the past we can all predict what will happen. The next area of specialization will be "OLFACTORY DISORDERS," and I am going to become an olfactory correctionist, therapist, clinician, or perhaps a pathologist. Think how exciting it will be!

Theories will emerge. We will have Guilboard's structure of the nose and Head's theory of nose assembly.

We will have to define the population in question, operationalize the definition, and translate theory into practice.

It will be necessary to develop screening devices and diagnostic tests. The American Psychological Association will insist on the right to administer certain tests, and because of the large number of referrals which will be received it may be a six month wait before a high risk child can be examined and sniffed out.

The learning disabilities people will devise remedial methods such as the Olesthetic Approach using sight, sound, touch, and smell simultaneously. In addition to directionality and laterality, we will have nasality.

We will have to decide which nostril is dominant and is the nose to the left or right of the midline?

The behaviorists will state that there is no such thing as an olfactory disability. If you cannot see it or measure it, it doesn't exist, even if you can smell it.

Speech pathologists will want to work with these children, because the sense of smell is related to the taste buds, which are located in the tongue.

Early childhood specialists will attribute Olfactory problems to developmental lags.

The culturally deprived group will insist that these children behave the way they do because they were deprived of Olfactory experiences such as smelling Chanel No. 5, chateaubriand, or popcorn.

The U.S. Office of Education will hold regional meetings to decide which professional group should work with Specific olfactory disability children (or SOD's as they are called for short). Mandatory laws will be written requiring states and local districts to serve these children, then fail to appropriate funds to implement the law.

Administrators will cope the best they can until the final rules and regulations are made available in printed form, and then they will become even more confused over the criteria for compliance, head count, accountability, and due process procedures.

Finally, when the children have been identified, assessed, and a multidisciplinary staffing held to determine if they are eligible as SODs and an IEP is written, they will be given to the regular classroom teacher as part of the local mainstream effort.

In conclusion, I want to emphasize the point that whether or not our learning disabled children will receive the kind of quality education, which they need and is their right under the law, is our responsibility—yours and mine. As for me, I am looking forward to the challenge of the 1980s.